Virtual Working

This book addresses the social and organisational dynamics which underlie recent technological and work developments within organisations, often referred to as 'virtual working'. It seeks to go beyond a mere description of this new work phenomenon in order to provide more rigorous ways of analysing and understanding the issues raised. In addition to providing accounts of developments such as web-based enterprises and virtual teams, each contributor focuses on the employment of information technology to transcend the boundaries between and within organisations, and the consequences this has for social and organisational relations. Issues include:

- the management of knowledge and organisational learning in dispersed networks
- understanding how team roles and processes are affected by virtual working
- managing the innovation process towards virtual forms of organisation
- maintaining commitment and managing culture in virtual work arrangements

Virtual Working offers new insights and perspectives on the dynamics presented by these emerging forms of work, and will help us to understand and, ultimately, to manage them.

Paul Jackson is Lecturer in Management Studies at Brunel University, UK. He has undertaken international speaking and consultancy assignments on new technology and flexible working, innovation and organisational learning. His previous publications include *Teleworking: International Perspectives* (with Jos van der Wielen, 1998), also published by Routledge.

The Management of Technology and Innovation
Edited by David Preece, University of Portsmouth, UK

The books in this series offer grounding in central elements of the management of technology and innovation. Each title will explain, develop and critically explore issues and concepts in a particular aspect of the management of technology/innovation, combining a review of the current state of knowledge with the presentation and discussion of primary material not previously published.

Each title is designed to be user-friendly with an international orientation and key introductions and summaries.

Other titles in this series include:

Technology in Context
Technology assessment for managers
Ernest Braun

Teleworking: International Perspectives
From telecommuting to the virtual organisation
Edited by Paul J. Jackson and Jos M. van der Wielen

Managing Technological Discontinuities
The case of the Finnish paper industry
Juha Laurila

Creative Technological Change
Configuring technology and organisation
Ian McLoughlin

Valuing Technology
Organisations, culture and change
*Janice McLaughlin, Paul Rosen, David Skinner
and Andrew Webster*

Virtual Working

Social and organisational dynamics

Edited by Paul Jackson

London and New York

First published 1999
by Routledge
11 New Fetter Lane, London EC4P 4EE

Simultaneously published in the USA and Canada
by Routledge
29 West 35th Street, New York, NY 10001

Routledge is an imprint of the Taylor & Francis Group

© 1999 selection and editorial matter, Paul J. Jackson; individual chapters,
the contributors

Typeset in Baskerville by Routledge
Printed and bound in Great Britain by Biddles Ltd,
Guildford and King's Lynn

British Library Cataloguing in Publication Data
A catalogue record for this book is available from the British Library

Library of Congress Cataloging in Publication Data
Jackson, Paul J.
Virtual Working: Social and organisational dynamics /
Paul J. Jackson
Includes bibliographical references and index.
1. Information technology – management. I. Title.
HD30.2.J325   1999   99-13724
658.4'038–dc21   CIP

ISBN 0–415–20087–3 (hbk)
ISBN 0–415–20088–1 (pbk)

Contents

Illustrations

Figures

Tables

Contributors

Louise M. Adami is a human resources practitioner working in the field of scientific research and development. She is currently researching the organisational and individual systems that facilitate and stunt career development and the potential benefits of flexible work arrangements on expanding career opportunities. Her other research has focused on industrial relations issues.

Charlotte Björkegren is a Ph.D. student at the Department of Information Science. She is also a member of the International School of Management and Engineering at Linköping University. Her current research is within project organising and the management of knowledge. Her thesis will be 'Learning for the next project – a study in knowledge transfer between projects'. She has a Masters degree in Business Administration and has been a visiting student at the University of Freiburg. Together with Professor Rapp she has written a report on Learning and working at a distance. For further information see www.ida.liu.se/labs/eis/people/chabj.html or e-mail *chabj@ida.liu.se*.

Alistair Campbell is a Lecturer in the Department of Computing and Information Systems at the University of Paisley, UK. He has presented at UK national and international conferences and published papers in the areas of electronic commerce, virtual organisations and business transformation. Current research interests are in network and web forms of enterprise, and organisational learning.

Anne-Marie Coles is a Research Fellow in the School of Business and of Management Studies, Brunel University, West London. She is currently working on a major research project sponsored by the European Commission entitled 'Building collaborative networks for new product development'. Her research interests include technology policy, inter-firm R&D collaboration, networking for new product development, and barriers to design innovation.

Astrid Depickere is a researcher at the Work and Organisation unit of the Department of Sociology, University of Leuven, Belgium. She is currently working on a project under the Medialab Action Program of the Flemish Government, focusing on organisational and personnel management aspects of teleworking.

Keith Dickson is Deputy Head of the School of Business and Management at Brunel University, West London. He is currently co-ordinating a major research project sponsored by the European Commission entitled 'Building collaborative networks for new product development'. His other research interests include the management of technological innovation, inter-firm collaboration and design procedures and technology processes in small firms.

Sean Galpin is a Masters graduate of the School of Business and Management, Brunel University. His 1997 Masters thesis is entitled 'Narratives, identity and space in flexible working and teleworking organisations'. He works for a multinational telecommunications company.

Lisa Harris is a Lecturer in Management Studies at Brunel University, West London. At present she is also working on a major research project sponsored by the European Commission entitled 'Building collaborative networks for new product development'. Her research interests include web-based marketing and networking for new product development. She is also involved in the design and development of multi-media study materials for teaching purposes. For further information contact: lisa.harris@brunel.ac.uk.

Paul J. Jackson lectures in Management Studies at Brunel University, West London. He holds a doctorate in Management Studies from Cambridge University. He has been a European Research Fellow at the Work and Organization Research Centre, Tilburg University, The Netherlands. He has undertaken international speaking and consultancy assignments on new technology and flexible working, innovation and organisational learning. He is also a co-founder of the International Workshops on Telework series and the International Telework Foundation. He is currently researching in the area of virtual organisations and Web-based learning.

Ian McLoughlin is Professor of Management Studies at the University of Newcastle. He is currently managing a major research project sponsored by the European Commission entitled 'Building collaborative networks for new product development'. He has written a number of articles and books, the most recent of which is entitled 'Creative technological change: shaping technology and organisation'. His current research interests include the management of innovation and organisational change and micro-political organisational processes.

Kiran Mirchandani is currently on a Social Science and Humanities Research Council of Canada (SSHRC) Postdoctoral Fellowship at St. Mary's University, Canada. She holds a Ph.D. in Sociology from McGill University and has published articles on gender, work and organisation. She is currently conducting a project on home-based business owners in Atlantic Canada.

Frank A. Morath earned his undergraduate degree from the University of Konstanz, Germany, and his Masters degree in public administration from the University of North Texas, Denton. He was recently involved in a five-year research project examining learning processes in public administrations. He is now working on his Ph.D., where he focuses on collective learning and knowledge management in network structures. His research interests are new public management, collective learning processes, knowledge management and the social dynamics of network societies. He has published several articles. He is also the co-author of a book on learning administrations (to be published in 1999).

Joe Nandhakumar is a lecturer in Information Systems at the University of Southampton. He received his Ph.D. in Information Systems from the University of Cambridge in 1994. His research employs an ethnographic approach to investigate the development and use of information systems in organisations. He has published widely on these issues. His recent paper received the 'best paper' award at the 18th International Conference in Information Systems held in Atlanta. He is currently investigating the emergence and social consequences of collaborative information technologies in global organisations.

Juhani Pekkola is Senior Researcher, Licentiate of Social Science at the Ministry of Labour, Helsinki. Since 1983 he has worked for the Ministry of Social Affairs and Health and for the Ministry of Labour on research and development activities in the area of labour relations and telework. During 1996 he was Project Co-ordinator for the National Workplace Development Programme and since 1997 has been Project Secretary of the Team for the Information Society.

Birger Rapp is Professor of Economic Information Systems, Department of Computer and Information Science, Linköping University. He is president of the board of the Swedish Teleworking Association, 'Distansforum' and Program Director in Management and Economic Information Systems at IMIT (Institute of Management of Innovation and Technology). He is also a board member of the Archipelago Office. He was an Expert for the 'Distansarbetsutredningen' ('The Public Investigation of Teleworking'). He has been the president of SORA, and was the second president of EURO. He has also been the vice president at large of IFORS, 1995–8. He belongs to the editorial (advisory) boards of, among others, the following international journals: EJOR, IJMSD, JORBEL and Omega. He is a senior consultant to many Swedish companies and was the first president of the Pronova Research and Development Board in Norrköping in Sweden. He is also one of the founders and the first president of the Association of 'Ekoparken' in Stockholm, the green area in an urban environment that has become the first National City Park in the world. Professor Rapp is the leader of the research group ITOS (Information Technology and Organisational Structure). He has recently written *Flexibla arbetsformer och flexibla kontor* (*Flexible forms of work and flexible offices*, in Swedish). He has also published books in investment theory, production planning and control, teleworking and principal agent theory, as well as many papers in international journals. For further information contact www.ida.liu.se/labs/eis/people/birra.html or e-mail *birra@ida.liu.se*.

Artur P. Schmidt has a Ph.D. in systems analysis of astronautics and aeronautics. He works as an author and journalist. He is the author of two books (*Endo-Management*, 1998; *Der Wissens-Navigator*, 1999) and many articles analysing new media, cyber-management and the creation of knowledge. He is currently researching the rules of the new knowledge economy. With endophysicist and chaos researcher Otto E. Rössler, he will co-author a book about the findings (*Die Wissens-Ökonomie*), to be published in 1999.

David Sims is Professor of Management Studies, Brunel University, and Head of the School of Business and Management and of the Graduate Business School. David has an academic background in operational research and organisational behaviour and has been a consultant in organisations in the oil, power, computer, publishing, airline, hotel and engineering industries, as well as in the public sector. His research interests are in management thinking and learning, in particular in agenda shaping, problem construction and managerial storytelling. He is editor of the journal *Management Learning* and author or co-author of some sixty books and articles (including the textbook *Organizing and Organization*) and a further forty or so international conference papers, though he cannot remember what they all say.

Reima Suomi is Professor of Information Systems Science at Turku School of Economics and Business Administration, Finland. His research interests focus on telecommunications management, including telework and telecommunication cost structures. He has published in journals such as *Information and Management, Human Systems Management* and *Information Services and Use.*

Preface

This book starts from the premise that recent developments in information technology (IT) and work design have given rise to new demands in understanding and managing organisational relations and processes. The developments in question are referred to in the book as 'virtual working'. These include instances where technologies such as the Internet, groupware and tele-conferencing allow for forms of dispersed interaction with co-workers, customers, allied enterprises and suppliers. In addition to the erosion of *spatial* barriers in the way work is organised, the book also addresses the relaxation of *organisational* boundaries (both within and between organisations). This later focus points to the fact that business processes are increasingly based around internal networks, or networks of (often small) organisations, which may use IT to work together across space to produce shared outputs.

The present volume carries forward a process that was started with the founding of an annual series of international workshops on teleworking by myself and Jos van der Wielen. These events – which began in London in 1996, moved to Amsterdam in 1997 and then to Turku, Finland, in 1998 – have brought together a network of scientists, researchers and consultants, all with interests in new ways of working. The first book to emerge from these endeavours was *Teleworking: International Perspectives*, edited by Jackson and van der Wielen and also published by Routledge.

In *Virtual Working* the aim is to build on this earlier work by focusing on the issues and dynamics brought about by the new ways of working. The theme of technology-supported dispersed working (the defining feature of teleworking) is thus still central to the book. However, we are also concerned herein with the growth in organisational networking and team working – developments which themselves often rely on new communications technologies. Virtual working in all of these cases presents organisations with new challenges in structuring, managing and generally coping with work. Put differently, it involves new *social and organisational dynamics*, an understanding of which may be the key to the effective implementation and management of the innovation involved.

Acknowledgements

In putting this book together I am deeply grateful to those who have supported our recent workshops, without whose help and advice this ongoing process of learning would not have been possible. I am particularly indebted, of course, to Jos van der Wielen for all his hard work in getting the workshop series off the ground, as well as to Victor de Pous. Our sponsors over the past few years deserve particular thanks. These include Maarten Botterman and Peter Johnston from the European Commission, DG XIII; Jeremy Millard and Horace Mitchel from the European Telework Development Initiative; Jan Tetteroo and Corly Bedacht from Nedernet, and Mike Maternaghan, Carol Maxwell and Diane Warne from BT. In putting the book together I would also like to thank Stuart Hay from Routledge and Lisa Harris from Brunel University.

For more details about virtual working developments, including workshops and publications, please visit the ITF Web site at www.TeleworkFoundation.org, or e.mail Paul J. Jackson at pauljjackson@compuserve.com.

1 Introduction

From new designs to new dynamics

Paul J. Jackson

As we stride across the threshold of the new millennium, many of us will find just cause to contemplate the world that lies ahead. A new millennium offers us all the chance to wonder and even dream how things may be different in the future – what changes may lie in store for the way we live and work; what new technologies may shape our lives. If we look just into our recent past, there is evidence that the scope and speed of change can be dramatic. Social and economic consequences of globalisation, for instance, have shown us how an increasingly interdependent world produces common problems and concerns that demand new forms of international management and new types of organisations. Developments, not least with the Internet, demonstrate how new technologies can spring, seemingly from nowhere, with pervasive consequences.

The introduction of new information technologies (IT), computer software and multi-media interfaces – particularly the World Wide Web – offer the possibilities of finding new ways of working and learning, new products and services, and even entire new industries. But this also comes at a time of heightened competition and of pressure on firms to be adaptive and innovative. The new possibilities are therefore tempered by uncertainty and anxiety. It is in this context that discussions of and developments in 'virtual working' are taking place.

The rise of virtual working

In one sense, virtual working is bound up with attempts to find ever more flexible and adaptive business structures. It addresses the need to break with old, bureaucratic ways of working, and to allow for rapid innovation and product development (Davidow and Malone 1992; Birchall and Lyons 1995; Hedberg *et al.* 1997). Business success, as Nonaka and Takeuchi (1995) have pointed out, increasingly relies not only on improving efficiency, but in embodying ideas and knowledge in products and services that are rapidly developed and deployed in the marketplace. But bringing new ideas and knowledge together may call for a change to traditional business practice, particularly where many different expert groups are involved (McLoughlin and Jackson, Chapter 11 this volume). Specifically, collaboration across functional boundaries, and even between organisations, may be required (Hastings 1993). In both cases, a need to transcend spatial barriers may also be pertinent, particularly where groups of experts are located in distant offices and countries (for example, see Lipnack and Stamps 1997 and Nandhakumar, Chapter 4 this volume). In this instance, then, the virtual working debate draws attention to the contrasts with old, 'Fordist' style organisations, which were generally vertically integrated, with all activities and skills housed within a single legal entity (see, for example, McLoughlin and Clark 1994; McGrath and Houlihan 1998; Harris 1998).

The breaking down of spatial barriers represents another key dimension of the virtual working debate. This has been given impetus in recent years by new forms of IT, particularly intranets and extranets, video-conferencing and mobile communications. Bridging distance with IT is a subject most closely associated with the idea of 'telework' (see Jackson and van der Wielen 1998). Of course for many people, telework has traditionally had a more restrictive meaning than that encompassed by virtual working, referring largely to flexible work arrangements. Here, individuals use IT to work (or telecommute) remotely from employers, at specially designed 'telecentres' or 'telecottages', at home or on the move (see also Nilles 1998).

As Jackson and van der Wielen point out, though, while telecommuting may provide a number of important benefits for both workers and their employers, the flexibility offered by the new technology provides for more than just doing the same or similar work tasks at a distance. As noted above, the opportunity to blend expertise across space, or the linking of enterprises to form collaborative networks, points to more powerful uses of the technology. This more strategic approach to virtual working (and the technologies that facilitate it) will be needed if contemporary business imperatives are to be addressed.

The basic premise of this book is that while these work structures and processes (inter-firm collaboration, flexible working, team working, knowledge management and organisational learning) are often treated in isolation, given the growing importance of IT and spatial flexibility to them, there are merits in examining their areas of connection. This will allow us to draw out points of contrast, as well as to see where lessons can be generalised. The new organisations and (virtual) ways of working that characterise the new millennium demand a systemic elucidating of these issues. Three reasons underpin this:

- The demand for more flexibility by individuals, combined with improvements in technological capabilities and cost-effectiveness, will make working arrangements, such as teleworking, increasingly viable and attractive.
- The need for organisations to improve innovation and learning will demand new knowledge management systems, making use of IT support, that help members to acquire, accumulate, exchange and exploit organisational knowledge.
- Because access to and transfer of knowledge and expertise will increasingly take place across boundaries (both organisational and spatial), internal networks and dispersed project groups, as well as inter-firm collaborations, will become more and more common.

From designs to dynamics

A whole new lexicon has arisen that seeks to capture the new ways of working described in this book, including 'Web enterprises', 'virtual organisations', 'virtual teams', 'teleworking' and so on. In many accounts of the new work configurations, attention is generally given over to *describing* the new forms or structures involved and what role the new technologies have played. Many of the experiences, achievements and benefits derived by the early adopters have been documented (Cronin 1995 and 1996; McEachern and O'Keefe 1998). These works are clearly important for illustrating new business models and working practices. However, this book seeks to move the debate a stage further by wrestling with the challenges involved in *migrating towards* and *managing* these new ways of working. In doing this, the book addresses two sets of concerns. The first recognises that in introducing forms of virtual working – from networking, to virtual teams and teleworking – particular problems and issues are faced by those charged with managing the change. The second points to the fact that such developments also bring with them a need for new skills, procedures, and even values and attitudes, on the part of workers, team members and managers. These two sets of concerns are what we refer to as 'social and organisational dynamics'. They are, it can be argued, the key challenges in virtual working over and above those of designing new work configurations or implementing the technologies that support them.

The problem here is that in introducing new ways of working, or in making sense of new work phenomena, there is danger of repeating the sort of mistakes made, for instance, in the world of information systems design. As Hirschheim (1985) pointed out, writers on and designers of information systems often addressed themselves to the 'manifest' and 'overt' aspects of organisations (technologies, information flows, work tasks, and formal structures and relationships), to the neglect of the 'cultural' and 'social' aspects. As Harris *et al.* (Chapter 3) and McLoughlin and Jackson (Chapter 11) note, the introduction of new technologies and corporate change strategies are still often looked upon as relatively non-problematical 'technical matters'.

One reason for this may be the complexity of the 'technical' knowledge involved (Attewell 1996). Few people have the business, technical and human resource expertise to grapple easily with such matters. It is not surprising, perhaps, that where new work concepts are produced (for example, by IT vendors or writers and consultants), and 'off the peg' software suites developed, they may stand in lieu of a thorough organisational assessment as to the strategic opportunities and implications of technology-supported change. There is also a danger here in the way successful cases of work innovation are documented and discussed, giving the impression that other firms could straightforwardly hope to emulate them. This may again downplay the complexity involved in managing the new work structures, as well as the know-how needed to appropriate benefits from the technologies (Stymne *et al.* 1996). Subtle differences – from market conditions and organisational cultures, to political agendas and expertise levels –

makes the transplantation of any technique or technology from one case to another fraught with difficulties.

New organisational thinking

One problem, of course, is that the rate of current technological and business change allows little time to get to grips with the intricacies of new devices and software, or for considered reflection on the sort of systems and competencies needed to manage the new work configurations based on them. The pace of change, and the pressure to innovate, thus presents two main challenges. The first is to embrace the 'potential' of new technologies in order to realise competitive benefits through new work structures and processes, as well as products and services. We can characterise this challenge as one of 'new practices'. The second and related set of challenges address 'organisational thinking'. This includes, for instance, the theories and concepts we use to describe and understand new practices (see also Checkland and Holwell 1998). It also encompasses the strategies and assumptions that guide decision making about them. Where new practices present particularly novel dynamics (such as 'remote management' in teleworking, or knowledge management in Web enterprises) the need for new organisational thinking (theories, strategies, attitudes) becomes sharper. This may also mean questioning fundamental assumptions about work and organisation – things that are often captured in the language and implicit metaphors we use when talking about organisational phenomena.

The main difficulty here, particularly where new technology is involved, is set out by Checkland and Holwell (1998: 56):

> In any developing field allied to a changing technology, there will be a relationship between the discovery and exploitation of technical possibilities ('practice') and the development of thinking which makes sense of happenings ('theory')...where the technology is developing very rapidly, new practical possibilities will be found and developed by users...they will not wait for relevant theory! Hence practice will tend to outrun the development of thinking in any field in which the technological changes come very quickly indeed, as has been the case with computing hardware and software.

The relation between domains of new organisational thinking, practices and technologies is shown in Figure 1.1.

Interpreting the significance of new technologies

First, it must be noted that existing ideas and assumptions about work and organisations, as well as corporate policies, business strategies and management philosophies, shape the way we think about new technologies – what role they might play, what new technologies would prove advantageous. Experience with previous technologies, then, may structure the way new ones are configured. For

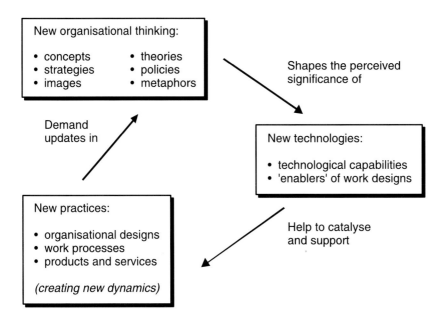

Figure 1.1 New organisational thinking, technologies and practices

example, new technologies may simply be used to *substitute* for old technologies rather than facilitate new ways of working (see also McLoughlin forthcoming).[1] This takes an implicit 'constructivist' approach to technology (Grint and Woolgar 1997): what technologies can and cannot do – and the sort of work configurations to which they lend themselves – rely on 'interpretive' skills on the part of those deploying new technologies. In other words, technologies may be 'read' in different ways, with many views on their possible uses.

New technologies in support of new ways of working

Second, where technologies are indeed interpreted and deployed to facilitate new forms of practice, then new organisational designs, new business processes and even new products and services *may* follow. But, as has been said, the ability to reconfigure organisational, technological and human resources is not straightforward and cannot be guaranteed. The problems involved here range from managing resistance and coping with different political agendas, to acquiring or developing the skills, values and attitudes needed to make the new configurations work (McLoughlin and Harris 1997). This is particularly so where radical changes are produced that demand new methods of supervision, new relationships between peers, and new sets of responsibilities (Badham *et al.* 1997). Such practices, then, are bound up with new social and organisational dynamics that demand some new organisational thinking.

Developing new organisational thinking

Third, virtual working often challenges the principles that underlie management strategies and practices, as well as our basic assumptions about organisations. Where organisational values and norms are out of 'sync' with the new ways of working, their success is likely to be jeopardised. In the management of telecommuting arrangements, for instance, control systems and attitudes that emphasise commitment and shared values may be required (see Depickere, Chapter 7 this volume). But new thinking may also be needed *to make sense of* the new dynamics – for example, in identifying the issues of significance in the new situation. So far as business networking is concerned, for instance, this may mean focusing on relationship-building, securing inter-firm trust, and handling uncertainty and ambiguity (see Harris *et al.*, Chapter 3 this volume).

Our deep-seated assumptions about organisations may also need rethinking. These often involve the way we think and talk about organisations. As Morgan (1997) has shown, we often tend to treat businesses as if they were 'machines' – particularly where tasks and workflows are routine and well-structured. Organismic or 'open system' metaphors, on the other hand, are also implicit when we seek to relate 'the organisation' to 'the environment' in which it operates. These basic metaphors are called into question by the sort of developments in business practice discussed in this book. The blurring of functional boundaries by internal networking, and their more fluid relationships and lateral communications, contrasts starkly with the structures implicit in the machine metaphor. Moreover, given the growth in inter-firm networking, it becomes increasingly difficult (in contrast to the organismic metaphor) to see where one organisation ends and the other begins (see, for example, Davidow and Malone 1992: 5–6). The need to create workgroups across organisations, to share, exchange and create new knowledge, is one reason for this. As such, the ideas embodied in the 'brain metaphor', which emphasises learning and knowledge flows, has become an increasingly important way of making sense of new forms of organisation – see also Campbell (Chapter 2), Björkegren and Rapp (Chapter 10), McLoughlin and Jackson (Chapter 11) and Morath and Schmidt (Chapter 12).

Setting the agenda for virtual working

In contemplating changes that involve new technologies, the above therefore identifies three key sets of challenges:

- to understand the 'capabilities' offered by new technology and the new work configurations they may provide;
- to reconfigure organisational designs and work processes to promote product innovation, flexible working, networking and improved knowledge management;

- to develop ways of understanding and managing the dynamics created by the new ways of working, as well as the concepts, theories, values and attitudes these demand.

The new work concepts that characterise virtual working certainly offer us ways of 'reading' the new technologies, as well as identifying innovation opportunities and prescribing solutions to problems. However, accounts of virtual working bring with them a range of perspectives, definitions and agendas. There is often little agreement as to what the 'virtual' in virtual working actually stands for, and in using this new language, many vendors, writers and consultants bring with them some simplistic and flawed assumptions about organisations and the human being at work. Before we try to redress this, let us first examine the key perspectives that characterise discussions on virtual working. Much of this debate has thus far occurred in the more 'popular' literature on organisations – particularly in American texts. As such, it often adopts an optimistic and even evangelistic tone (see, for example, Davidow and Malone 1992; Grenier and Metes 1995). However, it is exactly these discussions that have made concepts of virtual working a matter of common day parlance, at least in business circles.

Images and perspectives in virtual working

Five main images and perspectives are found in discussions of virtual working. These address: first, the growth in 'information processing' in organisations; second, the 'heightening of flexibility' issues; third, the 'disembodiment' of organisations; fourth, the 'erosion of boundaries' within and between businesses; and, fifth, the growth in 'electronic commerce'. We will begin with the 'information processing' view.

Virtual working as information processing

Debates on teleworking and virtual organisations, as well as the Information Society generally, are keen to play up the growing importance of *information* in work processes and products (see also Castells 1996). Many accounts of virtual working are premised on a belief that where work can be digitalised – or 'informated', to use Zuboff's (1988) term – novel work configurations can prevail. In digitalising or informating work, representations of the world are encoded in computer software, allowing people to interact in a 'virtual world' rather than the physical one (see Barnatt 1995: 15–16). This may take the form of computer-generated texts, pictures, diagrams, etc., or even more 'immersive' virtual reality technologies, such as head-mounted displays, that simulate the three dimensions of the real world (*ibid.*).

The growth in 'information workers' and 'knowledge industries' are often cited as testament to this. For instance, Davidow and Malone (1992: 65) observe, four decades into the computer age, that:

>...it is increasingly obvious that the very business itself is information. Many
>of the employees in any corporation are involved in the process of gath-
>ering, generating, or transforming information.

Grenier and Metes also point to the 'increasing role of information and information processing systems' in modern organisations (1995: 5). This is underlined by
Cronin (1995) in the context of the Internet, for whom information is the
'building block' of work processes. It is easy, here, to be seduced into a position
of viewing organisations *as nothing but* information processing systems and, moreover, that new forms of IT (involving computer-generated representations of the
world) can be used to 'virtualise' such systems, with work processes executed in
'cyber' rather than physical space. For instance, in a brochure by the electronics
giant Canon, entitled 'Work where you want' – a copyright synonym for telework
– we are told that:

>The time has come to revise our conception of what an office is. Gone are
>the days when it was a physical space where all employees gathered each
>day at an appointed hour. With the arrival of E-mail, voice mail, fax
>machines and teleconferencing equipment, *the office has been transformed into an*
>*electronic entity*. (Emphasis added.)
>
>   (Canon Corporation Europe 1995)

Here then, the imagery of the new technology – of computer networks and IT
devices – provides new modalities that enable us to represent work configurations in radical new ways. In many virtual work discussions, therefore, the
'machine' has been replaced by the 'information system' as the key metaphor in
thinking about organisations (see Jackson 1997).
   We should be careful, of course, not to become over-reliant on this view.
While it is important for reshaping organisational thinking, the model of the
information system is *only one* way of understanding the dynamics underlying
modern organisations. The more social and human aspects of work demand, as
we'll see in subsequent chapters, alternative sets of ideas. For now, let us examine
the importance of flexibility issues in virtual work discussions.

Virtual working as heightened flexibility

It is difficult today to open a book on management without hearing the call for
ever more organisational 'flexibility'. Exactly what flexibility means has been a
matter of considerable debate (for example, see Pollert 1991 and Adami,
Chapter 9 this volume). None the less, there is some consensus that organisations
need to rid themselves of bureaucratic constraints and allow for more fluid
working relationships in which overheads can be cut, lead times reduced, and
effectiveness and innovation improved. Three areas of flexibility can be identified here: workforce flexibility, de-bureaucratisation and organisational agility,
and flexibility in time and space.

First, then, flexibility often refers to a workforce strategy whereby employment relations are replaced by forms of outsourcing. According to Birchall and Lyons (1995), for instance, the increasing number of knowledge workers may herald a new organisational 'power shift', which will involve 'empowering individuals and encouraging them to manage themselves', and where the employment contract will be 'called into question, if not threat' (pp. 44–45). Of course, this may gloss over the nature of the labour market to some extent. While some (knowledge) workers may well be 'empowered' and able to manage themselves and defend their interests, lower skilled (operative) workers are likely to be in a much more vulnerable position (see Galpin and Sims, Chapter 6 this volume, for a discussion).

Second, in overcoming the constraints of bureaucratic structures, recent ideas, such as 'Business Process Re-engineering' (BPR) (for example, see Hammer and Champy 1993), have argued for an emphasis on processes and end products, over and above the structures which are set up to support them. For writers such as Tapscott, however, simply overcoming the dysfunctions of bureaucratic structures does not go far enough. This is because:

> …a far more comprehensive approach is urgently needed to handle the challenges of the new situation. What matters in every case is that the new technologies can transform not only business processes but also the way products and services are created and marketed, the structure and goals of the enterprise, the dynamics of competition, and the actual nature of the enterprise.
>
> (Tapscott 1995: 27)

In their discussion of virtual organisation, it is this need for agility and adaptability that is the focus of attention for Hale and Whitlam. For these authors, being virtual is bound up with the notion of 'continuous or institutionalised change' (1997: 3). This leads them to posit that:

> The virtual organisation is the name given to any organisation which is continually evolving, redefining and reinventing itself for practical business purposes.
>
> (*ibid.*)

This may be seen, for example, in the case of the 'dynamic networks' and 'Web enterprises' discussed by Campbell (Chapter 2 this volume). In these cases, the turbulence of the operating environment means that businesses need to react quickly and find new partnering possibilities if they are to seize the opportunities presented by the marketplace.

The third area of flexibility discussed in virtual working – *Time and space* – seeks to confront a further constraint on operating norms. This builds on the principles of teleworking, where IT is used to open up options as to where work is done, as well as to support remote, 'teleservices' (see Jackson and van der

Wielen, 1998; and Mirchandani (Chapter 5), Dickepere (Chapter 7) and Adami (Chapter 9) this volume). Barnatt (1995: 64) notes that while there is no agreement as to what binds together such concepts as virtual organisation, offices, corporations and factories, discussions on the subject:

> …are associated with the use of cybertechnologies to allow people separated by time and distance to work together cohesively. The concept of virtual organisation is therefore encapsulated in a desire to use information technology to enable a relaxation of the traditional physical constraints upon organisational formation and adaptation.

A focus on virtual working as heightened flexibility may even combine all three of the above: reducing bureaucratic, temporal and spatial barriers, and creating more dynamic enterprises that seek to go beyond established business models. In relying on cybertechnologies to do this, such ideas may also challenge our more 'reified', concrete sense of what organisations are.

Virtual working as disembodiment

In more reflexive accounts of virtual working, discussions often address the matter of their common adjective – in other words, what does it *mean* to be virtual? For many, the answer is that the entities and organisations involved are defined by the *absence* of the human components (colleagues, customers), as well as the non-human elements (buildings, offices). As Birchall and Lyons (1995: 18) put it, while such arrangements lack 'form', they are still capable of having 'effect', with the ability to have effects relying heavily on the use of IT. The virtual organisation is thus discussed as a counterpoint to images embodied in offices and factories, replete with regiments of workers. Morgan (1993: 5) captures this contrast well:

> Organisations used to be places. They used to be things…But, as information technology catapults us into the reality of an Einsteinian world where old structures and forms of organisation dissolve and at times become almost invisible, the old approach no longer works. Through the use of telephone, fax, electronic mail, computers, video, and other information technology, *people and their organisations are becoming disembodied.* They can act as if they are completely connected while remaining far apart. They can have an instantaneous global presence. They can transcend barriers of time and space, continually creating and re-creating themselves through changing networks of interconnection based on 'real time' communication…the reality of our Einsteinian world is that, often, organisations don't have to be organisations any more! (Emphasis added.)

For Barnatt (1995), too, disembodiment is one of the defining characteristics of virtual organisation. These include, he suggests: a reliance for their functioning and survival on the medium of cyberspace; *no identifiable physical form*, with only transient patterns of employee–employer connectivity; and boundaries defined and limited only by the availability of information technology (pp. 82–83, emphasis added).

This throws down a challenge to affirm what we take organisations to be if they 'don't have to be organisations any more'. For now, let us turn to the final point raised by Barnatt, and the issue of 'boundary-erosion' in virtual working.

Virtual working as boundary-erosion

As we have already seen, there are several themes that run through discussions of virtual working. One further set of issues and perspectives is revealed by those approaches that emphasise the matter of 'boundary erosion', either within or between organisations. For example, according to Grenier and Metes (1995: 5), virtual models of business occur where:

> …a lead organisation creates alliances with a set of other groups, both internal and external, that possess the best-in-the-world competencies…Such an alliance is 'virtual' in that it is really not one homogeneous organisation, but a hybrid of groups and individuals…whose purpose is not longevity, but bringing a specific, highest quality product or service to market as quickly as possible…as soon as the mission is accomplished, the alliance breaks up, and the organisations involved look for new teaming possibilities.

A similar stance is adopted by Davidow and Malone (1992: 5–6), who say of the virtual corporation that:

> To the outside observer, it will appear almost edgeless, with permeable and continuously changing interfaces between company, supplier, and customers. From inside the firm the view will be no less amorphous, with traditional offices, departments, and operating divisions constantly reforming according to need. Job descriptions will regularly shift, as will lines of authority – even the very definition of employee will change, as some customers and suppliers begin to spend more time in the company than will some of the firm's own workers.

The authors note that even in manufacturing, a 'blurring of functions' is increasingly needed to bring products to market. This, it is argued, will lead to a whole new meaning for 'organisation'. For example, it is suggested that a manufacturing company will no longer be an isolated facility of production, but rather a node in the complex network of suppliers, customers, engineering and other functions (1992: 6). (This reflects several of the dynamics found in inter-firm networking for product development, as developed by Harris *et al.*, Chapter 3 this volume).

For another set of authors (Hedberg *et al.* 1997), the blurring of boundaries demands a new way of looking at organisations – the 'imaginary organisation'. This involves (pp. 13–14):

> …a perspective revealing new enterprises which can utilise imagination, information technology, alliances, and other networks to organise and sustain a boundary-transcending activity; here the relevant organisation is predominantly imaginary.

Hedberg *et al.* give as an example the case of the Swedish men' clothes company, GANT. Behind the name GANT, they point out, is a company whose main job is to find designers, track trends, contract production, build a partner network, and engage in advertising and promotion. This arrangement relies heavily on the use of IT systems, which enables the business to manage and transmit data about customers, shipments and sales across space (1997: 6).

Given forms of IT, like the Internet/Web – and the access consumers have to information resources – the issue of boundary erosion also has consequences so far as *consumers* are concerned. This is not simply a matter of *how* businesses and their customers may interact, but may also reshape the *nature of* business-to-customer relations. For instance, Hagel and Armstrong (1997) point out that many companies have now gone beyond merely using the Web to provide electronic purchasing or product information; they also offer customers the opportunity to interact *with each other*. This, they say, allows businesses to build new and deeper relationships with their customers. Hagel and Armstrong refer to such arrangements as 'virtual communities'. In organising these communities to meet both social and commercial needs, the authors point to the new directions many businesses are seeking to go to embrace the new technologies. In addition, though, they illustrate the new mindsets needed, and again question the very divide between an organisation and its 'environment' (this time so far as *customers* are concerned). (This also illustrates the way the technologies may act as interfaces between 'endo' and 'exo' worlds, as described by Morath and Schmidt in Chapter 12, this volume).

In developing the link between businesses and their customers, let us now turn to the final perspective on virtual working and look at the debate on 'electronic commerce'.

Virtual working as electronic commerce

In highlighting the growing use of IT to blur the boundaries between organisations, partners, customers and suppliers, a whole new approach to business and commercial relations may be implied. Where new forms of financial transactions and credit transfers are included, such a system is commonly referred to as 'electronic commerce'. In this sense, electronic commerce is yet another perspective linked in with virtual working debates. According to Kalakota and Whinston, for instance, there are three types of electronic commerce (EC). The first two of these, they say, involve IT-supported 'inter-organisational' and 'intra-organisational' relations and transactions, and reflect many of the ideas set out above (in discussions of heightened flexibility and boundary erosion). The third type of electronic commerce embraces the issue of 'consumer-to-business' commerce (see Kalakota and Whinston 1997: 18–21). This is the terrain covered by discussions of 'online' or 'Web shopping', and has been a topic of popular interest for several years now (Cronin 1995, 1996; McEachern and O'Keefe 1998). One cited advantage of such developments is the reduced 'frictions', or transaction costs, that IT interactions provide for (cf. Gates 1995). In online business practice, say Kalakota and Whinston, the inefficiencies of conventional market structures and organisational designs can be overcome by a more effective combination of new technologies, business processes and customer interactions (1997: 5). In the 'information age', the authors argue, only by embracing such business models will organisations be able to succeed.

Virtual working: drawing out the themes

From the above, we can see that an airtight definition of virtual work or virtual organisation is likely to prove elusive. There are many interlinked perspectives, concepts and images. In most cases they address the same sort of real-world phenomena, although the boundaries of analysis may be drawn slightly differently in each case. Let us now clarify the key themes involved in these perspectives. There are nine main ones:

- the collapse of hierarchy and an erosion of boundaries, both within and between companies;
- a concentration on 'information processing', in which teams and individuals, using IT, create and manipulate information-based, 'virtual' products;
- the use of networked IT to empower consumers, providing new ways of interacting with businesses and greater access to information about their products;
- a movement away from employment relations, towards more arm's-length, contractual relationships with workers;
- transient, project-based work systems, involving networks of co-workers, suppliers and associated companies;
- flexibility in time and space, with interactions mediated by cyberspace;
- reduced use of 'centres', buildings and offices;
- a sense of disembodiment, with imagery emphasising a lack of physicality and corporeality;
- an emphasis on continuous innovation and learning, and a capacity rapidly to reinvent business models.

The themes and perspectives involved here reveal important dynamics that demand new ways of thinking about management and organisations. In order to have this debate, however, we need to identify areas of analysis and discussion.

More specifically, we can discuss the dynamics involved either by looking at different 'levels', or by different sets of 'issues'. In this book we will do both.

Levels and issues of analysis in the book

In Part I we will look at virtual working at the inter- and intra-organisational level. This includes organisational alliances, as well as cross-functional networks. In Chapter 2 by Alistair Campbell, for instance, the emphasis is placed on the emergence of 'Web enterprises' and the way organisations work together, with IT support, to pursue a common market opportunity. In Chapter 3 by Lisa Harris, Anne-Marie Coles, Keith Dickson and Ian McLoughlin, the discussion centres on collaborative networks (both internal and external) that support the process of product innovation. In both of these cases, the working practices may be manifested by the new types of *team working*, where groups work together, perhaps across space and time, by making use of IT support. It is the development of 'virtual teams' that is thus discussed in Chapter 4 by Joe Nandhakumar.

In Part II the experiences of *individuals* are the focus of attention. Teleworkers and other flexible workers, for example, in their dealings with colleagues and supervisors, face a number of problems and issues. In Chapter 5, by Kiran Mirchandani, the need to build relationships with onsite workers, build trust with supervisors and illustrate the cost–benefit of teleworking schemes are central items of concern. The issue of teleworkers' identity, and how it differs between skilled 'knowledge workers' and lower skilled 'operatives', is addressed in Chapter 6 by Sean Galpin and David Sims. The relation between the different levels of analysis and the 'forms' of virtual working these may take is illustrated in Table 1.1.

In Parts III and IV we move from levels of analysis to two sets of 'issues' that cut across these levels. Part III involves the problems of *managing* and *controlling* the forms of work involved. In Chapter 7, by Astrid Depickere, this is discussed in terms of the need for organisations to manage teleworkers by 'commitment' rather than bureaucratic surveillance and control. Reima Suomi and Juhanni Pekkola in Chapter 8 raise the issue of management rationalities in adopting teleworking, pointing to the cultural factors that may act against its promotion in organisations. Finally in this part, Louise Adami, in Chapter 9, points to the requirement for control structures that provide the autonomy needed to get certain types of work (in her research, journalism) done.

Part IV, the final part of the book, deals with *learning* and *innovation* issues. The

Table 1.1 Levels of analysis and forms of virtual working

Level of analysis	Form of virtual working
Inter-organisational	Inter-firm collaborations and alliances
Intra-organisational	Cross functional networks and virtual teams
Individual	Teleworkers, homeworkers and mobile workers

chapters in this part describe how, in moving towards and adopting virtual working, new forms of behaviour, knowledge management and organisational learning are required. In Chapter 10, Charlotte Björkegren and Birger Rapp address the need for a better understand of learning and knowledge issues in flexible organisations – particularly where these are characterised by dispersed project groups. In Chapter 11, by Ian McLoughlin and Paul Jackson, the link is made between learning and virtual innovations. Finally, Chapter 12 by Frank Morath and Artur Schmidt points to the need for completely new ways of understanding how new technologies link work communities to processes of learning and knowledge creation. The book's conclusion then attempts to draw together the different arguments and issues outlined in the preceding chapters.

But let us turn now to the first level of analysis, and look at the inter- and intra-organisational issues involved in virtual working.

Note

1 For instance, in World War I it was some time before the possibilities of using aeroplanes for bombing was recognised; initially, this new aviation technology was simply used for reconnaissance, thereby 'substituting' for hot air balloons.

Bibliography

Attewell, P. (1996) 'Technology diffusion and organisational learning', in Moingeon, B. and Edmunson, A. (eds) *Organisational Learning and Competitive Advantage*, London: Sage.

Badham, R., Couchman, P. and McLoughlin, I.P. (1997) 'Implementing vulnerable socio-technical change projects', in McLoughlin, I.P. and Harris, M. (eds) *Innovation, Organisational Change and Technology*, London: ITB Press.

Barnatt, C. (1995) *Cyberbusiness: Mindsets for a Wired Age*, Chichester: Wiley.

Birchall, D. and Lyons, L. (1995) *Creating Tomorrow's Organisation*, London: FT/Pitman.

Canon Corporation Europe (1995) *Work Where You Want* booklet.

Castells, M. (1996) *The Rise of Network Society*, Oxford: Blackwell.

Checkland, P.B. and Holwell, S. (1998)*Information, Systems and Information Systems*, Chichester: Wiley.

Cronin, M.J. (1995) *Doing More Business on the Internet*, 2nd edition, London: International Thompson.

Cronin, M.J. (ed.) (1996) *The Internet Strategy Handbook*, Cambridge, MA: Harvard Business School Press.

Davidow, W.H. and Malone, M.S. (1992) *The Virtual Corporation*, London: HarperBusiness.

Gates, B. (1995) *The Road Ahead*, London: Viking-Penguin.

Grenier, R. and Metes, G. (1995) *Going Virtual*, New York: Prentice-Hall.

Grint, K. and Woolgar, S. (1995) 'On some failures of nerve in constructivist and feminist analyses of technology', in Grint, K. and Gill, R. (eds) *The Gender-Technology Relation: Contemporary Theory and Research*, London: Taylor & Francis.

Hagel, J. and Armstrong, A.G. (1997) *Net Gain. Expanding Markets through Virtual Communities*, Boston: Harvard.

Hale, R. and Whitlam, P. (1997) *Towards the Virtual Organisation*, London: McGraw-Hill.

Hammer, M. and Champy, J. (1993) *Re-engineering the Corporation*, New York: Harper-Collins.

Harris, M. (1998) 'Rethinking the virtual organisation', in Jackson, P.J. and van der Wielen, J. (eds) *Teleworking: International Perspectives*, London: Routledge.

Hastings, C. (1993) *The New Organization: Growing the Culture of Organisational Networking*, London: McGraw-Hill

Hedberg, B., Dahlgren, G., Hansson, J. and Olve, N.G. (1997) *Virtual Organisations and Beyond*, Chichester: Wiley.

Hirschheim, R.A. (1985) *Office Automation*, Chichester: Wiley.

Jackson, P.J. (1997) 'Information systems as metaphor: innovation and the 3 R's of representation', in McLoughlin, I.P. and Harris, M. (eds) *Innovation, Organisational Change and Technology*, London: Thompson International.

Jackson, P.J. and Van der Wielen, J.M. (eds) (1998) *Teleworking: International Perspectives*, London: Routledge.

Kalakota, R. and Whinston, A.B. (1997) *Electronic Commerce: A Manager's Guide*, Reading, MA: Addison Wesley.

Lipnack, J. and Stamps, J. (1997) *Virtual Teams*, New York: Wiley.

McEachern, T. and O'Keefe, B. (1998) *Re-wiring Business: Uniting Management and the Web*, New York: Wiley.

McGrath, P. and Houlihan, M. (1998) 'Conceptualising telework: modern or post modern?', in Jackson, P.J. and van der Wielen, J.M. (eds) *Teleworking: International Perspectives*, London: Routledge.

McLoughlin, I.P. and Clark, J. (1994) *Technological Change at Work*, 2nd edition, Buckingham: Open University Press.

McLoughlin, I.P and Harris, M. (eds) (1997) *Innovation, Organisational Change and Technology*, London:Thompson International.

McLoughlin, I.P. (1999) *Creative Technological Change: Shaping Technology and Organisation*, London: Routledge.

Morgan, G. (1993) *Imaginization*, London: Sage.

Morgan, G. (1997) *Images of Organisation*, 2nd edition, London: Sage.

Nilles, J.M. (1998) *Managing Teleworking*, New York: Wiley.

Nonaka, I. and Takeuchi, H. (1995) *The Knowledge-Creating Company*, New York: Oxford University Press.

Pollert, A. (1991) (ed.) *A Farewell to Flexibility?*, Oxford: Blackwell.

Stymne, B., Carlsson, T. and Hagglund, P.B. (1996) 'Organisational innovation: a cognitive perspective', presented at the *Fourth International Workshop on Managerial and Organisational Cognition*, Stockholm, 28–30 August.

Tapscott, D. (1995) *The Digital Economy*, New York: McGraw-Hill.

Zuboff, S. (1988) *In the Age of the Smart Machine*, Cambridge, MA: Harvard University Press.

Part I

The inter- and intra-organisational level

In this part of the book we will look at virtual working issues displayed at the inter- and intra-organisational level of analysis. As we saw in the previous chapter, many conceptions of the virtual organisation take the blurring of boundaries between organisations and functions as a defining feature. The dynamics involved at this level are brought out by the following three chapters.

In Chapter 2, by Alistair Campbell, the focus of attention is placed on inter-organisational relations, with the issues of learning and knowledge management centre-stage. Campbell develops the notion of the Web enterprise – a form of virtual organisation where a number of partners come together around a core technology or service. Campbell distinguishes Web enterprises from three other main types of networked organisation: stable networks, as found in industries that are relatively unaffected by rapid technological change; dynamic networks, where environmental change is rapid; and internal networks, as found in relatively stable environments where a high need for knowledge transfer between participants exists.

For Campbell, Web enterprises not only depend on rapid learning and knowledge sharing between partners, they also occur in environments that are subject to uncertainty and change. The main rationale for such organisations is the creation of a new enterprise, whereby the value-added process is generated through ongoing collaboration and learning across the network. Here, partners need to recognise their mutual dependence and begin to share a common vision and strategy. The challenge in doing this is, says Campbell, to ensure that learning takes place, and that trust exists to permit knowledge sharing.

Campbell introduces the notion of 'communities of practice' to show how this might be done. Such communities, he notes, work and learn together in informal ways, and are bound together by similar beliefs and values. Such a community is thus a precondition for effective knowledge sharing. Moreover, it is only when members of the Web are engaged in mutual learning can a Web enterprise be said to exist.

Campbell concludes that while the new communications technologies provide the platform for such virtual organisations to develop, the need to create a dynamic sense of mutual learning and reciprocity between members of the Web is uppermost. This is possible, he notes, where communities of practice are formed.

In Chapter 3, by Lisa Harris, Anne-Marie Coles, Keith Dickson and Ian McLoughlin, the focus of attention is the issues involved in building collaborative networks for new product development. These authors point out that because product innovations rely on the ability to acquire and synthesise diverse forms of knowledge, it is often essential to work across traditional functional and organisational boundaries. This is particularly so where the knowledge is technically complex and where development lead times need to be kept short.

For these authors, the success of product innovations is significantly determined by the process of building and sustaining the requisite collaborative network. They place particular emphasis on the ability of organisations to enrol support, win resources and create and sustain high trust relationships among partners. Far from being a strictly 'technical' process, this demands both political and relationship-building skills. Strategies that seek to exploit potential network synergies are, say the authors, dependent to a large extent on the sense of trustworthiness, openness and fairness that network builders are able to engender. This may also include an ability to create a sense of shared goals and culture, as well as a commitment to the collaboration by all parties.

Harris *et al.* point out that while some firms may have explicit network strategies, much networking goes on in an informal way. In either case, investment in a relationship is essential if problems and conflicts between members are to be managed. Indeed, the authors note that the time and resources invested in forming collaborative networks, and building a working relationship, may mean that the pay-offs come not from initial product innovations but from those that take place in the more medium term.

In their discussions of the networking process Harris *et al.* also illustrate how new product development teams are often formed on the basis of requisite expertise rather than the location of their members. In these cases, extensive use is made of information technologies to support knowledge sharing across space. In these cases, too, the ability of teams to develop mutual trust and understanding is underlined. While this may rely initially on face-to-face contact between members, the authors point out that the evidence suggests that the need for this declines over time, once trust has been established.

Harris *et al.* warn us that despite the success of inter-organisational networking, particularly in spreading risks and managing uncertainty, such developments also leave organisations prone to new risks and uncertainties. For this reason they warn against seeing networking as any kind of 'quick fix'. Organisations, they conclude, need to recognise the political sophistication required for building and managing successful networks, as well as the interpersonal skills by which open and trusting relationships can be created.

In Chapter 4, by Joe Nandhakumar, collaborations across time and space are the focus of discussion. Nandhakumar notes that with the growth in global organisations, and the emergence of a range of information technologies, the need to share knowledge and expertise increasingly means that team working takes place despite members being separated in time and space.

The author draws upon research conducted with a multinational company to demonstrate the problems involved in working in such virtual teams. Here, one of the main technologies used to support team working was desktop video conferencing. Although certain communications barriers were reduced thanks to this system, Nandhakumar finds that a number of social and hierarchical constraints were still prevalent and placed particular limits on the interactions between hierarchical levels using the system.

Nandhakumar points to the importance of trust between team members as an antecedent to open and effective team collaborations. In so doing, he distinguishes between two sources of trust: the first, based on 'abstract structures', such as participants' knowledge about political legitimacy and systems of professional knowledge, and the second developed through personal relationships that were highly dependent on face-to-face encounters. In the latter, for example, an opportunity for socialisation in informal 'backstage' settings was seen as important for building trusting relationships and a sense of positive expectation.

Nandhakumar shows, however, that despite the benefits promised by the new technologies, many people feel anxious about being separated from other team members. In addition, despite efforts to engender trusting relationships, many team members did not feel sufficiently trusting and confident towards other members to make extensive use of the video-conferencing technology. He concludes, therefore, that personalised trust relationships are essential for continuous team working. Whereas for temporary team working, the abstract structures of the organisation may be sufficient to deal with specific problems, for more enduring arrangements, particularly where greater openness and knowledge sharing are required, opportunities for active social interactions need to be created.

2 Knowledge management in the Web enterprise

Exploiting communities of practice

Alistair Campbell

Introduction

The literature has identified a number of different forms of virtual organisation. The most radical of these forms is the Enterprise Web (Lorenzoni and Baden-Fuller 1995; Hagel 1996), which describes where a number of partners come together around a core technology or competence, to deliver new products or services into the marketplace. One of the most challenging aspects of the Enterprise Web is the issue of knowledge management and information transfer among the partners. The success of any Web enterprise will only come through optimising the learning processes of the Web to ensure the next generation of products and services. Although it is accepted that organisational Webs must create systemic learning systems to ensure innovation and future growth, our understanding of how this will be achieved is at present unclear (Drucker 1992; Amidon Rogers 1996). As a means of resolving this issue, some commentators are proposing that Enterprise Webs will in effect be *communities of practice* (Lave and Wenger 1991). Communities of practice describe social learning, where groups are bound together by similar values and beliefs to resolve a common set of problems. In a situation where an inherent tension is created between loyalty to the Web and the parent organisation, communities of practice may offer some insight into the learning processes and knowledge management of distributed enterprises. This chapter further explores the concept of Enterprise Webs, and the potential of communities of practice to resolve the problem of knowledge management across a virtual network.

Forms of network organisation

The explosive growth of the Internet in the early 1990s led to many commentators considering its impact on business structures, services, processes and management. It was argued that online electronic commerce heralded a new environment with a completely different set of business rules, which in fact reversed many long-standing business conventions (Rayport and Sviokla 1994). The virtual organisation was proposed as a radically different form of business enterprise that would take advantage of the Internet and the associated advances in computing and information technologies (Davidow and Malone 1992). The essence of the virtual organisation was a form of enterprise that focused on a small number of internal value-adding competencies or processes, supplemented by an extensive number of external partners to jointly bring forward a service to the marketplace. Although the concept of the virtual organisation sounded exciting and made a lot of business sense, it was apparent on further investigation that the main elements of the virtual organisation model were activities that many successful business organisations had been practising for years (Campbell 1996a). Similarly, the theoretical basis of the virtual organisation was not particularly novel, but simply an extension of ongoing research into network organisations, business strategy and management practices. A paper presented at the first Telework workshop, at Brunel University in 1996, described the different forms of virtual organisation identified in the literature (Campbell 1996b). These forms of virtual organisation are summarised in Table 2.1.

Stable networks exist in mature industries that are less affected by rapid technological change, such as car manufacturing and food retailing. Relationships in these networks are long term, contract based and driven primarily by cost factors. Dynamic networks operate in sectors such as computer manufacturing and fashion retailing, which are affected by a high degree of environmental change. Dynamic networks demonstrate the same form of outsourcing as stable networks, however the relationships are more flexible and responsive due to the turbulence of the commercial environment. Internal networks are similar to stable networks in that they operate in an environment that is less prone to change. The difference, however, is that there is a high need for knowledge transfer between the various elements of the network to leverage and fully

Table 2.1 Forms of virtual organisation

Form	Role	Relationships	Rationale
Internal	Independent business units responding to customer needs	Market and customer driven	Internal synergies
Stable	Outsourcing of non-core processes to provide limited flexibility	Static and contract driven	Lower cost
Dynamic	Extensive external relationships based on immediate opportunities	Short term and opportunistic	Market flexibility
Web	Community of partners that jointly delivers a service to the marketplace	Knowledge based	New enterprise

exploit the internal resources. Many successful multinational corporations (MNCs) and global management consultancies are examples of internal networks. The internal, stable and dynamic structures are based on the forms of network organisation defined by Charles Snow and Raymond Miles. Snow and Miles recognise that these three forms of virtual organisation are essentially transformations of existing business practices, in an effort to making existing business organisations more competitive in a turbulent and discontinuous environment (Snow *et al.* 1992).

The Web enterprise (Lorenzoni and Baden-Fuller 1995; Hagel 1996) is the final form of virtual organisation. The Web is probably closest to the early vision of the virtual organisation as a new form of business enterprise. The Web describes where a number of partners come together around a core technology or competence, to deliver new products or services into the marketplace. It is influenced by operating in an environment with a high degree of change, and by the need to transfer knowledge throughout its network relationships. There are three principal elements that distinguish the Web enterprise as being different from other forms of network organisation.

1   *Mutual strategy.* The resources and competencies of each partner in the Web are critical to the success of the whole enterprise. Web enterprises create strategy and structure at the same time, resulting in the network of relations within the Web becoming a guide of, and for, strategic action (Lorenzoni and Baden-Fuller 1995; Barley *et al.* 1992). Web strategies further contradict conventional strategic thinking which dominates the other forms of network organisation. Members of enterprise Webs accept that the Web strategy comes before the firm's own strategy. If the company places its own interests first before that of the Web, the company may benefit in the short term. The Web however may be weakened, which will ultimately affect the company in the long term. Conversely, if the company places its immediate interests as secondary to the Web, then it may lose in the short term, but ultimately will benefit as the Web prospers (Hagel 1996).

2   *Knowledge exchange.* Webs are ultimately shaped by their information flows, as information is distributed more widely and more intensely than in conventional business structures (Hagel 1996). By recognising the mutual interdependence in the network, organisations are willing to share information, and cooperate fully with each other to maintain their relative position (Miles and Snow 1992; Hagel 1996). Knowledge exchange, and jointly developing internal competencies through external linkages, suggests that these forms of company networks may offer a new form of industrial order (Powell and Brantley 1992).

3   *New enterprise.* The whole rationale behind the Web is to innovate and create new forms of enterprise. In some technological sectors, enterprise Webs are being recognised as a necessity. Technological innovation almost certainly requires some form of network, as few companies possess all the necessary knowledge and resources to develop and exploit the innovation (Powell and

Brantley 1992; Shan 1990; Noren *et al.* 1995). With competencies spanning multiple organisations, the external network becomes the primary focus. Any advantage from the innovation benefits the network (or Web), rather than just individual firms (Powell and Brantley 1992; Fairtlough 1994).

There are limitations on the extent to which this chapter can cover all the issues raised, therefore the remainder of the chapter will only address the issue of knowledge management within the extended Web enterprise. It could be argued that of the three elements listed, knowledge management will be the most critical, and the most difficult to achieve for successful Web enterprise. Returning to the original justification for the creation of virtual forms of business, it was argued that two of the key factors affecting business organisations at the end of the twentieth century were the degree of environmental change affecting business organisations (Handy 1989; Scott Morton 1991; Kanter 1992; Peters 1992) and the need for effective learning processes within organisations (Senge 1990; Drucker 1992; Argyris 1993; Garvin 1993). To illustrate the importance of knowledge management for the Web enterprise, the four forms of virtual organisation identified earlier can be mapped against these two dynamics; the degree of environmental change and the requirement for learning. This is shown in Figure 2.1.

Stable and dynamic networks are in effect the same organisational model based on the strategic outsourcing of non-core activities. In both cases, the host organisation can focus on what it does best, while at the same time reducing costs and increasing competitiveness. The only difference between the two is the rate of change in the commercial environment that might demand more flexible and responsive relationships. In neither case is there a great demand for knowledge transfer between the host organisation and the external partners. In the dynamic form of network there may be some limited exchange of knowledge; however, all the members of the network are aware of the contractual nature of their relationships. Although the potential for mutual benefit exists if the business partnership prospers, the basis of stable and dynamic networks is what is in the best interests of the host organisation, rather than all the partners who are involved in the enterprise.

The sharing and exchange of knowledge is a critical element of internal and Web enterprises, however there are different knowledge management factors affecting the two forms of organisation. Many companies have made major investments in new or upgraded IS and applications, only to find that people still do not want to collaborate to share and develop new knowledge. Interconnectivity begins with people who want to connect, thereafter tools and technology can make the connection. The key to this transition is when people have compelling reasons for finding others with knowledge to share, who in turn have compelling reasons to share their knowledge when asked (Manville and Foote 1996b). This transition will happen where companies secure strong individual commitment to the corporate vision and objectives, so that all personal energies and ambitions are put to the use of the corporate goal (Bartlett and Ghoshal 1990).

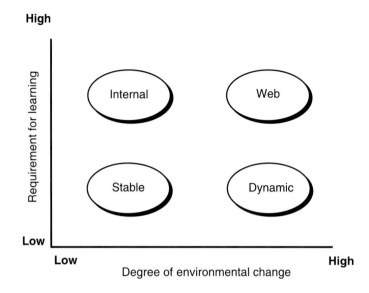

Figure 2.1 The degree of organisational learning in the virtual organisation

In addition to internal networks being easier to create and manage, the dynamics behind transaction cost theory may also encourage managers to internalise their activities. Transaction cost theory argues that the cost of market governance increases when the terms of exchange are surrounded by uncertainty. This uncertainty arises when the variables affecting the execution of the agreement are complex and difficult for trading partners to understand, predict or articulate. The hazards of entering repeatedly into contractual agreements that involve uncertainty and transaction specific assets, provide an incentive for vertical integration. Firms must assess the trade-off between the transaction costs of using the market and the organisational cost of using internal hierarchies (Williamson 1975).

The result has been that much that we know about organisational learning has focused on the individual learner and the single organisation (Senge 1990; Drucker 1992; Argyris 1993; Garvin 1993). The Web enterprise throws up a new series of challenges to the concept of the learning organisation in its broadest sense. How is it possible for different organisations with different attitudes and perspectives to come together to share and exchange knowledge? How does the process start? How is it managed? What form of control is there to ensure that no one member abuses the knowledge that is freely given by another partner? The second part of the chapter will look at some of these issues and examine whether the concept of *communities of practice* offers some insight to these difficult questions.

Knowledge management in the Web enterprise

In a business economy of collapsing product development times and life cycles, successful business organisations must be skilled at devolved decision making, high-speed capital and technology transfer, accessing the most cost-effective labour and strategically managing their supply chains. In the new environment, competitive advantage will no longer arise from ownership of fixed physical assets, but in terms of ownership of, or access to knowledge-intensive, high value-added, technology-driven systems (Amidon Rogers 1996). The external relationships in Web enterprises are more visible and explicit in their nature, in that the level of performance that is expected from each partner can be measured and compensated for. The underlying dynamic of these 'network' structures is *voluntarism*, where partners are free to withdraw from relationships which they believe are unfair. Unless this is present, the openness and explicitness of the structure is compromised. It could be argued that voluntarism is the true test of the structure, as any action that reduces it within a network, poses an overall threat to the future success of the network (Miles and Snow 1992). By recognising the mutual interdependence in the Web network, organisations are willing to share information, and cooperate fully with each other to maintain their relative position in the network (Hagel 1996). Jarvenpaa and Ives (1994) describe a number of assumptions inherent in this proposition. First, it is assumed that if information is available and in the right format to be used, it will be shared and exchanged within the network, and not controlled by one of the partners. It is also assumed that workers will know how to use that information, and that subsequent actions are retained in the organisational memory of the network. As Davenport (1994) points out, the presence of a technological infrastructure in itself, will not change an organisation's existing behaviour, attitude and action towards information sharing. New technology may only reinforce those attitudes that already exist. It is wrong to assume that, providing the technology to share and exchange information is present, information sharing behaviour will follow automatically. As information becomes the key organisational currency, it becomes too valuable to be simply given away.

Davenport *et al.* (1992) describe five models of information politics and suggest that companies choose a preferred information model, and then move continually towards it, irrespective how long it takes. They argue that a business culture dominated by widespread participation and empowered members, should adopt a 'federal' information model which promotes a consensus and negotiation on the key information and reporting requirements of the organisation. Jarvenpaa and Ives (1994) point out that gaining consensus across a distributed enterprise could be a time-consuming process, which restricts the very agility that the enterprise intended in the first place. Davenport *et al.* admit this possibility and propose that those organisations which decide that information federalism is not a suitable option should consider a 'benevolent monarchy' as a model that is as effective and possibly easier to implement. In the 'benevolent monarchy', the lead partner defines information categories and reporting structures, and then makes them available to the other partners. The overall aim is to facilitate information flows throughout the enterprise, and that the information model should match the enterprise culture. Open information flows will only happen through open organisational cultures (Davenport *et al.* 1992). The lead firms in Enterprise Webs aggressively source in new ideas. Lorenzoni and Baden-Fuller term this *Borrow–Develop–Lend*. The original concept is brought in by the lead partner, where it is then developed by the other Web partners who add varying degrees of value before it is relaunched as a new product or service (Lorenzoni and Baden-Fuller 1995).

Establishing relationships with companies who may be direct competitors in other areas, may mean providing access to each other's core value-adding capabilities. It is obvious that trust between the partners is a key determinant of success and that relationships should be seen as a 'win–win' situation, rather than some form of zero-sum game (Cravens *et al.* 1994; Rai *et al.* 1996). Within Silicon Valley, intense competition helps to spur the technological innovation within the region. Lawsuits and arguments over intellectual property rights are relatively common, with some competitive rivalries becoming highly personalised. Despite these intense pressures, the overall sense of network commitment to technological excellence and development unifies the membership (Saxenian 1990). The lead firm or firms in a Web have a pivotal role in developing a dynamic sense of trust and reciprocity throughout the Web (Lorenzoni and Baden-Fuller 1995). In a Web, behaviour is not limited to the restrictions of a formal contract. The actions of Web partners are structured for the future unknown, with each promising to work positively to solve challenges and problems as they arise. The focus in overcoming these difficulties is in providing a timely solution for the customer. Any discussions about liabilities and uncertainties will be resolved after the customer has been satisfied. If one party extends its commitment to the Web to resolve any short-term problem, this will be remembered by the others and reciprocated at a later date (Lorenzoni and Baden-Fuller 1995). One of the ways in which trust is developed throughout the network is to ensure that the partners receive suitable rewards for their efforts. In some instances, this may result in the partners receiving more of the profits of the enterprise than the lead organisation. This acceptance of others receiving a larger share of the profits is not altruism on behalf of the lead firm; it is recognition that the stronger the Web becomes, then the stronger the lead firm's own position will be in the long term (Lorenzoni and Baden-Fuller 1995).

Communities of practice

There are clearly significant knowledge management issues in the Web enterprise. Organisational learning in the distributed enterprise is threatened through difficulties in building an organisational memory of previous actions, effectively transferring knowledge throughout the enterprise, and problems in appreciating synergistic opportunities when they arise. Conflicts between individual and personal objectives can also harm the intellectual capital retained by the organisation (Jarvenpaa and Ives 1994; Handy 1995). Knowledge management is clearly one of the greatest challenges affecting the Web enterprise, and will demand an uncommon level of professionalism and rigour in management decision making (Jarvenpaa and Ives 1994).

Knowledge management posits that the core competencies of the organisation represent the collective knowledge, based on the skills and experience of people who do the work. The power of these competencies is harnessed by creating informal networks of people who do the same or similar kinds of work, often in different or geographically dispersed business units. These informal networks have been called *communities of practice* and are defined by Lave and Wenger (1991) as a:

> Set of relations among persons, activity, and world, over time and in relation with other tangential and overlapping communities of practice. A community of practice is an intrinsic condition for the existence of knowledge, not least because it provides the interpretive support necessary for making sense of its heritage.

Brook Manville and Nathaniel Foote (1996a) of McKinsey & Company define a community of practice more simply as

> A group of professionals, informally bound to one another through exposure to a common class of problems, common pursuit of solutions, and thereby themselves embodying a store of knowledge.

Communities of practice form intellectual communities in areas that are central to competitive advantage. A vibrant learning community gives an organisation an ownership stake in its marketplace (Manville and Foote 1996a). The notion of *practice* is a critical element within communities of practice. The members of the community may be drawn together through some common set of values or beliefs, or joint mission. If, however, nothing results from the community, then the whole process is wasted. The practice element is the result of the community, whereby learning is only achieved through actually practising one's craft. The individual learner (or organisation) does not gain a discrete body of abstract knowledge, to be applied later in different contexts. The learner acquires the skill to perform by actually engaging in the process, under the attenuated conditions of legitimate peripheral participation (Lave and Wenger 1991). Legitimate peripheral participation sees learning as a process within a framework of participation, rather than individual minds. The learner becomes an insider, learning to function within a community. The central issue in learning is *becoming* a practitioner, rather than learning *about* practice (Brown and Duguid 1991). The different perspectives of the community members mediate the process of learning, and it is the community, or at least those participating in the learning context, who learn under this definition. Legitimate peripheral participation argues that learning is not merely a condition for membership of the community, but is itself part of an evolving form of that membership (Lave and Wenger 1991).

Peripherality is an important concept in the learning process within communities. It does not mean being on the 'outside' or 'disconnected' from the practice of interest. It is a dynamic term that suggests an opening or a way of gaining access to sources, through increasing involvement. Learners need legitimate access to the periphery of communication (electronic mail, informal meetings, stories, etc.) which gives them not just information, but also the manner and technique of the community. The periphery becomes not only an important site of learning, but also a place where innovation occurs (Brown and Duguid 1991; Lave and Wenger 1991).

The learning curriculum of the community is that which may be learned by newcomers who have legitimate peripheral access, and this learning activity appears to have a characteristic pattern. A learning curriculum consists of situated opportunities for the improvisational development of new practice. The learning curriculum differs from a teaching curriculum through seeing learning resources, in everyday practice, from the perspective of learners. A teaching curriculum, on the other hand, is developed to instruct newcomers to the community, not all members. Learners, as peripheral participants, develop a perspective of the purpose of the whole enterprise and what there is to be learned. The learning process and the curriculum are not specified as a set of canonical practices; it is an improvised process whereby the learning and the curriculum unfold in opportunities for engagement in practice (Lave and Wenger 1991). Communities of practice recognise that learning, transformation and change are elements of the same system, and that managing the status quo is as complex as managing change. Change is an important attribute of any community, as communities of practice are necessarily engaged in the process of generating their own future (Lave and Wenger 1991).

The theory behind communities of practice was initially developed to help understand the process of individual learning. There are, however, elements of the theory that appear pertinent to the issue of knowledge management within Web enterprises. Communities of practice exist solely so that all members of the community can *learn*. The Web form of enterprise exists for precisely the same reason. If the members of the Web are not engaged in mutual learning, then the Web as such does not exist. The participants are simply involved in standard commercial relationships that exist in all forms of inter-enterprise alliance. Learning in the community of practice occurs through *participation*. Members must be actively involved in the Web for learning to occur. Passive membership of a Web cannot occur. The learning process is for all members of the Web, not simply to pass on an existing body of knowledge to new members of the community. This holistic nature of learning involving all members of the community recognises the dynamic nature of the knowledge base, and the automatic need for change within and among the community members.

The active process of learning represents an ongoing part of the membership and duties within the Web. Participation in learning is also *peripheral*. This recognises that there is no natural centre or boundary to the Web. Hierarchies are eliminated. Simply being part of the Web is sufficient for the learning processes to occur. The theory also suggests that being on the periphery is a naturally desirable position. Being on the periphery of a community or a number of different communities is often where innovation occurs, and that ultimately is why the Web enterprise exists. Innovation is what produces the next generation of products and services, and wealth creation.

Conclusions

This chapter has tried to develop further our understanding of the virtual business organisation, in particular the Web enterprise and the critical role of knowledge management in this form of organisation. The internal, stable and network forms of virtual organisation, discussed earlier, arose through conventional organisational structures being reconfigured to handle the complexity of delivering services to individual customers. Business managers were pointed either in the direction of a complete absence of organisational design and 'thriving on chaos', or led towards defining a new organisational structure (Nohria and Berkley 1994). Defining concrete examples of any new organisational form are elusive and may ultimately prove counterproductive. Seeing organisational change in terms of perspectives rather than structures is far more valid in capturing the essence of the environmental change affecting companies (Nohria and Berkley 1994). The Web enterprise can therefore be seen as a series of value-adding processes and capabilities, rather than a structure of functional units. One of these capabilities is clearly the ability to create and manage a distributed knowledge base that is accessed by all the members of the enterprise. Conventional theories of organisational learning do not fully explain how learning will occur and be managed in a distributed enterprise involving numerous independent partners. A brief overview of communities of practice suggest that there is merit in further examining how this theory of individual and organisational learning can be applied to manage the process of learning in the extended Web enterprise.

Communities of practice recognise the systemic nature of commerce, where many of the real benefits are realised (Mukhopadhyay *et al.* 1995). This perspective is often ignored through focusing on the operational efficiencies of individual firms. Networks require the cooperation and commitment of all the network members, which may be complicated further by the complex business relationships that exist between some members (for example, see Harris *et al.*, Chapter 3 in this volume). The effective operation of the network is therefore affected by a number of variables including social, political and economic factors (Premkumar and Ramamurthy 1995). Judging the operation of electronic networks solely on the effectiveness by which they handle internal and external transactions, may not provide a rich enough picture.

The communication networks that link organisations will do more than simply act as a conduit for commercial transactions. They will act as the platform that allows new forms of enterprise to appear. The most successful networks will be those that exhibit inter-organisational characteristics beyond overlapping workflows, to an actual sharing of organisational missions. Communication networks will allow the different organisations to share and exchange knowledge, and to build up a collective knowledge base. Out of this knowledge base will come the forms of innovation that will set the enterprise apart from its competitors. The ultimate aim of this networked enterprise will be to deliver new forms of value to customers and clients.

Bibliography

Amidon Rogers, D.M. (1996) 'The challenge of fifth generation R&D', *Research Technology Management*, July/August: 33–41.

Argyris, C. (1993) *Knowledge for Action: A Guide to Overcoming Barriers to Organisational Change*, San Francisco: Josey-Bass.

Barley, S.R., Freeman, J. and Hybels, R.C. (1992) 'Strategic alliances in commercial biotechnology', in Nohria, N. and Eccles, R.G. (eds) *Networks and Organisations: Structure, Form and Action*, Cambridge, MA: Harvard Business School Press.

Bartlett, C.A. and Ghoshal, S. (1990) 'Matrix management: not a structure, a frame of mind', *Harvard Business Review*, July/August: 138–44.

Brown, J.S. and Duguid, S. (1991) 'Organizational learning and communities of practice: toward a unified view of working, learning and innovation', *Organization Science*, 2, 1: 40–57.

Campbell, A.M. (1996a) 'The virtual business: creating the effective business organization', *Business Change and Re-engineering*, 3, 4: 45–53.

—— (1996b) 'Creating the virtual organisation and managing the distributed workforce', *Proceedings of Workshop on the New International Perspectives on Telework*, UK: Brunel University: 79–89.

Cravens, D.W., Shipp, S.H., Cravens, K.S. (1994) 'Reforming the traditional organization: the mandate for developing networks', *Business Horizons*, 37, 4: 19–28.

Davenport, T.H. (1994) 'Saving IT's soul: human centred information management', *Harvard Business Review*, 72, 2: 119–31.

Davenport, T.H., Eccles, R.G. and Prusak, L. (1992) 'Information politics', *Sloan Management Review*, Fall: 53–65.

Davidow, W.H. and Malone, M.S. (1992) *The Virtual Corporation: Structuring and Revitalizing the Corporation for the 21st Century*, New York: HarperBusiness.

Drucker, P.F. (1992) 'The new society of organizations', *Harvard Business Review*, 70, 5: 95–104.

Fairtlough, G. (1994) 'Organizing for innovation: compartments, competencies and networks', *Long Range Planning*, 27, 1: 88–97.

Garvin, D.A. (1993) 'Building a learning organisation', *Harvard Business Review*, 71, 4: 78–91.

Hagel, J. III (1996) 'Spider versus spider', *The McKinsey Quarterly*, 1: 5–18.

Handy, C.B. (1989) *The Age of Unreason*, London: Century Hutchison.

—— (1995) 'Trust and the virtual organisation', *Harvard Business Review*, 73, 3: 40–50.

Jarvenpaa, S.L. and Ives, B. (1994) 'The global network organisation of the future: information management opportunities and challenges', *Journal of Management Information Systems*, 10, 4: 25–57.

Kanter, R.M. (1992) *When Giants Learn To Dance*, London: Routledge.

Lave, J. and Wenger, E. (1991) *Situated Learning: Legitimate Peripheral Participation*, Cambridge: Cambridge University Press.

Lorenzoni, G. and Baden-Fuller, C. (1995) 'Creating a strategic center to manage a web of partners', *California Management Review*, 37, 3: 146–63.

Manville, B. and Foote, N. (1996a) 'Harvest your worker's knowledge', *Datamation*, 42, 13: 78–82.

—— (1996b) 'Strategy as if knowledge mattered', *Fast Company*, May: 66.

Miles, R.E. and Snow, C.C. (1992) 'Causes of failure in network organizations', *California Management Review*, Summer: 53–72.

Mukhopadhyay, T., Kekre, S. and Kalathur, S. (1995) 'Business value of information technology: a study of electronic data interchange', *MIS Quarterly*, 19, 2: 137–54.

Nohria, N. and Berkley, J.D. (1994) 'An action perspective: the crux of new management', *California Management Review*, 36, 4: 70–92.

Noren, L., Norrgren, F. and Trygg, L. (1995) 'Product development in inter-organisational networks', *International Journal of Technology Management*; Special Edition on Emerging Technological Frontiers to Increasing Competitiveness: 105–18

Peters, T. (1992) *Liberation Management: Necessary Disorganisation for the Nanosecond Nineties*, London: Macmillan.

Powell, W.W. and Brantley, P. (1992) 'Competitive cooperation in biotechnology: learning through networks', in Nohria, N. and Eccles, R.G. (eds) *Networks and Organisations: Structure, Form and Action*, MA: Harvard Business School Press.

Premkumar, G. and Ramamurthy, K. (1995) 'The role of interorganizational factors on the decision mode of adoption of interorganizational systems', *Decision Sciences*, 26, 3: 303–36.

Rai, A., Borah, S. and Ramaprasad, A. (1996) 'Critical success factors for strategic alliances in the information technology industry: an empirical study', *Decision Sciences*, 27, 1: 141–55.

Rayport, J.E. and Sviokla, J.J. (1994) 'Managing in the marketspace', *Harvard Business Review*, 72, 6: 141–50.

Saxenian, A. (1990) 'Regional networks and the resurgence of Silicon Valley', *California Management Review*, 33, 10: 89–112.

Scott Morton, M.S. (ed.) (1991) *The corporation of the 1990s; Information Technology and Organisational Transformation*, Oxford: Oxford University Press.

Senge, P. (1990) *The Fifth Discipline: The Art and Practice of the Learning Organization*, New York: Doubleday.

Shan, W. (1990) 'An empirical analysis of organisational strategies by entrepreneurial high-technology firms', *Strategic Management Journal*, 11:129–39.

Snow, C.C. and Miles, R.E. and Coleman, H.J. Jr (1992) 'Managing 21st century network organizations', *Organizational Dynamics*, Winter: 5–20.

Williamson, O.E. (1975) *Markets and Hierarchies: Analysis and Antitrust Implications*, New York: Free Press.

3 Building collaborative networks

New product development across
organisational boundaries

*Lisa Harris, Anne-Marie Coles, Keith Dickson and
Ian McLoughlin*

Introduction

One set of developments that can be considered under the ambit of virtual working is the growth in *intra-* and *inter*-organisational networks. These are often found, for example, in the form of cross-functional and project-based teams whose activities increasingly transcend and cut across not only internal organisational boundaries but external ones too. There is evidence that this way of working is becoming increasingly widespread as a means of facilitating new product development, because such networking allows acquisition and synthesis of particular forms of knowledge across traditional internal and external organisational boundaries. Networking in relation to new product development is also a particularly interesting area of investigation because the innovation networks that arise – whether they are substantially mediated through electronic means or not – frequently seek to transcend spatial and temporal boundaries. In particular, such networking is frequently predicated on a desire to reduce product development lead times and integrate dispersed expertise into the development process.

This chapter draws upon data emerging from a study of four case study networks. The research forms part of a major ongoing international research project that is examining collaborative networking in three European countries (UK, Germany and Denmark) and it is data from the UK project which is referred to here. Of particular concern to the research programme is the manner in which new product development collaborations are built and sustained over time. Rationalist approaches such as that of Porter (1980) view product innovation as a relatively unproblematic and straightforward aspect of corporate behaviour. Our perspective suggests, however, that this process is a more complex, longitudinal, dynamic, messy and uncertain activity, dependent for success, *inter alia*, on a high level of political sophistication on the part of organisational actors seeking to manage the development processes. We can therefore see innovation managers as needing to enrol and re-enrol support, win resources, create and sustain high trust relationships with a wide variety of stakeholder interests, and achieve and maintain legitimacy for new product developments. Indeed, it is this network-building activity which is crucial to the successful implementation of any networking strategy.

This highlights an interesting paradox resulting from the development of innovation networks. On the one hand, they can be understood as an effort to reduce and spread risks involved in developing new products in uncertain and rapidly changing markets. However, on the other hand, such behaviour exposes the organisation to new risks and uncertainties associated with the complexities of forging collaborative relationships and potentially radical organisational arrangements that may arise. Thus while being a source of risk reduction, innovation networks may expose collaborators to new sources of vulnerability associated with building and managing network relationships and organisational forms. In order to consider *how* membership of a network facilitates innovation and hence new product development, the meaning of the term 'network' needs to be clarified. These issues are considered in the next section. We then consider what we see as the crucial issues of network building and the politics of trust.

Innovation networks

The term 'network' may be understood in many ways, and networks can take a number of forms. Networking is generally regarded as a process through which firms can develop both technological and managerial competence and such activities appear to be increasingly common in innovative firms. The role of such linkages has been highlighted in the literature as a specific factor in the success of new product development, in terms of the effectiveness of alliances *within the firm* (Moenart and Caeldries 1996; Dougherty and Hardy 1996; Tidd *et al.* 1997), as well as by participation in *external* networks (Szarka 1990; Steward and Conway 1996; Hakannson 1998). A firm may have an explicit networking strategy, together with a formal system of accessing network partners; it may choose to network in a more implicit, or informal fashion, or it may combine both methods.

Various types of external networking relationships relevant to the innovation process have been identified, with a number of attempts made to classify them (see, for example, Freeman 1991). Lundgren (1995) claimed that while external networks can be restrictive and constrain innovative activity, they also provide opportunities to forge new technological links with other firms involved in the development of related technologies. Pisano (1990) described how membership of a network can facilitate the process of knowledge acquisition for new product development from sources external to the firm, while Cohen and Levinthal (1990) showed how a firm might use networks to 'absorb' or 'internalise' external information (cf. Campbell, Chapter 2 in this volume). Emphasis has been placed on the value of informal information exchange networks (von Hippel 1987), and also the involvement of research and development staff in professional communities through which they gain access to new technical knowledge (Rappa and Debackere 1992). The ongoing process of informal networking, therefore, may be equally important in the pursuit of innovation as is the actual membership of a formal network. In other words, belonging to a network of firms in order to develop new products implies that the innovation strategy of the members also includes emphasis upon the *process of networking* in order to find, join and participate fully in the activities of the *network* itself.

The type of networking favoured by a particular firm has implications for innovation success, as it will affect access to ideas about possibilities for future product development, and offer opportunities to become a partner in closer relations concerned with specific innovations. The influence of specific local, regional and national settings, together with other factors in the business environment such as sector, industrial relations and propensity to innovate, also have a role in shaping network dynamics. Lundvall (1988), Kogut (1993) and Lawton Smith (1995) emphasised the particular influence that these factors could have on the processes of technology transfer and the sharing of 'know-how' between network partners.

Since the pioneering work of Burns and Stalker (1961) it has been accepted that unpredictable market and technological environments may require 'organic' organisational structures rather than the more traditional 'mechanistic' forms best suited to more stable conditions. In terms of new product development, 'organic' structures are exemplified by the creation of cross-functional project teams in response to particular market and technological conditions. Hence the assumption is that such organisations can generate a high degree of 'fit' between the external environment and the internal organisational form.

But the scenario of organic structures which enables matching with changing external conditions is also problematic, and does not appear to reflect organisational experience any more than the classical viewpoints that it displaced. First, the capacity to 'read' the requirements of the external environment is seen as relatively straightforward. Second, the boundary between the external environment and the organisation is taken as relatively clear and distinct. Finally, it is assumed that the achievement of optimum fit between the external environment and internal organisational forms is a stable and sustainable configuration. Miles and Snow (1986) criticised this model by noting how the 'external' environment has recently become a far more dynamic, complex and 'difficult to read' phenomenon. At the same time, boundaries between the organisation and its environment are becoming increasingly blurred.

The concept of more flexible, or 'network' forms of organisation seeks to address these drawbacks. Both Aoki (1984) and DeBresson and Amesse (1991) note the growth of inter-organisational forms of innovation such as networking and strategic alliances, especially in terms of risk-reduction strategies in increasingly unstable global markets. Many other analysts have introduced the concept of networking as an essential aspect of a successful innovation strategy. For example, Vergragt *et al.* (1992: 244) state that technological development:

> is made possible through the creation of internal coalitions or networks and by extension of these networks to include other organisations in the environment.

The focus on networking means that organisational and economic factors within the firm are considered to be fundamental factors in strategic decisions about the development of new products. Ford and Thomas (1997) go so far as to suggest that a new product development strategy is now inevitably a networking strategy. They consider suppliers, subcontractors, partners and distributors as possible major network participants, although this list is not definitive. Hislop *et al.* (1997) note that effective strategies for the development of a new product depends on good communication between internal and external organisational networks.

Findings such as these show that in a number of industry sectors network organisational forms have emerged in response to the new complexity and rate of product innovation required by external environments. Van Rossum and Hicks (1996) claim that over time this also supports the emergence of collaborative networks for new product development, comprising loosely coupled and autonomous organisational units both internal and external to the firm. In these circumstances boundaries within and between organisations become blurred, and resource flows between different network elements are based upon contractual mechanisms or even informal exchanges.

Bringing the focus of analysis of innovation strategy from macro-considerations to the level of specific firms highlights the particular factors affecting network design and implementation in individual cases. While networking strategies are becoming increasingly common, it is by no means clear how such intentions are translated into practice in organisational terms. For example, crucial issues highlighted by a move to networking are likely to be the appropriateness of the internal organisation of a firm, the managerial expertise that is used to formulate strategy, and the ability to harness external sources of technological expertise. Morgan (1997) notes how firms participating in a network for the first time face a double challenge of managing their own organisational change while at the same time adapting to changes taking place within the broader network environment. This means that communication problems between network members can jeopardise the implementation of a firm's strategy for new product development despite its own best efforts.

Developing a strategy for innovation can therefore be regarded as a much more complex process than is suggested by the rationalist approach noted at the beginning of this chapter. The innovation process may be profoundly affected by change external to the firm, and depend on success in network building as much as on technological competence.

Network building

The term 'network building' implies the participation of individuals who are engaged in an *active process of network development and management*. The issue of partner choice is pertinent to building networks, and management actions such as enrolling support, winning resources, gaining legitimacy, trust building and so forth will be important means through which collaboration is brought about and network strategies implemented. In addition, consideration will need to be given to the flow of technological and other information throughout the network, and the exchange of 'tacit' knowledge has been identified as a particular difficulty in the context of technology transfer across firm boundaries (see Senker and Faulkner 1992). Another factor crucial to consideration of the process of network building is the means by which new products are selected for development within a network. As Firth and Narayanam (1996) found, firms appear to make very clear distinctions between the type of new product development suitable for internal development and those suitable for collaboration with external partners. Dodgson (1993) notes that loss of vital technological knowledge is one of the risks faced by a firm when entering an external collaboration. Biemans (1998) comments on the critical networking role played by key individuals within the partner firms as 'project champions'. These people are prepared to spend time building up working relationships with their counterparts based on trust that could be drawn upon if problems arose in the future. Hagedoorn and Schakenraad (1991) also note how successful networking requires considerable energy and resources extending well beyond the signing of the original agreement. Pfeffer (1992) argues that innovation in firms is increasingly a matter of being able to mobilise power resources in order to 'get things done'.

Lane (1989) demonstrates that differing approaches to organisational design and management style are significant sources of variation in relationships within networks. It is, therefore, important to investigate the dynamics of the network-building process. Such a study must incorporate many complex facets such as inter-personal relationships, the manner in which the politics of different stakeholder interests are manifested and managed, methods of knowledge transfer and such like, all of which can affect both the nature and eventual outcome of the network. The crucial role of inter-personal negotiations in building successful innovative teams is also identified by Anderson *et al.* (1994). In addition, management issues such as communication, control and development of trust are factors that existing research has shown to be critical in network formation (see for example Hakansson 1987; Hagedoorn 1990; Dickson *et al.* 1991; Biemans 1992; Sako 1992).

The innovation and change management literature also points strongly to the critical nature of the political expertise and competencies of 'change agents' (Buchanan and Boddy 1992). Indeed, our perception is that the vulnerability of networking as an innovation strategy makes such expertise crucial if the potential for disruption and disturbance that it involves are to be effectively managed. Network builders, we would suggest, will need to confront and resolve issues arising from the political interactions and conflicts arising between the different interest groups involved if network collaborations are to be built and sustained over time. This complex milieu is what Buchanan and Boddy term the 'process agenda' of change (as distinct from the technological 'content' and project management 'control' agendas).

The significance of attending to the process agenda is being illustrated in one of our case studies. Here, an independent 'network broker' has played a crucial role as 'project champion' in developing and sustaining the network, both through his ability to develop and maintain the appropriate contacts and in managing a diverse range of problems. The participating firms in the network are united by the need to address a common threat to their livelihood. This means that concerns over confidentiality are given a lower priority, and to a large degree are mitigated by the agreement of all parties to the strict terms of a formal networking agreement arranged by the network broker. In this case it appears that the role of the broker as network builder is vital to the ultimate success of the business venture being undertaken by the network members.

Participants in another of the case study networks also place great reliance upon formal networking agreements and active management of the network relationships. This strategy is justified by the long time span of typical projects in the industry (defence electronics), which means that an alliance can extend over different stages of the business cycle and cover a number of management changes within the partner firms. As a result, operating conditions for the network partners could change considerably from those envisaged in the early 'honeymoon period' of the relationship. This case also illustrates the need for active management of inter-firm relationships well beyond the signing of any formal collaboration agreements (see Hagedoorn and Schakenraad 1991).

The managing director of one of the firms involved in the network stressed the value of negotiating a deal that is *fair* to each firm, both in terms of the financial return and the amount of development work required. This is considered important because the short-term benefits of holding an unreasonable advantage can be lost if one partner harbours a grudge at being 'stitched up'. He seeks fairness by putting himself in the position of the proposed partners, by asking whether the situation is *equitable* enough for him to accept the terms if he was in the partner's position. He emphasised the need to remember that access to a partner's expertise could be a deciding factor in giving the combined operation the necessary *competitive advantage* to win a contract that neither could have attained by himself. In other words, if properly managed, synergy can be created within the network that renders it greater than the sum of the parts. Effective management of the relationship is therefore a critical issue. For example, it was agreed that profits from the sale of products developed as part of a network would be shared among the participants. This gives an incentive to the partner firms to pass on subsequent technical improvements that will enhance the product they have developed together, because it is in the interests of both parties to maximise customer satisfaction and hence generate more sales over the longer term. The prospect of additional income being generated after the end of the collaborative period may also 'leave a warm glow', hence serving to remind the partners on a regular basis of the benefits of working together. Such a strategy attempts to formalise and quantify the synergy that the partners seek by working together, while at the same time reinforcing the advantages in a more subliminal way. The crucial point of this particular story in the context of network building is *that a positive pay back from the networking is not expected to be seen immediately, or indeed at any time during the first project*. This is because of the degree of effort that has to be made by all the parties to overcome the obstacles encountered when working together. It may well be two or three projects before a significant financial return on the investment is made, which in the timescales operating in the defence industry could mean several years of work. If the relationship breaks down in the early stages, or even after completion of the first project, then the effort will not have been worthwhile.

By acknowledging and acting upon the need to work on the relationship building process over a long period, the evidence we are gathering from the two cases mentioned in this section illustrates to us the crucial importance of *interpersonal and political skills* when managing collaborative relationships over the length of time necessary for them to become profitable.

Managing networks: the politics of trust

The maintenance of inter-organisational trust has been identified as a pertinent network management issue by Lewicki and Bunker (1996). Blomqvist (1998) shows how firms that are using a strategy of networking to gain access to external technologies and expertise must accept a certain visibility within the network. This demands that attention be paid to maintaining and promoting a trustworthy reputation for good business practice. The onus is also on collaborating firms to develop and protect good levels of trust between the network participants in the project. The development of trust is one area that can bring into focus the relationship between internal and external networks, as there is no guarantee that good external relationships will be reflected in good internal relationships or vice versa. Fox (1974) postulates the concept of 'low' and 'high' levels of trust in terms of intra-organisational employment relationships. He characterises low-trust situations by opportunistic relationships, close supervision, the discouragement of information exchange and internal power struggles, and high trust relationships by commitment and identification with the organisation. Bruce *et al.* (1995) suggest that specific management skills are then necessary to progress networks in circumstances where trust is felt to be lacking. This is because trust is difficult to establish, and talking to competitors does not come naturally for UK firms. Kreiger (1998) shows that developing relationships built upon trust is a crucial aspect of network building, although he recognises that the issue may affect different parts of the organisation in different ways, with associated implications for management.

Kay and Wilman (1993) focus on the role of trust between internal departments involved in innovation, while others have investigated the consequences of low trust in external networks (see, for example, Lorenz 1991; Buckley and Casson 1988). Dodgson (1993) shows that low levels of trust in external relationships are regarded as a problem to be managed and controlled, while not necessarily preventing the development of working links with other organisations. He notes that high-trust situations are deemed more crucial for networks where there is a high level of specialised knowledge to share.

If trust is regarded as a problem to be overcome in inter-firm relationships, it must be recognised as one with many aspects. Zucker (1986) identifies a number of areas in which the process of trust building takes place. These include a mixture of organisational and personal factors such as reputations, shared goals and the quality of interaction in terms of communication, competencies and behaviours that unfold as the relationship develops. Dasgupta (1988) claims that 'trustworthiness' is as much part of the intangible assets of the organisation as is knowledge and expertise. Trust, however, is partly a manufactured component of the image and reputation of the firm. Miell and Duck (1986) show that inter-firm collaborations can develop much stronger bonds if the relationship is tested through satisfactory resolution of particular difficulties, but this process may be interpreted as undesirable in a commercial situation if the team involved have their individual institutional loyalties tested.

The above discussion also highlights the length of time necessary for trust to be built up between network participants. In what can be regarded as a direct reflection of this finding, Buckley and Casson (1988) noted that *distrust* may be in evidence in short-term inter-firm collaborative networks. In one of our case studies, a large electronics firm ran into difficulties when lack of in-house technical expertise left a gap in the company's product range. A small specialist firm was engaged to provide a quick solution to this problem, and it was able to negotiate very favourable contract terms after discovering 'on the grapevine' that the matter was particularly urgent. As a result of being held to ransom in this way, the electronics firm was reluctant to build a long term relationship with its partner and therefore did not make use of its services again.

Evidence exists to support the theory that firms can attain significant *long-term* benefits by participating in specific networking projects. For example, Dickson *et al.* (1997) show that firms which have long experience in inter-firm innovation may develop a specific competence in managing the problems of network building, and become 'strategic collaborators', based on the learning acquired over time by experience and adaptation to change. This finding is supported by Cohen and Levinthal (1990) and Lyles (1988) who show that such firms go through a process of learning over time based on technological, managerial and organisational change. Other studies of innovative ventures also identify such learning issues as crucial factors in inter-firm innovation success (see, for example, Schill *et al.* 1991). We would suggest that one of the key learning processes is that concerned with identifying who to trust and who not to trust; categories whose membership is unlikely to be fixed for the duration of any collaborative relationship.

In one of our case study networks, the development of trust between the members over time allowed learning to occur through a process of communication and shared problem solving that would previously have been impossible. The legal safeguards incorporated into a formal network model sowed the seeds for the establishment of a degree of trust, which then led to further informal networking between members in both related and entirely new contexts. As a direct result of their successful involvement in the network, one of the partner organisations has since set up a new network of local firms designed to use the shared resources of participants to improve the competitiveness of businesses in an entirely different industry context. In another of our case studies the issue of determining who to trust and not trust has considerable resonance and the political judgements on these points made by network builders appears to mark distinct stages in the development of the collaboration.

Networks as virtual organisations

Lyles (1988) noted that the extent of learning and adaptation within a network over time can, in some cases, overcome initial problems in cross-boundary linkages. The eventual result is that the independent organisational boundaries may become blurred and it is this phenomenon that has given rise to the term 'virtual organisation' in the context of intra- and inter-firm networks. McLoughlin and Jackson (Chapter 11 in this volume) note how networks can be created to perform specific tasks, resulting in what may be termed 'Web' organisations composed of individuals from a number of different firms. Recent advances in communications technologies have had a significant and positive impact on the viability of these entities in practice, in particular in relation to their capacity to transcend constraints of time and space in the way in which the network interacts.

One of our case studies relates to an organisation drawn from three very different types of firm that have come together to develop data analysis tools for retail industry suppliers. The network consists of a major computer hardware manufacturer, a data broking firm, and an IT consultancy. The make-up of the new product development team is governed by the particular skills required rather than geographical location or company affiliation of the staff, who are physically located throughout Europe. After early meetings to establish contact and assess each other's abilities, the project team has increasingly been able to work remotely, relying upon sophisticated communications technologies and project management software tools to interact with fellow team members. The need for face-to-face contact has reduced over time as trust has been developed among the team members and they have learned how to work together effectively. Structure and discipline are enforced on the team by rigorous project management techniques that include detailed documentation of requirements and transparent communication of responsibilities. Specific guidelines of the output required and the deadlines to be met by the different teams are written down, in order that everyone working on the project is aware of what is expected of them. Suitably embroiled in a web of virtual formality, the team members are then left to manage their time and resources as they see fit in accordance with the goals set.

As a result of this strategy, the inter-organisational project team developed its own specific culture and way of doing business that transcended specific company affiliations. The focus of management is now upon the team unit rather than on the employees of a particular organisation. The manager responsible for recruiting new staff for the project relies extensively upon both his own and his employees' network of contacts in recruiting individuals with the appropriate skills and attitudes to meet project requirements. This means that people who have worked together in the past for a previous employer form a large part of the overall group. In a market characterised by chronic shortages of labour, financial incentives are offered to newcomers who encourage suitable erstwhile colleagues to join them. As well as providing a good example of how virtual organisations can overcome spatial constraints, this case seems to raise significant issues concerning the manner in which network builders may set about 'managing what they cannot see' (Handy 1995) when it comes to collaborative product development initiatives of this type.

Conclusion

This chapter has drawn upon the early findings emerging from a major ongoing research project on building collaboration in new product development. This research is focusing on the manner in which such collaboration is increasingly based on network forms of organisation as a response to complex and changing markets, demanding reductions in product development lead times and increasing product sophistication which may well extend beyond a firm's existing knowledge base. However, while this offers a potential means of reducing uncertainty and risk, it is our contention that such collaborative networking also brings with it new problems. This arises from the inherent vulnerability of the network-building process as attempts are made to forge new and novel links within and between organisations. Such developments highlight the skills and competencies of network builders as they engage with the content, control and especially process agendas of creating and sustaining collaborative relationships which cut across existing organisational boundaries and may even support new organisational forms. We have sought to emphasise the importance of such activities to the longevity of network forms of organisation. In contrast to the examples of networking discussed elsewhere in this volume, therefore, the network relationships we have examined are expected by their participants to endure rather than to act as a 'quick fix'. It can be concluded that an explicit approach to network building, in terms of the significant effort required over a long time period to manage relationships and build trust, will be a function of the political sophistication of network management in the firms studied. In the context of new product development, therefore, the existence of technical capability is merely the starting point.

Acknowledgement

This work is being funded by the European Commission under contract number PL97-1084 of the Targeted Socio-Economic Research (TSER) Programme.

Bibliography

Aoki, A. (1984) *The Co-operative Game Theory of the Firm*, Oxford: Clarendon Press.
Anderson, N., Hardy, G. and West, M. (1994) 'Innovative teams at work', in Mabey, C. and Iles, P. (eds) *Managing Learning*, London and New York: Open University/Routledge.

Biemans, W. (1992) *Managing Innovation Within Networks*, London: Routledge.

—— (1998) 'The theory and practice of innovative networks', in During, W. and Oakey, R. (eds) *New Technology-based Firms in the 1990s*, Vol. IV, London: Paul Chapman Publishing.

Blomqvist, K. (1998) 'The role and means of trust creation in partnership formation between small and large technology firms: a preliminary study of how small firms attempt to create trust in their potential partners', in During, W. and Oakey, R. (eds) *New Technology-based Firms in the 1990s*, Vol. IV, London: Paul Chapman Publishing.

Buchanan, D. and Boddy, D. (1992) *Expertise of the Change Agent*, Hemel Hempstead: Prentice Hall.

Burns, T. and Stalker, G.M. (1961) *The Management of Innovation*, London: Tavistock.

Bruce, M. *et al.* (1995) 'Success factors in collaborative product development: a study of suppliers of information and communication technology', *R&D Management*, 25, 1: 33–44

Buckley, P.J. and Casson, M. (1988) 'A theory of co-operation in international business', in Contractor, F. and Lorange, P. (eds) *Co-operative Strategies in International Business*, Lexington, Mass.

Cohen, W.M. and Levinthal, D.A. (1990) 'Absorptive capacity: a new perspective on learning and innovation', *Administrative Science Quarterly*, 35: 128–52.

Conway, S. and Steward, F. (1998) 'Mapping innovation networks', *International Journal of Innovation Management*, 2, 2, Special Issue: 223–54.

Dasgupta, P. (1988) 'Trust as a commodity', in Gambetta, D. (ed.) *Trust; Making and Breaking Co-operative Relations*, Oxford: Basil Blackwell.

DeBresson, C. and Amesse, F. (1991) 'Networks of innovators: a synthesis of research issues', *Research Policy*, 20, 5: 363–79.

Dickson, K., Lawton Smith, H. and Lloyd Smith, S. (1991) 'Bridge over troubled waters? Problems and opportunities in inter-firm research collaboration', *Technology Analysis and Strategic Management*, 33, 2: 143–56.

Dickson, K., Coles, A.-M. and Lawton Smith, H. (1997) 'Staying the course: strategic collaboration for small high-tech firms', *Small Business and Enterprise Development*, 4, 1: 13–21

Dodgson, M. (1993) *Technological Collaboration in Industry*, London: Routledge.

Dougherty, D. and Hardy, C. (1996) 'Sustained product innovation in large mature organisations: overcoming innovation to organisation problems', *Academy of Management Journal*, 39, 5: 1120–53.

Firth, R.W. and Narayanam, V.K. (1996) 'New product strategies of large dominant product manufacturing firms: an exploratory analysis', *Journal of Product Innovation Management*, 13, 4: 334–347.

Ford, D. and Thomas, R. (1997) 'Technology strategy in networks', *International Journal of Technology Management*, 14: 596–612.

Fox, A. (1974) *Beyond Contract: Work, Power and Trust Relations*, London: Faber.

Freeman, C. (1991) 'Networks of innovators: a synthesis of research issues', *Research Policy*, 20, 5: 499–514.

Hagedoorn, J. (1990) 'Organisational modes of inter-firm co-operation and technology transfer', *Technovation*, 10, 1: 17–30.

Hagedoorn, J. and Schakenraad, J. (1991) 'The economic effects of strategic partnering and technology co-operation', *Report to the Commission of European Communities*, September, EU R13150EN.

Hakansson, H. (1987) *Industrial Technological Development: A Network Approach*, London: Croom Helm.

Hakansson, H. (1998) 'Managing co-operative R&D: partner selection and contract design', *R&D Management*, 23, 4: 273–85.

Handy, C. (1995) 'Trust and the virtual organisation', *Harvard Business Review*, 73, 3: 40–50.

Hislop, D., Newell, S., Scarborough, H. and Swann, J. (1997) 'Innovation and networks', paper given at *British Academy of Management Conference*, London, September.

Kay, J. and Wilman, P. (1993) 'Managing technological innovation: architecture, trust and organisational relationships in the firm', in Swann, P. (ed.) *New Technologies and the Firm*, London: Routledge.

Kogut, B. (ed.) (1993) *Country Competitiveness: Technology and the Organising of Work*, London: Oxford University Press.

Kreiger, E. (1998) 'Trust and management: as applied to innovative small companies', in During, W. and Oakey, R. (eds) *New Technology Based Firms in the 1990s*, Vol. IV, London: Paul Chapman Publishing.

Lane, C. (1989) *Management and Labour in Europe*, Cheltenham: Edward Elgar.

Lawton Smith, H. (1995) 'The contribution of national laboratories to the European scientific labour market', *Industry and Higher Education*, 9, 3: 176–85.

Lewicki, R. and Bunker, B. (1996) 'Developing and maintaining trust in work relationships', in Kramer, R.M. and Tyler, T.R. (eds) *Trust in Organisations: Frontiers of Theory and Research*, New York: Sage.

Lorenz, E.H. (1991) 'Neither friends nor strangers: informal networks of subcontracting in French industry', in Thompson, G., Frances, J., Levacic, R. and Mitchell, J. (eds) *Markets, Hierarchies and Networks*, London: Open University/Sage.

Lundgren, A. (1995) *Technological Innovation and Network Evolution*, London, Routledge.

Lundvall, B. (1988) 'Innovation as an interactive process', in Dosi, G. (ed.) *Technical Change and Economic Theory*, London: Pinter.

Lyles, M.A. (1988) 'Learning among joint-venture sophisticated firms', in Contractor, F. and Lorange, P. (eds) *Co-operative Strategies in International Business*, Lexington, Mass.

Miell, D. and Duck, S. (1986) 'Strategies in developing friendships', in Valerian, J. and Winsted, B. (eds) *Friendship and Social Interaction*, Springer, New York.

Miles, R.E. and Snow, C.C. (1986) 'Network organisation: new concepts for new forms', *The McKinsey Quarterly*, Autumn.

Moenart, R.K. and Caeldries, F. (1996) 'Architectural redesign, interpersonal communication and learning in R&D', *Journal of Product Innovation Management*, 13: 296–310.

Morgan, G. (1997) *Images of Organisations*, 2nd edition, London: Sage.

Pfeffer, J. (1992) *Managing with Power: Politics and Influence in Organisations*, Boston, Mass.: Harvard Business School.

Pisano, G.P. (1990) 'The R&D boundaries of the firm', *Administrative Science Quarterly*, 35: 153–76.

Porter, M. (1980) *Competitive Strategy*, New York: Free Press.

Rappa, M. and Debackere, R. (1992) 'Technological communities and the diffusion of knowledge', *R&D; Management*, 22, 3: 209–20.

Sako, M. (1992) *Prices, Quality and Trust: Interfirm Relations in Britain and Japan*, Cambridge: Cambridge University Press.

Schill, R.L., Bertodo, D.G. and McArther, D.N. (1991) 'Achieving success in technology alliances: the Rover Honda strategic collaboration', *R&D Management*, 24, 3: 261–77

Senker, J. and Faulkner, W. (1992) 'Networks, tacit knowledge and innovation', in Coombs, R., Richards, A., Saviotti, P. and Walsh, V. (eds) *Technological Collaboration: The Dynamics of Co-operation in Industrial Innovation*, Cheltenham: Edward Elgar.

Steward, F. and Conway, S. (1996) 'Informal networks in the origination of successful innovations', in Coombs, R., Richards, A., Saviotti, P. and Walsh, V. (eds) *Technological Collaboration: the Dynamics of Co-operation in Industrial Innovation*, Cheltenham: Edward Elgar.

Szarka, J. (1990) 'Networking and small firms', *International Small Business Journal*, 8, 2: 10–22.

Tidd, J., Bessant, J. and Pavitt, K. (1997) *Managing Innovation: Integrating Technological, Market and Organisational Change*, Chichester: Wiley.

Vergragt, P.J., Groenewegen, P. and Mulder, K.F. (1992) 'Industrial technological innovation: interrelationships between technological, economic and sociological analysis', in Coombs, R., Richards, A., Saviotti, P. and Walsh, V. (eds) *Technological Collaboration: the Dynamics of Co-operation in Industrial Innovation*, Cheltenham: Edward Elgar.

Van Rossum, W. and Hicks, E. (1996) 'Processes of innovation: combined insights from network and systems theory', paper presented at *COST A3 Conference, Management of New Technology*, Madrid.

Von Hippel, E. (1987) 'Co-operation between rivals: informal know-how trading', *Research Policy*, 16, 4: 291–301.

Zucker, L.G. (1986) 'Production of trust: institutional sources of economic structures 1840–1920', *Research in Organisational Behaviour*, 8: 53–111.

4 Virtual teams and lost proximity

Consequences on trust relationships

Joe Nandhakumar

Introduction

The concept of virtual teams has gained considerable attention in recent years. Within global organisations virtual teamworking involves collaboration and teamwork between a geographically and temporally separated workforce (Hammer and Champy 1993; Lipnack and Stamps 1997). Such collaboration may also extend outside the organisational boundary, with partners in joint ventures and contractors who are in various locations. Emerging information and communication technologies such as groupware, Internet and desktop video conferencing systems are seen by global organisations as facilitating such collaboration and enable the workforce to share knowledge and expertise (Orlikowski 1996; Lipnack and Stamps 1997). For example, Lipnack and Stamps (1997: 18) claim that with the use of Internet, 'teams can virtually collocate all the information they need to work together'.

While virtual teamworking is seen as potentially necessary for global organisations, many authors (e.g. Handy 1995; Lipnack and Stamps 1997) argue that 'virtuality' requires trust relationships to make it work. However little is understood on how the loss of physical proximity in virtual teamworking affects trust relationships among participants.

This chapter describes the findings of a field study carried out in a large multinational company, which examines various forms of interactions enacted by the use of information technology in virtual teamworking and discusses the consequences of the absence of collocation in virtual teams on trust relationships. The chapter argues that personalised trust relationships established through face-to-face interactions and socialisation are essential for continuous virtual teamworking. The use of information and communication technologies appears to be inadequate for establishing and reproducing such trust relationships. Trust relationships may also be based on the abstract structures of organisations for temporary virtual teams. Such impersonalised trust relationships are not psychologically rewarding for individuals.

Trust relationships

In recent years, the role of trust in organisations has gained increasing attention from management researchers (e.g. Kramer and Tyler 1996; Rousseau *et al.* 1998). The notion of trust is often seen by researchers as the most difficult concept to handle in empirical research because of the diverse definitions of trust used in each discipline and the multitude of functions it performs in the society (Misztal 1996).

Giddens (1990: 34), for example, defines trust as 'confidence in the reality of a person or system, regarding a given set of outcomes or events'. Giddens therefore conceptualises trust as being a property of both individuals and 'abstract' social systems. He argues that with globalisation and the restructuring interactions across undefined spans of time–space, trust which is traditionally secured by community, tradition and kinship is increasingly vested in abstract capacities characteristic of modern institutions. Apart from these two categories of trust (personal and abstract systems), Giddens also refers to 'basic' trust. He sees basic trust as our confidence in the continuity of personal identity together with the building of trust in others (ontological security). The routines of everyday life and predictability of social order contributes to such basic trust.

Sociologists claim that trust performs a multitude of functions. For example, it can be a silent background, sustaining a smooth-running of cooperative relations (Misztal 1996). It can help individuals to reconcile their own interests with those of others. Trust is therefore seen as fundamental for all aspects of social life. By drawing on social theories, many organisational researchers commonly view trust as an expression of confidence in organisational 'exchange' which leads to cooperative behaviour among individuals and groups within and between organisations (e.g. Jones and George 1998).

Research study

The findings discussed here are part of a larger study that investigated virtual teamworking in a large multinational company (Xeon)[1].

Research approach

The research approach adopted in this study is interpretive (Schwandt 1994) involving a collection of detailed, qualitative data on virtual teamworking practices in a specific context. To interpretivists, all human action is attached with 'meanings' and these meanings are enacted through numerous symbolic actions and interactions such as ceremonies, folklore and rituals (Nandhakumar and Jones 1997). Prasad (1997) argues that the researcher can understand the social situation only through appreciating the meaning they hold for people in a given cultural context. The validity of interpretive research depends on gaining sufficient access to the knowledge and meanings of actors to enable a plausible, credible, and relevant representation of their interpretations to be generated (Altheide and Johnson 1994).

The study employed ethnographic techniques (Van Maanen 1979) such as observation of participants in their context, social contact and unstructured and semi-structured interviews with virtual teamworkers, during 1997–1998. The study specifically focused on participants of two virtual teams: members of the knowledge management team who were also the early adopters of virtual teamworking; and managers from a large construction project, who were seen as the 'champions' of virtual teamworking at Xeon. Within each team, the interviewees were identified by following their social network. The author also spent time interacting with team members and observing the actual practices of virtual teamworking by being with participants at Xeon. Documents have also been examined, including documentation on benchmarking, training manuals and internet-based support documents and also documents on frequently asked questions. Detailed field notes were maintained during the study period to record observations and events during each visit. Most of the interviews were recorded and transcribed.

The focus of this research is to derive theoretical interpretations from data (Glaser and Strauss 1967), rather than to test theory against data as is traditionally the case. During the analysis, the interview and field notes were read several times, and coded systematically to identify key issues and concepts. These initial issues and concepts were analysed and aggregated to articulate a set of common or recurring themes. Extracts from the interviews are used as examples in this chapter to illustrate the incidence, which led to the development of some of our interpretations.

Research site

Xeon is a large multinational company with operations in over 70 countries. It has an annual operating revenue of over $50 billion with over 50,000 employees world wide. Xeon introduced the virtual teamwork project by mid-1990s to foster collaboration both within and among Xeon's business units and between their contractors and partners in joint ventures. The virtual teamwork facilities consisted of a high-power desktop personal computer (PC) which included desktop video conferencing and scanning facilities, and multimedia email and groupware (including internet/intranet, and file transfer) applications (VTPC).

During 1997, management of the virtual teamwork project was taken over by a newly formed knowledge management team. By the end of 1997, virtual teamworking had also spread to senior executives at Xeon. Although the initial intention of the virtual teamworking project was to improve communication between employees, by 1997 the desktop video-conferencing facilities were seen as helping users to overcome the 'barriers' for collaboration and knowledge sharing. The VTPC technologies were integrated, delivered and supported as part of Xeon's IT infrastructure. Users were trained to work with VTPC and to develop skills on virtual teamworking.

Research findings

The discussion of results highlights various forms of interaction enacted by the use of information technology at Xeon and the effects of loss of proximity on trust relationships among the virtual teamworkers.

Forms of interactions

With the introduction of VTPC, participants began to experience the emergence of various forms of interaction around the VTPC technology. A senior participant from the construction team noted:

> We had a number of locations with people…and that is always a communication problem…the first experience we had [with VTPC] was the added dimension in communication.

One way the new forms of interaction took place within the team was through on-line sharing of documents such as contractual documents, presentations, planning documents, engineering drawings. For example, contractors from the construction site and other managers in other locations were able to work on the same document held in a central repository in the headquarters.

Through such on-line interactions enabled by the use of VTPC, senior managers extended their authority over subordinates, for example, by making their presence more visible in the remote sites. Participants found it more difficult to reject senior managers' idea when VTPC was used to communicate with them. This is reflected in one of the team members' comments:

> Our project manager in particular is a very strong body language person…in the meetings exceptionally so…you can really tell the mood by how he is holding his body, shoulders, sitting forward or back…on [VTPC] screen…[he is] a lot more effective than just on the phone, or just an email.

The interactions with senior managers also enabled junior participants to reinforce their relationship with powerful figures by allowing them to participate in their meeting. The participation of senior managers in virtual team meetings enabled the team members to draw on resources of authority to legitimise their activities. One of the participants explained:

> [VTPC] allows more senior people to be able to look in, if you like, more junior meetings a week. We have meetings and we have been in with somebody quite senior for 15 minutes, it just costs them 15 minutes of time but it has brought a level of authority and significance to our workshop, which we couldn't otherwise have had.

Another form of interaction enacted with the use of VTPC was through 'task-based' temporary teams. Specialist consultants from Xeon and from contracting companies often interacted using VTPC to deal with problems on remote sites, without having all the specialists permanently located on those sites. For example, a participant explained:

> Traditionally that [a problem] would have meant people flying up to site…but we found that by showing people those pictures, you could get to resolve problems a lot quicker, not always…sometimes you do need to physically see the thing but quite often skilled people could say, 'Well I could see by the way that failed [and] what caused it'.

Many of such alliances were therefore formed temporarily as and when needed to resolve problems. For example, a participant noted:

> Like you have a shoal of fish swim around an object, they [experts] swim together [with project team members] in perfect unison then they split and rejoin.

Despite efforts to promote the use of VTPC to overcome the 'barriers' such as the strong hierarchical norms for sharing expertise, such barriers continuously constrained interactions across various hierarchical levels. Any attempts by junior employees to interact with senior managers were marked by the imbalance of authority between them. Many sought to overcome such imbalance of authority relationships through various mechanisms. For example, one of the junior managers explained that he reduced the size of images of other participants appearing on the VTPC by resizing the windows. He suggested:

> …make important people smaller and make yourself bigger on screen, so that it helps the balance. If you see yourself on the screen…'I'm a big person'.

The knowledge management team tried to address the effects of cultural norms and value systems on limiting interactions through the training programme. In addition to providing the necessary technical skills for working with VTPC, the trainer coached participants a 'new virtual work behaviour'. This involved training on how to establish the first contact with other experts and appropriate use of body language in VTPC-mediated interactions to help users to overcome the limitations imposed by technology and cultural norms. The findings indicated, however, that the norms and value systems were resistant to transformation, at least in the short term. One of the knowledge management team members observed:

> For some people it [training programme] did stick and they are very much into it, these are the people who have really changed the way they work,

[but] there are others that are kind of on the edge that really didn't buy into the whole story, that will have dropped it [VTPC].

The findings suggest that the use of VTPC within Xeon enacted various forms of interaction. Social constraints such as the strong hierarchical norms continuously limited interactions across different organisational levels. The participants however used the VTPC in ways that were not originally intended. For example, VTPC enabled experts who were working with Xeon from contracting organisations to video conference with their other clients, who were often Xeon's competitors. By not having to physically go to their clients to deal with their problem, the experts were able to get back to the contract work at Xeon after the video-conferencing session.

Formation of trust relationships

We now explore how the absence of collocation has affected trust relationships at Xeon.

VTPC technology was continually reshaped and redesigned by the members of the knowledge management team – who were also early adopters of the technology – and other users at Xeon. The knowledge management team saw this technology as not only allowing dispersed teams at Xeon to 'see, hear, and speak with others around the globe as they were collocated' but also enabling participants to develop 'trusting relationships'.

My observation indicated that many temporary virtual teams formed to solve specific problems often exhibited behaviour that presupposed trust. Many of these teams often depended on an elaborate body of collective knowledge and diverse skills for solving problems; however, they had no history of working together. With the finite life span of the team, the participants had little time to share experience or reciprocal disclosure, which was traditionally seen as sources of trust relationships between participants. This indicated that the trust relationships in this context were mainly based on the abstract structures of Xeon, such as participants' knowledge about political legitimacy and systems of professional knowledge. Lipnack and Stamps (1997) also illustrate a similar form of trust relationships in many of their examples of 'effective' virtual teamworking. Such trust relationships were therefore more abstract forms, based on legitimacy and guarantees of expectations, which were reinforced and reproduced by previous interactions with different participants.

The team members at Xeon, however, did not want to rely only on such impersonalised trust; rather they actively sought to establish personalised trust relationships for continuous teamworking. They deliberately cultivated face-to-face relationships to establish personalised trust. This was reflected in participants' emphasis on the need to establish 'working relationships' in the conventional way before virtual teamworking. For example, a participant noted:

> ...to start establishing a relationship I think you do need to have the physical contact more because you have this indefinable thing about relationships and body language and you don't get it in the same way...so...as you do the team building you need to have some physical contact.

Such reflections revealed that participants perceived the trust based on abstract systems as not providing emotional satisfaction and sought to establish trust relationships through face-to-face encounters. Even if such personal relationships were established, in the absence of collocation the team members might have found it difficult to maintain them. One member from the knowledge management team observed:

> We are having a global team meeting in two weeks time...the big joke is – 'can't you do this virtually?'...I say no we can't do it virtually, we can get so far virtually but until we have a real good drink and a good meal and a good social chat at length we are not going to be a 'real team'....We can then use technology to maintain it [relationship] and obviously it's going to slide.

Such socialisation processes enabled participants to get behind the 'official activities' and to participate in activities happening at the 'backstage' (Goffman, 1990) where participants exchanged and shared feelings and emotions. The participants saw such involvement as helping to develop attitudes towards the other reflecting the other as a trustworthy party.

In addition to being psychologically rewarding for the participants, establishing personalised trust relationships was also seen as helping to maintain the relationships and positive expectations. For example, one of the participants expressed:

> If I need to get real alignment of vision I would definitely go to that person...anything that is going to raise emotion – it seems totally natural for me to go and be there...any strong emotional feedback where I need assurance that people are really getting it they understand the issue....I would struggle to get that via [VTPC].

This indicated that the use of VTPC, however, was seen as inadequate for maintaining and reproducing trust relationships. In fact there were high levels of anxiety among the virtual teamworkers, especially among those who were stationed in remote locations and relied exclusively on VTPC technology for their interactions with other members. One of the participants noted:

> In my team some people [are] based in [x], some people based in [y] and then odd ones kind of all over...slowly people started to migrate to the biggest centre for the meetings. It was classic...instead of going to my base office which was in [x], I would go to [y] because I knew the boss was going to be there for a start,...but then there was the deep scare that if the

[VTPC] broke down I will be where the action is....I'm not going to be left out.

This indicated that participants perceived the modes of interaction enabled by the VTPC as 'unreliable'. This led to unpredictability of the continuity of their routine interactions and meetings. The participants therefore had a constant fear of isolation. In the absence of a shared daily working life together with the rest of the team, remote members found it hard to develop positive attitudes towards others and felt uneasy about the activities of the rest of the team. It was therefore difficult to maintain trust relationships in this situation. This particular virtual team was therefore gradually transformed towards a collocated team.

The inadequate conditions for maintaining mutual trust relationships among the virtual members in remote locations also led participants to look for ways of keeping formal records of every exchange. Participants raised concerns about the limitations of VTPC to maintain records or minutes of what was said during virtual meetings. This is reflected in one of the participants' comments:

> The downside of virtual teamworking is – no audit trail, there is no record of what happens unless you take notes...no back up...a month ago – and it costs me nothing – everything...in an email somewhere and I could recover it.

The lack of mutual trust also limited informal exchange between dispersed team members by using VTPC. Such informal exchange among collocated team members 'around coffee machines and corridors' was seen as important venues for exchange of ideas and to reproduce trust relationships. Participants were unable to secure trust in abstract structures of Xeon for informal interactions, as they were able to do so in task-based temporary teams. For example, one member of the knowledge management team noted:

> We try to have what we call virtual coffee sessions, which were dreadful...all around the world we tried to get together and have a cup of coffee and sit down and look at each other, and you can't be spontaneous now, you can't do it, you can't force it.

This indicated that in the absence of collocation and shared social context, however, participants lacked confidence in sharing their feelings and informal knowledge of the organisation during 'virtual coffee sessions'.

At the individual level, there were links between participants' inner traits and the ability to trust and more general trust attitudes. Despite efforts by the knowledge management team to establish trust relationships among participants, many of the participants could not develop confidence in each others' values and trustworthiness and hence could not make use of the VTPC technology. One of the knowledge management team members who was very frustrated about this noted:

>...you can use all the technology in the world to connect people and make them transparent and make them accessible at work, but if they don't want to see...or...if they don't want to share...that is the critical part.

He further stated that:

>We even toyed with the idea of randomly reconnecting two people once a day. Almost a lottery. You don't know if you might find yourself connected to somebody you don't know. We decided not to do that in the end.

Summary of findings

The above discussion indicates that various forms of interactions were enacted among the geographically dispersed team members with the use of VTPC. The team members sought to interact on-line using the technology. The on-line participation of senior managers in virtual team meetings enabled the junior participants to draw on resources of authority to legitimise their activities. This also enabled stretching of formal authority relations across geographical boundaries. Temporary on-line alliances were formed with specialist consultants to deal with problems on remote sites. The participants also used the VTPC in ways to develop interaction patterns, which were not originally intended.

While some authors, such as Sproul and Kiesler (1996), suggest that information technologies can overcome constraints on interaction between different organisational levels, the findings suggest that social constraints such as the strong hierarchical norms continuously limited interaction with senior managers.

In the absence of collocation, trust relationships were based on the abstract structures of the organisation for temporary virtual teams. Such systems of trust depended on the legitimacy and expectations which themselves were sustained through the continuous reproduction of this kind of interaction with other participants.

The team members, however, actively sought to establish personalised trust relationships for continuous teamworking. Face-to-face relationships were deliberately cultivated within the organisation to establish trust. Such relationships also enabled participants to involve together in activities at the 'backstage' where the exchange of feelings and emotions took place. The participants saw such personalised trust relationships as psychologically rewarding and helping to exchange favourable attitudes and positive expectations.

The use of VTPC, however, was seen as inadequate for maintaining and reproducing such trust relationships. The virtual team members, therefore, made significant investments into the maintenance of trust relationships through face-to-face interactions and socialisation, to sustain reciprocal support.

Any informal exchange between dispersed team members was limited by the lack of mutual trust. In the absence of collocation, participants lacked confidence in sharing their informal knowledge of the organisations.

Individual participants' inner quality and the ability to trust seemed to influence their more general trust attitudes. Many of them could not engage in virtual teamworking because they were unable to develop confidence with others in different locations to enable continuous interactions.

Conclusions

In this chapter I have sought to illustrate various forms of interactions enacted with the use of information technology in virtual teams and to discuss the effects of the absence of collocation in virtual teamworking for building trust relationships among the participants in a large multinational company.

The findings suggest that personalised trust relationships are essential for continuous virtual teamworking. Such personalised trust relationships are normally established through face-to-face interactions and socialisation. The use of information and communication technologies appears to be inadequate for establishing and reproducing such trust relationships owing to their inability to provide access to the 'backstage' of participants' activities. These technologies may have potential in temporary virtual teams formed to solve specific problems. In such teams, trust relationships may be based on the abstract structures of the organisation rather than at a personal level. These structures are sustained by their continuing reproduction through participants' interactions.

The insights gained from this study may be of value to practitioners involved in virtual teamworking or in managing such teams, in broadening their understanding on the trust relationships in virtual teams and also for developing policies to foster and strengthen trust among virtual teamworkers in organisations. The findings that trust relationships based on both abstract systems and other participants are sustained by their continuing reproduction would seem to suggest that there is a need for organisational policies to create conditions for socialisation and construct opportunities for active interactions. This can be achieved, for example, by providing individuals with: resources in terms of expertise, time and skills to become effective contributors; opportunities in terms of autonomy and authority; and motivation to take the practice of good organisational citizenship seriously in terms of performing duties, which they owe to the other colleagues.

Acknowledgement

I wish to thank the participants of the company in which the field study was carried out, for their collaboration in this project. This study was funded by a research grant (R000221855) from the UK Economics and Social Research Council.

Note

1 Xeon is a pseudonym. Throughout this chapter actual job descriptions of employees have been disguised to protect anonymity.

Bibliography

Altheide, D.L. and Johnson, J.M. (1994) 'Criteria for assessing interpretive validity in qualitative research', in Denzin, N.K. and, Lincoln, Y.S. (eds) *Handbook of Qualitative Research*, London: Sage: 485–99.

Giddens, A. (1990) *The Consequence of Modernity*, Oxford: Polity Press.

Glaser, B.G. and Strauss, A.L. (1967) *The Discovery of Grounded Theory: Strategies for Qualitative Research*, New York: Aldine Publishing Company.

Goffman, E. (1990) *The Presentation of Self in Everyday Life*, London: Penguin.

Hammer, M. and Champy, J. (1993) *Reengineering the Corporation: A Manifesto for Business Revolution*, New York: HarperCollins.

Handy, C. (1995) 'Trust and the virtual organization', *Harvard Business Review*, May/June.

Jones, G.R. and George, J.M. (1998) 'The experience and evolution of trust: implications for co-operation and teamwork', *The Academy of Management Review*, 23, 3: 531–46.

Kramer, R.M. and Tyler, T.R. (1996) *Trust in Organizations: Frontiers of Theory and Research*, Thousand Oaks, CA: Sage.

Lipnack, J. and Stamps, J. (1997), *Virtual Teams: Reaching Across Space, Time and Organizations with Technology*, New York: Wiley.

Misztal, B.A. (1996) *Trust in Modern Societies*, Oxford: Polity Press.

Nandhakumar, J. and Jones, M. (1997) 'Too close for comfort? Distance and engagement in interpretive information systems research', *Information Systems Journal*, 7: 109–31.

Orlikowski, W.J. (1996) 'Learning from notes: organizational issues in groupware implementation', in Kling, R. (ed.) *Computerization and Controversy'*, San Diego: Academic Press.

Prasad, P. (1997) 'Systems of meaning: ethnography as a methodology for the study of information technologies', in, Lee, A.S., Liebenau, J. and, DeGross, J.I. (eds) *Information Systems and Qualitative Research*, London: Chapman & Hall, 101–18

Rousseau, D.M., Sitkin, B.B., Burt, R.S. and Camerer, C. (1998) 'Not so different after all: a cross-disciplinary view of trust', *The Academy of Management Review*, 23, 3: 393–404.

Schwandt, T.A. (1994) 'Constructivist, interpretivist approaches to human inquiry', in Denzin, N.K. and, Lincoln, Y.S. (eds) *Handbook of Qualitative Research* , London: Sage: 118–37.

Sproull, L. and Kiesler, S. (1996) 'Increasing personal connections', in Kling, R. (ed.) *Computerization and Controversy*, San Diego: Academic Press.

Van Maanen, J. (1979) 'The fact of fiction in organizational ethnography', *Administrative Science Quarterly*, 24: 539–50.

Part II

Individual experiences of virtual working

In this part we look at the issues involved in teleworking from the level of the individual. We can learn much from the experiences that virtual workers themselves have of the new ways of working. Of course, because of individual and occupational differences, such experiences may vary widely.

In Chapter 5, by Kiran Mirchandani, discussion draws upon the study of professional and managerial home-based teleworkers in Canada. The author argues that such research offers important insights into the ways organisations are using virtual working, the role it can play in offering employee-centred workplaces, but also in challenging attitudes and discrimination that exist in company hierarchies.

To overcome many traditional prejudices about working away from the office, Mirchandani suggests we need to reconceptualise organisations in terms of a set of relationships. In many respects, she notes, organisational culture is seen by its members as spatially bound. Given the importance of work identities and relationships to individuals and work processes, it is these aspects that must be addressed for virtual working to succeed. The importance of building relationships – often remotely – is seen as important by many teleworkers in getting their job done, exchanging ideas and transferring expertise. Indeed, more than just the communications infrastructure, it is the cultural and relationship infrastructure that supports work collaborations and knowledge exchange.

Mirchandani also addresses the issue of teleworking cost–benefits. These come, she notes, in both economic and non-economic forms. So far as economic cost benefits are concerned, however, many organisations expect to see benefits from teleworking arrangements before they commit themselves to incurring costs. As such, the uncertainty and risk involved in teleworking may cause many businesses to be conservative towards it. Mirchandani shows that the perceived risks associated with telework vary significantly depending on individual managers.

Differences between managers' behaviour and attitudes is also important for teleworking developments so far as the way arrangements are managed. Whereas many younger managers are willing to engage in trusting relations with teleworkers, as manifested in both supervisory norms and methods, Mirchandani notes that many older managers are not. Indeed, she argues that remote supervision demands a new style of management, involving participation – something that itself is to some degree personality dependent. The teleworkers studied also point to the motivational benefits gained from being trusted to do their work at home, as well as the pride such trust brings.

By looking through the prism of individual experiences, Mirchandani is able to reveal the sense of vulnerability felt by some teleworkers. This may well result where the arrangements involved are often not publicly recognised as accepted modes of working, and have not been formalised in company practices. Commitment towards the arrangement from the organisation is seen to be important for the individuals involved. Having their working mode valued, and feeling part of the organisation, is thus essential for commitment and motivation. This underscores the need for such arrangements to be voluntary.

Mirchandani concludes that where organisations are willing to challenge management styles and working norms, and unlearn the bad habits that have grown up around conventional ways of working, we are likely to see many potential benefits from teleworking.

In Chapter 6, by Sean Galpin and David Sims, we look specifically at the experience of identity in flexible working. The authors argue that, in today's world, one's identity is bound up with one's job of work. However, the sense of identity that arises from this does not happen in an unmediated way. Rather, argue the authors, such an identity is constituted, maintained and expressed through narratives and story telling. How we structure the stories we tell about ourselves reveals much about our identities.

The authors use this approach to illuminate the contrasts in experiences and identities between two groups of virtual workers: operatives and knowledge workers. Whereas the latter group are viewed as being highly skilled, flexible workers, the former work in lower-skilled and highly structured work environments, even though these may involve technology-supported, teleworking arrangements. By focusing on the capacity of each group to assemble narratives about themselves, the authors show that while knowledge workers are able to construct a strong sense of identity, and express this across a number of projects and relationships, operatives, because they are isolated from other workers, find it hard to construct a coherent identity for themselves.

Access to stories and opportunities for story telling also has important implications for organisational culture, as well as the capacity for individuals to gain access to such cultures. While operators may find difficulty in connecting what they do to wider organisational processes, and exchange jokes, stories and conversations about the organisation, knowledge workers have no such problems. Because of the nature of their roles and relationships, they are able to connect their experiences, roles and identities to the broader organisational picture. This is especially so, the authors show, where such workers occupy 'boundary-spanning' roles. This is often the case, of course, in virtual organisations, where individuals may need to work with others from different departments and functions, as well as separate organisations. In such cases, an ability to manage multiple identities may be needed.

Galpin and Sims use their approach to illustrate the need for flexible workers to learn new methods of communication in order to tell and sell their stories effectively in virtual working situations. This may include visual performances, but also written communications. Not all workers, they point out, are in a position to learn these crafts, thus frustrating the ability to develop new narratives. For instance, the actions and even conversations of operatives may be heavily circumscribed – as illustrated by the 'scripts' that must be followed by call centre employees. Moreover, because of the effort to enforce standards in such work, careful and intrusive monitoring (of calls and tasks) may also go on. Hence, opportunities for self-expression are curtailed. This may also be exacerbated by the limited induction into organisations enjoyed by operatives, as well as their physical isolation – reducing still further their capacity to assemble their own networks, and thus to build narratives.

5 Re-forming organisations

Contributions of teleworking employees

Kiran Mirchandani

Introduction

A number of scholars have focused on the ways in which the proliferation of virtual work impacts existing organisational structures. Given that so much of organisational life is assumed to be created and maintained within the physical boundary of a workplace, virtual workers can pose a considerable challenge to the cultures of organisations (Jackson and van der Wielen 1998). In this chapter I focus on one group of virtual workers – home-based professional or managerial employees (salaried teleworkers). I argue that these employees can provide significant insight on the ways in which organisations can use the growth of virtual work to develop employee-centred workplaces and challenge structures of discrimination often embedded in traditional organisational hierarchies. The lived experiences of teleworkers not only provide useful individual-level feedback on the effectiveness of work-at-home programmes and policies currently in place but also highlight the ways in which it is organisations, and their own treatment of telework, which determine the long-term effects of the proliferation of virtual work. With reference to qualitative interviews with fifty women and men (in Canada) who work at home, this chapter serves to highlight the contributions they make to ways in which organisations can be re-formed (for both virtual and non-virtual workers) through the introduction of telework. The discussion in this chapter is focused around two areas on which organisational concern about telework is often situated: economic and non-economic cost–benefit analyses and analyses on the organisational readiness for telework. The experiences of teleworkers reveal that while they are 'virtual' workers in that they are distanced from their organisations, they continue to be embedded in a physical environment (in their case, the home). Given the historical definition of the home as a private, extra-organisational space, teleworkers are seen to be working 'outside' organisational boundaries; they highlight the lack of trust, the need for visibility and the assumption of physical presence underlying knowledge-exchange within their organisations. This analysis reveals that the move towards virtual work would require a fundamental rethinking of the notion of organisation itself and necessitate its reconceptulisation as a set of relationships rather than as a physical site.

Methodology

Open-ended qualitative interviews were conducted between July 1993 and June 1994 with thirty female and twenty male teleworkers living in Toronto, Ottawa and Montreal. The teleworkers included in the present sample were highly skilled and well-paid 'knowledge workers' rather than operatives (see Galpin and Sims, Chapter 6 in this volume). Respondents were asked about their experiences of working at home and at the central office; interviews lasted between 1 and 2½ hours. Rather than providing answers to a defined set of questions, respondents were asked to discuss why they became teleworkers and to describe the ways in which telework impacted their work and family lives. Such a qualitative method of enquiry is particularly suitable for gaining knowledge about a phenomenon such as telework, given that many of the dimensions and implications of virtual working are as yet unmapped in the literature. Participants in the study were assured that their identities and the names of their employers would remain anonymous, which allowed them to discuss some of their frustrations with organisational responses to telework without jeopardising their own individual work-at-home arrangements. Overall, however, all of the teleworkers interviewed saw telework as a privilege and spoke about their experiences of working at home in largely positive ways.

The teleworkers in this sample should not be seen as representative of all virtual workers. Rather the teleworkers interviewed for this project are part of the small percentage of virtual workers who are organisationally powerful (occupying the core workforce) while being spatially peripheral (working outside the traditional organisational site). This dual location in the 'margin' and 'centre' (Hooks 1984) gives teleworkers an important and unique angle into the development of virtual work forms such as telework.

A snowball method was used to locate teleworkers, and individuals who met certain criteria were included in the study. Only those who are salaried employees of companies were interviewed; these criteria ensured a homogeneity in the employment conditions of the respondents. In addition, the sample for the present study was limited to individuals who were in occupations that were traditionally office-based; this allowed respondents to compare their experience of working at home and working in a central office (for example, academics or real estate agents were excluded). Teleworkers doing overtime work at home were also excluded from the sample; only those who work at home in lieu of office-based work were interviewed. About half the teleworkers in the present sample work at home four or more days of the week. The remainder spend between one and four of their work days at home. Teleworkers from eighteen different organisations in Canada (in both the public and private sectors) were interviewed; they perform a variety of jobs in management, administration, natural and applied sciences and sales. All interviews were transcribed verbatim and coded in-depth. A computer software package (The Ethnograph) was used to aid in the latter part of the data analysis.

Telework: cost–benefit analysis

There have been several studies attempting to assess the impact of telework on companies by using various forms of cost–benefit analyses (Ford and Butts 1991; Kroll 1984; Alvi and McIntyre 1993; Goodrich 1990; Filipczak 1992; Weijers *et al.* 1992). Financial costs to the organisation can include the installation of equipment in homes and the cost of training for both the teleworker and the supervisor. Financial benefits can accrue from the reduced need for office space, overheads and parking costs. Gordon, for example, estimates that it costs between $1,500 and $6,000 per employee per annum for office accommodation (1988: 115). Cote-O'Hara (1993: 104) notes that one large company based in Ottawa saved approximately one million dollars a year on real estate costs (see also Gray *et al.* 1994: 136).

Several of the costs and benefits of telework, however, are said to be *non-economic*. By offering the option to telework, organisations can attract and retain highly qualified employees, thus reducing recruitment and training costs (Gordon 1988: 144; TBS 1992: 13; Christensen 1992; Kugelmass 1995: 10; Pitt-Catsouphes and Morchetta 1991: 13). Often, with telework, work productivity increases since employees take less informal breaks during the day, and work in an environment over which they may have more control over interruptions (Olson 1989: 218; TBS 1992: 13; Schepp 1990: 3). Telework is also said to alleviate the conflict employees experience between their work and family responsibilities (Duxbury 1995). Work-at-home programmes can potentially enhance an organisation's corporate image; a company which offers this work option may receive favourable publicity for its progressive work styles (Olson 1989: 218). Other benefits can arise from the fact that instead of taking sick days or family leave days employees often continue to do their work from home (Filipczak 1992: 55; Gray *et al.* 1994: 136). These non-economic benefits may have a direct economic impact; JALA Associates has estimated that increased employee productivity with telework saved their company $4,000 per employee (Pitt-Catsouphes and Morchetta 1991: 24). Weiss notes that some telecommuting managers in Bell Atlantic recorded 200 per cent increases in output (1994: 51).

At the forefront of organisational costs is the possible threat to the coherence of the organisation, the repercussions of less frequent face-to-face communications and the difficulties associated with managing remote employees. There is a realisation that 'remote supervision' often requires different management styles from on-site supervision (Olson 1989: 221). As Christensen and Staines note, telework 'encourages a more participatory style of supervision – one that relies on planning and coordination rather than on monitoring' (1992: 462). Remote supervision can sometimes even be more time consuming (Olson 1989: 221).

Teleworker responses

Teleworkers frequently describe working at home as 'the ultimate' (Respondent 7, Woman) and 'a benefit for both [the individual and the organisation]'

(Respondent 20, Man). Some say they would not trade telework for a higher salary or a more senior job in another organisation. This does not imply that teleworkers do not note any difficulties associated with working at home; rather many see telework as the best of their available choices.

Within the context of this strong endorsement of telework, these employees make two sets of contributions to the debates around the organisational costs and benefits of telework. Through their experiences they provide invaluable direction on the gaps in the development of telework policy to date. First, teleworkers note that once a cost–benefit analysis is carried out, and telework is found to be beneficial to the organisation, the costs should be included in the operating budget of the company. A number of teleworkers note that although the commitment to telework programmes may exist, obtaining the correct infrastructure is often an 'uphill battle' (Respondent 24, Man). Teleworkers note:

> [The organisational policy is] that they will support people working at home. [That] does not mean that they are willing to start putting out money to make it possible.
>
> (Respondent 41, Woman)

> It is not expensive but in a big company there is so much bureaucracy…it took me six months to get my laptop [after my telework arrangement was officially approved]…there is a lot of politics [on]…who gets what and sometimes it is dependent on who you know instead of what you need.…I felt that I was running against a brick wall.…It frustrated me because I knew I could do a better job…but I was not given the tools to do it and I knew the tools were there. Look – there is a laptop PC that sits in this drawer [in a common room] seven days a week. Nobody uses it.
>
> (Respondent 24, Man)

A few teleworkers work for organisations within which telework is a well-developed programme and, as one woman says:

> They have provided us with the right equipment to do this job the right way. And that has been fundamental…you can't do it half way. You either have to do it properly or not at all. And the company that I work for has chosen to do it properly.
>
> (Respondent 42, Woman)

A second contribution that teleworkers make to the cost–benefit debate is to emphasise the central role of employee motivation, and its effect on the long-term organisational impact of telework. These workers recognise that if the work-at-home programme is well constructed, the organisation can reap many benefits from its employees. Teleworkers identify themselves as highly motivated employees who quickly embrace the opportunity to increase their contribution to the organisation. Teleworkers say:

If a person has to spend twelve hours doing one task, and you can get [that task] accomplished in three hours, there is a big savings…in dollars for my boss.

(Respondent 1, Man)

My boss trusts me and I think this is number one. If you don't have the trust, it is not good being a self starter and being disciplined.

(Respondent 9, Woman)

The primary source of this higher productivity, however, is teleworkers' own work motivation:

My boss told me – 'I won't keep track of your hours if you don't keep track of your hours.' Now why would he say that?…Because he knew that I already put in more than my expectation was and I had demonstrated that for years.

(Respondent 23, Man)

Teleworkers derive their work motivation from being recognised as a valuable part of their organisations. Accordingly, they stress that telework should be used as a way of *enhancing* this motivation, first, through a formal recognition of the organisational value of the teleworker, and second, through ensuring that telework remains a purely voluntary arrangement whereby an employee continues to feel connected to, and a vital part of, the corporation.

Teleworkers note that organisations should recognise the contributions of employees at home in ways which are attentive to the physical remoteness of these workers. One man notes:

I'm working around the company as opposed to the company being sensitive that this [telework] is a blessed program – it has got benefits to the company.…No-one in personnel…has given this thing one iota of respect.…[We should be] treated as a fully endorsed, vibrant, essential…part of the organisation.…If I were a manager of people [who telework] I think it would be important…to call them once a week to say: 'How's it going…keep up the good work.' Just so that the person knows that he [sic] is still part of the fold, there is still the umbilical cord.…I mean the President (of the company) should come out and say: 'Hey, this is great. We trust our employees…we will cater to them and we will do the following things and build a culture.'

(Respondent 44, Man)

Jackson argues that 'the formal view of organisation, which sees "real work" as being *task centred* not *relationship building*, neglects the social and network dynamics through which unanticipated problems are solved' (1997: 15). Teleworkers frequently do 'relationship building' remotely; discovering ways of maintaining virtual relationships forms part of their often invisible 'emotion work' (Fineman 1994). As one woman says:

> When you transfer expertise...to other individuals and go back and forth, you're giving them ideas creatively...that's kind of a hidden thing but I could see that being a potential problem [of working at home]....I decided one day, maybe it's up to me, so I started phoning and asking questions...[even for small things]...and they got used to me phoning.
>
> (Respondent 7, Woman)

This relationship building is, however, conceptualised as a set of individual tasks which teleworkers need to do to maintain their connection to the corporate culture. Teleworkers' comments reveal the prevalence of the belief that the organisation is a physical location (*within* the boundaries of which 'cultures' are created) rather than a collective endeavour (Jackson and van der Wielen 1998: 12) or a 'community of practice' (Campbell, Chapter 2 in this volume). As a result, teleworkers often see themselves as working outside a corporate culture rather than being part of its very definition:

> There's a certain community atmosphere in the [office] that...I'm no longer really a part of....You have to be able to build a relationship and a rapport with your colleagues if you want them to help you, or if you want to help them...that's one of the reasons why I'm trying to come into the office once a week.
>
> (Respondent 50, Man).

> I miss being part of a corporate culture. It's difficult to do that at home. You're not part of that corporate culture.
>
> (Respondent 30, Woman).

Galpin and Sims (Chapter 6 in this volume) challenge the notion that knowledge workers are developing 'new' forms of communication. Instead, they suggest that these workers may in fact be making greater use of traditional forms of relationship building in addition to the time they spend working at home. The experiences of teleworkers in the present sample point to the difficulties of building non-visual relationships within groups that do not, as yet, form 'communities of practice' (Campbell, Chapter 2 in this volume). Teleworkers operate within organisational norms which equate visibility with hard work, and work sites with the public sphere. The woman quoted above accordingly goes on to talk about why she does not feel part of the organisational culture at home. She says it is because of:

The place itself…There's definitely an environment that you know exists and its different than your home environment. And when you work at home you don't have that.

(Respondent 30, Woman)

This analysis suggests that virtual workers such as teleworkers feel the need to develop a particular 'environment' for work. Such an environment would allow teleworkers to use forms of relationship building with which their peers and customers are comfortable, and which are conducive to the transmission of 'tacit knowledge' (Nandhakumar, Chapter 4 in this volume). Teleworkers stress that setting up such an environment should be seen as an organisational responsibility:

One of the things that the company has to look at…[is] providing the umbilical cord to the corporation and make sure that it is never severed.…If people…have a job that allows them…to telecommute, it is really a benefit for the company. But the company has to recognise where their responsibilities are.

(Respondent 23, Man)

Part of the maintenance of the organisational coherence is the need to recognise that telework should not be a way of cutting employee costs by requiring individuals to work at home as independent contractors:

You have to be careful about that group atmosphere. It's very, very important.…..It's hard to work together and to develop comraderie and respect…if [telework] is overdone. I think it would be more detrimental than beneficial…that group thing would be lost.

(Respondent 26, Man)

The fact that teleworkers perceive this form of organisational support as not being present is clear in that they fear that working at home will be detrimental to their career advancement:

I may be cutting my own throat in that there may be less advancement for me.

(Respondent 34, Woman)

If you are actively seeking a promotion or you're looking for a new direction, the home is not the best place to be.…If you're working under the direction of the manager…they are seeing you everyday and you're socializing and you're talking and you're on their mind when it comes to promotions.

(Respondent 20, Man)

Teleworkers stress, therefore, that while companies frequently carry out cost–benefit analyses of telework, many expect to see the benefits *before* incurring the costs. They note that all the benefits frequently noted in the literature on the organisational advantages of telework depend primarily upon the high motivation of these employees. Structures must therefore be put into place to support and bolster this motivation, within a framework of volunteerism (see also Campbell, Chapter 2 in this volume, on knowledge management in the Web enterprise). As discussed in the next section, organisations often expect to implement telework programmes without having to fundamentally rethink how they *see themselves*. The creation of specific structures to maintain employee motivation need to be accompanied by challenges to the physicality assumed to be required in the creation and maintenance of organisations and their cultures.

Organisational readiness for telework

Several studies have focused on what makes organisations 'ready' for telework. Theorists note that some organisations may turn to telework as a means of immediate cost reduction which is achieved by changing workers' status from 'employee' to 'independent contractor'. There has been some research, however, which indicates that this form of restructuring poses significant problems in the long run. Korte notes that when the primary objective of telework is the externalisation of labour, employee dissatisfaction tends to be high (1988: 169). Leidner argues that such a policy can be directed only to employees without any other work options (1988: 74). Steinle notes that telework can only be used to reduce or eliminate employee benefits only when employee tasks are highly standardised (Steinle 1988: 12; Christensen 1988: 76). Accordingly, Gordon (1988: 124) summarises that 'it makes poor business sense' to convert employees into independent contractors (see also Galpin and Sims. Chapter 6 in this volume).

Other theorists note that organisations move towards telework in order to retain qualified and trained employees who are valuable members of the company. These are often highly paid employees who do not need direct supervision and whose work is evaluated in terms of long-term goals (Leidner 1988: 80; Olson 1989: 218; Goodrich 1990: 33; Kraut 1987: 119).

An organisation may also be 'ready' for telework when there is a recognition that its employees face significant work/family conflict which has a detrimental effect on their work. Accordingly, telework is seen as one of a number of work/family initiatives (others include flexitime, job sharing, compressed work weeks and part-time work). For example, the Canadian Federal Government's telework policy objective is to 'allow employees to work at alternative locations, thereby achieving a better balance between their work and personal lives' (TBS 1992: 3).

Teleworker responses

The literature on organisational readiness for telework has primarily stressed the advantages of telework for the company; the assumption is made that an organisation is 'ready' for telework when it can reap benefits from the introduction of this work arrangement. While these organisational advantages of telework are all mentioned by teleworking employees, several note that the most significant factor that indicates an organisation's readiness for telework is one that is seldom mentioned in telework policy. Teleworkers note that only in organisations which have mechanisms in place which acculturate, endorse and support norms which foster trust of remote workers, can the work arrangement be successfully introduced. While some telework policies recognise the need for these mechanisms for work-at-home programmes to be successful, it is often assumed that they already exist. For example, the Canadian Federal Government telework policy states that 'telework is based on the belief that mature, responsible adults do not need constant, close supervision in order to perform their work' (TBS 1992: 1). However, there is little focus in the policy on how this 'belief' is manifest, or developed in organisational practices.

Teleworkers note that such a culture of trust in fact frequently does not exist in organisations. One man says:

> I've seen a number of employers…[whose] definition of an employee is…someone you cannot trust. Whereas basically an employee is usually someone who works pretty darn hard for you and given the chance will work a hell of a lot harder.
>
> (Respondent 4, Man)

Faced with this focus on visibility, several teleworkers have had to lobby their organisations for years to introduce work-at-home policies:

> Nobody really wanted to talk about the subject at all…it went back and forth for two years…people [would say] the same thing over and over again – what if she falls down the stairs, what if the equipment causes a fire.
>
> (Respondent 7, Woman)

> The 'what-ifers' will get you every time. Those things…become things to hide behind for the people who are too afraid to take the step. (Respondent 11, Man)

Rather than changes in corporate culture, teleworkers attribute the work-at-home policies that they have in place to their individual supervisors:

> I did approach [my earlier boss]…and gave him my rationale for wanting…[to telework]. He sort of hummed and hawed a bit. He didn't

give me any reason why I shouldn't but he didn't support it....[Now I am] fortunate to be reporting to a relatively young, risk-taking boss.

(Respondent 38, Woman)

It's always been very...dependent on whomever you work for trusting you sufficiently to see that you actually can work away on your own and produce some sort of results.

(Respondent 4, Man)

Recognising the possibility of changes in the organisational hierarchy and supervision chains, teleworkers see the work at home option as being in a precarious position. As one woman says:

Sometimes I wish they'd just commit themselves....I don't dare cancel my parking [at the central office] because it could take me three months to get it back.

(Respondent 34, Woman)

Not only is the individual teleworker harmed in this situation, but the organisation, too, is not able to capitalise on employee motivation:

You can't commit to a company that does not commit to you....I think that is a message for employers that if you really want the best of your employees you have got to let them...take responsibility because when they do that they're probably going to do better than when you tell them what to do.

(Respondent 6, Woman)

Teleworkers who do work within organisations which attempt to foster a culture of trust are careful to point to this fact as the key to successful telecommuting:

It gives me some pride at being different from the rest of the crowd....I find that my company trusts me....It has given me a sense of pride and ownership to be able to say that I am working from home.

(Respondent 50, Man)

Rather than assuming that this culture exists, or will develop automatically, teleworkers stress that it is necessary for a company to actively and continuously foster cultures which are created within, and support 'dispersed organisations' (van der Wielen *et al.* 1993: 150). Several strategies are proposed on ways in which corporations can acculturate, endorse and support telework within their organisations.

Acculturation

The 'acculturation' of telework would involve a recognition that remote work is part of the culture of the organisation. While many work practices are based on present and visible employees, telework challenges companies to rethink the equation that is often drawn between being visible and working hard. In fact, teleworkers note that a culture which supports remote interactions would allow all employees, both office and home based, to benefit. Teleworkers say:

> [With telework] work got better for everyone because rather than those dreadful ad hoc meetings…it required a bit more discipline of everyone to say, 'OK, at one o'clock, I'll find B— and we'll phone you at home.'
>
> (Respondent 11, Man)

> When you're right there they [your colleagues] are more apt to check their little problem out with you and your peer and the next person. [When I am at home] they have to phone me…what that really does for the company is that it helps people make better decisions on who they are going to get input from and how frequently they are going to interrupt you.
>
> (Respondent 38, Woman)

Teleworkers see the need for a balance between remote and face-to-face contact between employees. Achieving this balance would be beneficial to the organisation and should, as such, be recognised as an organisational responsibility. Accordingly, the acculturation of telework would involve setting up structures which support remote interaction in conjunction with the provisions of opportunities for face-to-face meetings. To achieve this balance, teleworkers suggest strategies such as training sessions for telephone meetings, the formation of 'information loops' that are viable alternatives to memos in mailboxes, prearranged meeting times and regularly organised gatherings. Galpin and Sims (Chapter 6 in this volume) discuss the ways in which narratives play a role in the formation of workers' identities. This suggests that the acculturation of virtual work would require opportunity for the remote creation of organisational narratives. In effect, the creation of cultures which support remote interactions may necessitate the rigidity rather than the flexibility of organisational processes (Jackson 1997).

The acculturation of telework would involve the challenging of norms which underlie the cultures of many of today's organisations. Rather than assuming that decentralised forms of working will automatically lead to the 'unfreezing' of the culture of an organisation (Schein 1994: 142), teleworkers' comments discussed above suggest that they remain embedded within norms which equate visibility with career advancement and home-based work with leisure. These norms are gendered in that they assume that paid work is separable from family responsibilities and has first claim on workers (see Mirchandani (1999) and Mirchandani (1998a)). The widespread prevalence of these norms requires organisational change which far exceeds the introduction of individual work/family policies or telework programmes for selected employees.

Endorsement

As noted in the discussion above, telework is often situated within a rhetoric of precarious privilege. As one woman says:

> I don't know whether to play it [telework] up or just keep quiet….I try not to say too much about anything…[so as not]…to jeopardise the programme.
>
> (Respondent 7, Woman)

Teleworkers stress that this precariousness is related to the lack of formal organisational endorsement of telework; only with such endorsement can the full benefits of the work arrangement be reaped. Such endorsement would involve a public recognition of the existence and value of this work arrangement. This may involve, for example, training on telework for support staff, switchboard operators and human resource personnel. The organisational endorsement of telework would also necessitate the standardisation of protection for the teleworker.

Most of the individuals interviewed for the present study do have some form of written contract around telework. There are, however, vast differences in what these contracts include, and which levels of the organisation they involve. For one teleworker, for example, the contract was a negotiation which involved the tele-worker, the supervisor, the union and the President of the company. For another, the contract was a letter in the employee's file, approved by the manager. Telework contracts also differ greatly in terms of what they include. For a few teleworkers, a comprehensive contract is used; this contract includes the days and times work is to be done at home, the job content and how it is to be evaluated, the equipment to be provided, the insurance coverage, and the safety standards to be maintained in the home. Some contracts include a clause that identifies telework as a voluntary arrangement; employees have the option to return to the central office at any time. The development of such standardised contracts would ensure a basic level of employee protection and allow the employee's tele-work performance to be measured against certain collaboratively predetermined yardsticks. Table 5.1 shows eight dimensions which telework contracts can address; while formalising telework arrangements for individuals doing piece-work at home may in fact mean that their work is further routinised and deskilled, such contracts are likely to benefit home-based knowledge workers.

It is interesting to note that many teleworkers in the present sample report that they themselves did much of the research in developing business plans and telework contracts. This research work is often unrecognised, suggesting a need for organisations to acknowledge the research being done by pioneering tele-workers. As part of the endorsement of telework, the development of

Table 5.1 Formalisation of telework contracts

Nature of contract		
Dimension	Informal	Formal
Type of contract	Verbal	Written
Level of approval	Immediate supervisor	President of company
Union involvement	Union not informed	Included in Union negotiations
Detail included in contract	None	Information about telework days/times
Worker protection	Assumed; handled on case by case basis if problem arises	Insurance and compensation predetermined
Job evaluation	Assumed to be same as on-site work	Established work goals and methods of evaluation.
Equipment	Employee provided or requested on an ad hoc basis	Automatically provided by employer as part of telework package
Voluntarism	Unstated	Guaranteed

programmes and contracts should be seen as primarily an organisational, rather than an 'unpaid' employee, responsibility.

Support

Clearly the ability to work at home depends on access to the technology and infrastructure commonly available in the workplace. Among the present sample of teleworkers, there are vast differences in the extent to which the arrangement is supported within the organisation. There is little standardisation of equipment and infrastructural support with which employees are provided while they work at home. Almost all teleworkers cover part of their work costs themselves, especially for furniture and maintenance (such as electricity bills). Teleworkers are rarely compensated for the fact that part of their home is dedicated to organisational activities.

Support for telework clearly involves more than just an endorsement of the potential advantages of this work arrangement for the company. Such support requires a coordinated effort to standardize the equipment provided to all workers at home, and to align this equipment with the infrastructure of the central workspace. Accordingly, through technology, and some capital investment, remote interactions can be made feasible.

Conclusion

In light of the seemingly numerous teleworker demands, it is perhaps useful to return to the question of why an organisation would initiate a telework programme. The advantages for individual companies can be numerous and are well documented in the literature cited in this chapter. Employees working at home, however, stress that telework forces an organisation to rethink work styles which are traditionally accepted as business norms. Challenging these business norms, as one teleworking manager notes, has led him to realise that:

> One of the things that working in an office has done is that it has bred a bunch of bad habits...ninety per cent of what you get dragged into are totally inconsequential issues.
>
> (Respondent 11, Man)

Telework, if successfully implemented, can therefore provide a reflective critique of the work norms within an organisation, thus providing the impetus through which effective organisational change can occur.

Noting advantages and drawbacks of telework do not, however, provide strategies for ways in which organisations can maximise on the benefits and minimise on the disadvantages of telework; these strategies can most clearly be seen through the lived experiences of teleworking employees. The long-term impact of telework on the organisation, these employees suggest, can be overwhelmingly positive. This is so, however, only if the introduction of this work arrangement is recognised not as a benefit given to a handful of valuable employees with progressive supervisors, but as a tool through which the organisations can move towards cultures and work styles which allow all employees (both home and office based) to reach a fuller work potential.

Bibliography

Alvi, Shahid and McIntyre, D. (1993) 'The open collar worker', *Canadian Business Review*, 20, 1: 21–4.

Christensen, K. (1988) *Women and Home-Based Work: The Unspoken Contract*, New York: Henry Holt & Co.

Christensen, K. (1992) 'Work restructuring as a result of family responsive policies', paper presented at the *Boston University Work and Family Roundtable*, 14–16 October, Montreal.

Christensen, K. and Staines, G. (1992) 'Flexitime: a viable solution to work/family conflict', *Journal of Family Issues*, 11, 4: 455–76.

Cote-O'Hara, J. (1993) 'Sending them home to work: telecommuting', *Business Quarterly*, Spring: 104–9.

Duxbury, L. (1995) 'Balancing work and family: impact on the bottom line', presentation at the *International Association of Business Communicators Conference*, Toronto, June.

Filipczak, B. (1992) 'Telecommuting: a better way to work?', *Training*, May: 53–61.

Fineman, S. (ed.) (1994) *Emotion in Organisations*, London: Sage.

Ford, R. and Butts, M. (1991) 'Is your organization ready for telecommuting?', *SAM Advanced Management Journal*, Autumn: 19–23.

Goodrich, J. (1990) 'Telecommuting in America', *Business Horizons*, 33, 4: 31–7.

Gordon, G. (1988) 'The dilemma of telework: technology vs tradition', in Korte, W.B., Robinson, S. and Steinle, W.J. (eds) *Telework: Present Situation and Future Development of a New Form of Work Organization*, Amsterdam: Elsevier.

Gray, M., Hodson, N. and Gordon, G. (1994) *Teleworking Explained*, Chichester: Wiley.

hooks, b. (1984) *Feminist Theory: From Margin to Centre*, Boston: South End Press.

Jackson, P. and van der Wielen, J. (1998) 'Introduction: actors, approaches and agendas: from telecommuting to the virtual organisation', in Jackson, P. and van der Wielen (eds) *Teleworking: International Perspectives – from Telecommuting to the Virtual Organization*, London: Routledge.

Jackson, P. (1997) 'Flexibility and rigidity in new forms of work: individual versus organisational issues', *EAWOP Symposium*, Verona.

Korte, W.B. (1988) 'Telework: potential, inception, operation and likely future situation', in Korte, W.B., Robinson, S. and Steinle, W.J. (eds) *Telework: Present Situation and Future Development of a New Form of Work Organization*, Amsterdam: Elsevier.

Kraut, R.E. (1987) 'Predicting the use of technology: the case of telework', in Kraut, R.E. (ed.) *Technology and the Transformation of White-Collar Work*, New Jersey: Lawrence Erlbaum Associates.

Kroll, D. (1984) 'Telecommuting: a revealing peek inside some of industry's first electronic cottages', *Management Review*, November: 18–21.

Kugelmass, J. (1995) *Telecommuting: A Manager's Guide to Flexible Work Arrangements*, New York: Lexington Books.

Leidner, R. (1988) 'Homework: a study in the interaction of work and family organization', *Research in the Sociology of Work*, 4: 69–94.

Mirchandani, K. (1998a) 'Protecting the boundary: teleworker insights on the expansive concept of "work"', *Gender and Society*, 12, 2: 168–87.

—— (1998b) ' "The best of both worlds" and "Cutting my own throat": Contradictory images of home-based work', presented at American Sociological Association Annual Meetings, San Francisco, August.

—— (1999) 'Legitimizing work: telework and the gendered reification of the work–nonwork boundary', *Canadian Review of Sociology and Anthropology*, 36,1: 87–108.

Olson, M.H. (1989) 'Organizational barriers to professional telework', in Bosis, E. and Daniels, C.R. (eds) *Homework*, Urbana: University of Illinois Press.

Pitt-Catsouphes, M. and Morchetta, A. (1991) *The Coming of Age: Telework*, Boston University, Center for Work and Family, November.

Schepp, B. (1990) *The Telecommuter's Handbook*, New York: Pharos Books.

Schein, E.H. (1994) 'Innovative cultures and organizations', in Allen, T.J. and Morton, M.S.S. (eds) *Information Technology and the Corporation of the 1990s*, New York: Oxford University Press.

Steinle, W.J. (1988) 'Telework: opening remarks on an open debate', in Korte, W.B., Robinson, S. and Steinle, W.J. (eds) *Telework: Present Situation and Future Development of a New Form of Work Organization*, Amsterdam: Elsevier.

TBS (1992) *Telework Pilot Program in the Public Service*, Treasury Board Secretariat (Canada), Personnel Policy Branch.

van der Wielen, J.M.M, Tallieu, T.C.B., Poolman, J.A. and van Zuilichem J. (1993) 'Telework: dispersed organizational activity and new forms of spatial-temporal co-ordination and control', *European Work and Organizational Psychologist*, 3, 2: 145–62.

Weijers, T., Meijer, R. and Spoelman, E. (1992) 'Telework remains "made to measure": the large scale introduction of telework in The Netherlands', *Futures*, December: 1048–55.

Weiss, J.M. (1994) 'Telecommuting boosts employee output', *HR Magazine*, February: 51–3.

6 Narratives and identity in flexible working and teleworking organisations

Sean Galpin and David Sims

Introduction

It has long been recognised that work and identity are intimately bound up with each other. On presenting yourself to someone you have not met before you are likely to tell that person at an early stage something about how you earn your living. As Sims *et al.* (1993) point out, the question 'What do you do?' is clearly understood in our culture to be about work occupation, not about eating or personal habits. Adults getting to know a child will often ask some variant of the question: 'What do you want to do when you grow up?' This is not because they need some prediction of occupation. It is because the answer to that question, even in childhood, gives some impression of identity. The question is based on the premise that, if you want to know what sort of people children expect to be, they will best tell you by talking about the future occupations they have in mind.

Studies of redundant managers and workers have led to the same conclusion; identity is closely bound up with work. But how do we express and maintain our identity? We shall be arguing that this is done principally through narratives and storytelling. We construct events into a story, both for others and for our own consumption. The stories we tell about ourselves reveal the aspects of ourselves and our lives that we think are worth telling people about, and the narratives by which we structure and connect the elements of those stories show something of the way we think the world works.

In this chapter, we argue that narratives both reveal and constitute the identities of workers, and we apply this argument to a study of the narrative accounts of people in flexible working and teleworking arrangements. At the same time, narratives reveal something important and basic about the contrasting experience of work for two different groups of workers in our study. One group is referred to as 'operatives'. They are isolated from other workers and unable to construct a coherent identity for themselves. Their identity and experience of working life is constructed for them by others, or by the structure of their jobs. The other group we refer to as 'knowledge workers', using Bell's (1973) term and applying it specifically to highly skilled flexible workers. We suggest that knowledge workers are able to construct an identity for themselves, and to show the strength of that identity as it persistently reveals itself across the range of projects with which they are involved.

Narrative and identity

A much-quoted phrase of Christie and Orton (1988) was that human beings are '*homo narrans narratur*' – that is, they are storytellers and the subjects of stories, both their own stories and those of others. We are narrators and narrative. Boland and Tenkasi (1995: 357) make a bold claim for the scope of narrative understanding:

> The importance of narrative has not gone unnoticed in organisational research.…Myth and saga are important, but they can distract our attention from the way that human cognition operates almost continuously in a narrative, storytelling mode.

Some authors give even greater scope to a narrative approach. For example, Hardy (1968: 5) says:

> We dream in narrative, daydream in narrative, remember, anticipate, hope, despair, believe, doubt, plan, revise, criticise, construct, gossip, learn, hate and love by narrative.

Widdershoven (1993: 6–7) argues that 'experiences have little value as long as they are not connected to, or as Proust says, fused with stories' (6–7). We do not turn an event into an experience – something that we might remember and learn from – until we have connected it with a story. This is supported by Kelly's (1955) theorising about experience, that experience is not simply colliding with events; we experience only to the extent that we are changed by the events that we collide with, and this change is revealed by a change in our constructs. We would suggest that what Kelly does not offer is a mechanism for making or retaining the change in constructs, and that narrative does more to explain how and where we learn from experience.

This leads us on naturally to the notions of memory and identity. Funkenstein (1993: 23) says:

> The identity of an individual and the identity of a group consists of the construction of a narrative, internal and external.

Funkenstein (p. 24) says that the holocaust is characterised by the surprising inability of survivors to construct anything other than very fragmented memories of the events:

> The Nazis robbed them of their identity, of their capacity to construct a narrative, of investing the events of their lives with meaning and purpose.

Memory is carried through stories and narrative, and there is nothing to remember unless people have constructed a narrative and thus gained meaning and purpose.

It would, of course, be utterly meaningless to insist that everything is narrative, but it may be that everything we can remember is narrative, that narrative *is* sense-making and vice versa. Weick (1995: 128) says:

> The requirements necessary to produce a good narrative provide a plausible frame for sensemaking. Stories posit a history for an outcome. They gather strands of experience into a plot that produces that outcome. The plot follows either the sequence beginning–middle–end or the sequence situation–transformation–situation. But sequence is the source of sense.

As different people pick up and retell stories, so those stories become vehicles or carriers of their teller's own identity, as well as possibly re-shapers of that identity. As O'Connor says, stories are one of the ways in which we talk to ourselves, and shape and remember events for ourselves. The role that we cast for ourselves within the stories is one of the means by which we construct ourselves. As MacIntyre (1981: 216) puts it:

> I can only answer the question 'What am I to do?' if I can answer the prior question, 'Of what story or stories do I find myself a part?'.

Bruner (1990: 111) summarises Spence (1984) thus:

> Spence addressed the question of whether a patient in analysis *recovered* the past from memory in the sense in which an archaeologist digs up artefacts of a buried civilisation, or whether, rather, analysis enabled one to *create* a new narrative that, though it might be only a screen memory or even a fiction, was still close enough to the real thing to start a reconstructive process going. The 'truth' that mattered, so went his argument, was not the historical truth but the *narrative* truth.

However, there may be more than one narrative truth. Several writers on narrative emphasise the multiplicity of narratives and identities attached to a single individual. Neisser (1994) states that an individual does not tell a single story from which a coherent identity is constructed; rather 'there is a multiplicity of selves' (p. 9). The stories an individual tells and the identity they present vary with the individual's mood, the audience to which the story is being 'sold' (Ochberg 1993b) and the occasion.

So far we have considered the relationship between narrative and identity at the individual level. However, there is also evidence that identity construction via narrative extends beyond the individual to the organisation. Johnson's (1988) study of a large men's clothing retailer gives an insight into the process by which narratives are exchanged, agreed and protected from change within organisations. Meanwhile Cook and Yanow's (1993) study of the organisational culture of hand-crafted flute-making firms in Boston suggests that culture 'is reflected, for example, in the company's stories and myths' (p. 384).

O'Connor (1997: 304) gives a general version of this argument, and illustrates something of the way that stories interact with identity at the organisational level:

> To discover how anything happens in an organisation, we ask people to tell us stories. To convince others that we know something about how things happen in organisations, we construct and tell stories about those stories. As others react to our stories, they tell stories about the stories we have told – and so on.

Thus storytelling would appear to be at the centre of the organisation, providing both collective and individual cognition and identity. However, as Boje (1991) reminds us, stories in organisations do not get told in their entirety by one person. They are often multi-authored, and parts of them are left implicit as a teller assumes that the audience will know part of the story from other sources. Boje (1995: 1030) comments 'the storytelling organisation consists of many struggling stories, each a particular framing of reality being chased by wandering and fragmented audiences'. This 'plurivocality' (Boje 1995: 1030) is emphasised by Curt's (1994) concept of narrative 'tectonics'. Curt suggests that new stories 'never arise entirely spontaneously, but are crafted out of existing ones or the discursive spaces between them' (p. 12). It is the 'dynamic interplay' (p. 9) between existing narratives which not only creates new ones but also enables existing stories to be 'marketed…muted, adapted, reconstructed and disposed of' (p. 12).

Before considering storytelling and identity within flexible working arrangements it is worth while briefly discussing a point of difference in narrative literature. This revolves around the exact way in which narratives create identity. Two views may broadly be delineated. The first is that narrative is something which is constantly performed, and it is this performance which creates identity. The second is that it is the text, rather than the performance of a story, which creates identity.

The performance view is typified by Ochberg (1993a). As we have already seen, in order to create and sustain identity individuals must tell their stories to themselves and to others. However, Ochberg points out that, despite the storied character and feel of life in organisations, in reality the complete process of telling a story can be observed comparatively rarely. This leads him to argue that people do not just tell stories about their lives, 'they live out their affairs in storied forms' (p. 116); they 'perform' (p. 117) their lives with reference to the narrative and identity which they have constructed for themselves. Thus everything an individual does is done with reference to a narrative 'script' and the performance of this script creates and sustains identity.

The second school of thought is based on the argument that people tell stories about their experiences rather than performing narratives. In other words, identity is formed from text not performance. This line is taken by Ricoeur (as cited by Widdershoven, 1993: 5) who argues that 'it is only in the story that the meaning of life really takes form'.

This conflict is perhaps reconciled by Barthes (1974) who distinguishes between two kinds of texts that authors may write, *scriptible* texts (translated by Roe (1994) as 'writerly') and *laisible* ones (translated by Roe as 'readerly'). The distinction between 'readerly' and 'writerly' narratives is based on the way they are intended to be heard by others. 'Readerly' narratives invite passive reception on the part of listeners, and may be equated with the view of narrative as text. Meanwhile 'writerly' narratives offer the hearer the opportunity to participate as a writer or co-author of the narrative and may perhaps be equated with the performance view of narrative. Roe suggests that some storytellers involve their audience in more participation, and are more likely to build their storytelling partly from narrative elements supplied by their audience, than others. In this way the distinction between narratives as text and as performance may depend on the individual's storytelling preference. Perhaps it is simplest to conclude that 'text and performance can be viewed as two sides of the same coin' (Boje 1991: 110).

People spend their time narrating, and this includes narrating themselves. We are continuously telling each other whom we wish to be taken to be in the stories in which we have parts. Any meeting could be used to illustrate this, as we present ourselves in particular role identities. We have argued elsewhere (Sims 1995) that the identification of different types of narrative plot with which we construct our stories about ourselves can be helpful in understanding this. So we see that narratives are the means by which we understand the story of how we come to be in our present situation, and give ourselves a place and a role within that story. They are also the means by which we create an image of a future for ourselves, and of the identity that we are to carry in to that future. They are the means by which we remember our sense of who we are, and by which we communicate that identity to others.

Experiences of different groups of flexible workers

Flexible workers 'are by no means an homogeneous group' (Huws *et al.* 1990: 103). It may be expected that the experience of an elite flexible worker, able to dictate terms to his or her employer, would be very different from that of a parent teleworking in order to try to combine work and family obligations. Our data suggest that flexible workers may be divided into two groups, each with its own concerns, narratives and issues of identity. In this section the nature of the two groups is explored.

The argument is based on the work of Burrell (1997), that Taylorism may be seen as 'essentially an assault upon the peasantry' (p. 107). By 'peasantry' he is referring to the vast numbers of European agricultural emigrants to the United States in the late nineteenth and early twentieth centuries. Burrell argues that the innovation of Taylorism is breaking work down into simple repetitive tasks so that a worker need not possess any industrial skills, nor indeed have a strong grasp of English in order to perform the tasks required. New immigrants were taken out of their cultural and family contexts and set to work in environments where their colleagues could be expected to speak different languages and possess very different cultural identities. As Burrell puts it, 'Taylorism has to be understood therefore, as an assault on the peasantry by making their origins, beliefs and values meaningless and immaterial. It does not socialise the peasantry; it circumvents them' (p. 105).

While Taylorism was destroying the identity of industrial peasants, it may be argued that it was creating identity for another group. Industrial mass production saw the development of a new type of worker, the professional manager. Foucault (1975) comments that mass production required 'intense, continuous supervision which ran throughout the production process' (p. 174). For the first time this supervision was carried out by paid supervisors rather than a 'master' working side by side with workers. As Foucault says, 'a specialised personnel became indispensable, constantly present and distinct from the workers' (p. 174). He goes on to suggest that intensive supervision by paid employees was necessary because the economies of scale involved in mass production meant that seemingly minor infringements of rules could multiply into major losses. Constant supervision by paid staff became an economic necessity. With the development of professional managers came the creation of new narratives which evolved into a management discourse (Knights and Morgan 1992). Thus in terms of narratives and identity Taylorism created clear 'winners' and 'losers' – those who could construct a narrative and thus an identity for themselves, and those who could not.

According to Burrell, today 'peasants exist across the planet' (p. 84). He goes on to say that 'the history of corporate growth has been marked by successful assaults on the peasantry' (p. 103). 'Peasants' in some form continue to exist within organisations today, and their identity continues to be subverted. This argument is supported by other writers. Garson (1975) states that 'the methods of Ford and Taylor, division of labour and stop watch supervision, which were applied to factories at the turn of the century, are now being applied to offices' (p. 150). Meanwhile Donkin (1997) quotes work on Microsoft by Stross (1997). Stross suggests that in attempting to recruit the most able individuals, companies such as Microsoft are creating a widening division between elite workers who might be termed 'knowledge workers' and others which Burrell might refer to as 'peasants'. This line of argument reflects the large volume of work available on the model of the labour market as core and periphery (Atkinson 1989).

The existence of an 'elite' and a 'peasantry' within contemporary labour markets is also addressed by Robert Reich (1997) who states that in America 'all the rungs on the economic ladder are now further apart than a generation ago, and the space between them continues to spread'. He supports this assertion with a variety of statistics including the statements that 'between 1979 and 1995, the income of the richest fifth of American families grew by 26 per cent in real terms, while the income of the poorest fifth fell by 9 per cent', and 'between 1980 and 1995, the real weekly earnings of [US] workers in the top tenth rose by 10.7 per cent…workers in the bottom tenth saw their pay drop 9.6 per cent'. Thus there is evidence to suggest that a division continues to exist today, indeed exists perhaps more than ever, between a group of affluent, valued, skilled workers and a group which Burrell might refer to as 'peasants'.

Most pointedly, the European Commission (1994) suggests that a division of the type outlined above may be observed among flexible workers. The Commission places teleworkers into two groups: 'middle class, self-motivated independent individuals', and low wage relatively unskilled workers who are 'desperate for work and, therefore, open to exploitation'. Quinn (1992) also supports the view that in a technologically advanced 'intelligent' enterprise there will be distinct groups with very different experiences. This leads to the argument of this chapter, that flexible workers may be divided into two groups, a skilled, elite 'core' which will be referred to as 'knowledge workers', and an unskilled 'peasant' group which will be referred to as 'operatives'. We have chosen to use the term 'operative' since it is devoid of many of the emotive and pejorative associations of the word 'peasant', and also appears to be appropriate to the type of data entry work commonly performed by this group.

It might be expected that operatives and knowledge workers have different experiences of flexible working, and in the next section we detail these differences. Before doing this, however, it is worth noting that these experiences are based in part on the way in which electronic space is constructed for each group. Samarajiva (1993) states that 'Perhaps the most important idea taken from the cyberspace literature is the conceptualisation of the Internet as a space, rather than as a conduit, or as a system of conduits' (p. 36). The conceptualisation of IT and telecommunications networks as 'electronic space' is important since space is where narratives and identities are constructed and reconstructed. As Wagner and Kompast (1998) state 'places are specific settings for interaction; they provide a context for social activities' (p. 96). They further suggest that flexible workers 'not only have to make transitions between multiple work sites; they also make extensive use of electronic spaces for communication and work. These spaces are different from the places we are familiar with' (p. 99). They allow 'for disrupting and reassembling narratives' (p. 99) in new ways. This is supported by Jackson's (1997) observation that the very nature of what is constructed as work is determined in part by spatial parameters. It is to the construction of narratives and identity by knowledge workers and operatives in the context of electronic space that we will now turn.

The knowledge worker's experience of storytelling and identity formation

The constantly changing identity of the knowledge worker

McKinley (1996) suggests that in 'virtual' organisations many more employees will hold boundary-spanning positions than has previously been the case. It may be argued that this is particularly true of skilled knowledge worker roles. Meanwhile, Wagner and Kompast (1998) state that flexible working is often related to project working; particularly for highly skilled, valuable knowledge workers, and cite Perin (1996), who suggests that employees in companies organised around projects, experience different levels of 'project density' (Wagner and Kompast 1998: 436). Some projects they work on will be more significant than others, both organisationally and personally. In some they will take a more central role, and each project will have a different expected output, some of which will be more easily measured and thus rewarded than others. For all these reasons 'each project puts employees into different spaces' (Wagner and Kompast 1998: 436). Accordingly it may be argued that identity will be constructed differently in each space so that an employee will assume different identities when working on different projects. Thus, we argue that the boundary-spanning project-based nature of much knowledge work encourages knowledge workers to construct multiple identities – depending on which part of their organisation or a partner organisation they are dealing with and the nature of the projects they are working on.

The above is supported by Wetherell and Potter's (1989) role theory of identity which assumes that 'the individual is like a chameleon with not one stable consistent personality or set of traits but the ability to play many parts and assume many guises' (p. 207). Berger and Luckmann (1966) follow a similar line with the theory of alternation, again suggesting that in industrial societies individuals assume different identities in different situations.

The suggestion that the knowledge worker identity is shifting is also supported by writers on narrative. The point has already been made above that individuals tell multiple narratives (Ochberg 1993b; Curt 1994), and on this basis we would expect identity to shift with shifts in narrative. As Neisser (1994: 9) comments: 'there is a multiplicity of selves'.

The requirement to learn new methods of storytelling

As we have seen, telling and 'selling' narratives is vital in constructing identity for oneself and communicating it to others (Ochberg 1993b). There is evidence to suggest that flexible workers are required to learn new methods of communication in order to effectively tell and sell stories in electronic space (Finholt 1997, Costigan Lederman 1986). Davies (1995) suggests that flexible workers must learn new methods of storytelling which rely less on visual performance and more on written and spoken eloquence and presentation. This suggestion is supported by Sproul and Kiesler (1991) who state that in electronic communication individuals focus on the words in the message; therefore, skilful writing is required to communicate a message persuasively.

We argue that opportunities to learn these skills are not available to all flexible workers, they are often only available to knowledge workers. It has already been shown that knowledge workers are increasingly occupying boundary-spanning positions. The nature of these positions may offer a powerful justification for learning the new skills of communication and presentation associated with electronic space. However, the boundary-spanning nature of operative work is often either severely circumscribed or non-existent. A data entry operative will generally not be expected to have any contact with partner organisations or customers, and will work within clearly defined organisational boundaries. Meanwhile a teleworking agent in a virtual call centre will have contact with customers, but this contact is often severely circumscribed by the 'script' that the agent is expected to follow in order to capture information from callers. In such situations, boundaries between those inside and outside the organisation are clearly defined, and there is little or no requirement for creativity in communicating across organisational boundaries. Therefore we argue, first, that organisations often do not view training operatives in the subtleties of new communication methods as a necessity and, second, that learning new methods of communication is vital in order to tell stories effectively in electronic space. Thus operatives are effectively prevented from constructing and communicating narratives and identity in electronic space.

The operative's experience of storytelling and identity formation

The flexible working narrative told to operatives

Before considering operatives' experience of organisational storytelling and identity construction it is worth while briefly reviewing the way in which flexible working is presented to operatives and, in particular, why it is that despite its drawbacks operatives continue to enter into flexible working arrangements. It may be argued that a very particular narrative is told about flexible working via television, the popular press (Gooding 1993, Houlder 1994) and advertising, which focuses largely on its benefits. Although this narrative is not aimed solely at operatives it may be expected to influence their choices to work flexibly.

Boje (1995: 1025) refers to a story which appeals to a 'fundamental essential of human character' as an 'essentialism'. It may be argued that the essentialisms in the narrative of Taylorist production told to European agricultural immigrants concerned the offer to earn more money than they had ever done before, to be able to provide for themselves and their families, and to buy into the 'American dream'. In the same way the essentialism within the story of flexible working told to the operative would appear to concern the opportunity to combine work and family commitments; the offer of increased freedom and leisure time. Burrell's (1997) work illustrates very fully that the experience of Taylorism can be presented in very different terms from those of the essentialisms associated with it; and in the same way an alternative account of the experiences of flexible working operatives can be constructed from that above. Such a view is outlined below.

The isolation of flexible working operatives from organisational storytelling

The suggestion that operatives are excluded from learning new methods of storytelling associated with electronic space has already been discussed above. However, operatives may also be excluded from fully understanding more traditional methods of storytelling. Limited induction and lack of contact with colleagues may prevent operatives from completely understanding major organisational narratives, and accepted storytelling practices which must be followed in order to sell a narrative to others (Miller 1994). Boje (1991: 110) comments: 'Part of knowing how to behave in a storytelling organisation is knowing who can tell and who can be told a particular story.' The argument here is that operatives may be isolated from learning these 'entitlement rights' (p. 110) and other storytelling practices and customs.

The isolation of flexible working operatives from organisational storytelling is exacerbated by the nature of operative work. 'Unlike factory hands, clerical workers usually can't talk while they work and there is nothing cooperative about their tasks' (Garson 1975: 152). Hamper's (1991) account of working on a General Motors production line shows the rich possibilities for informal storytelling and identity construction on a car production line. This may be contrasted with Machung's (1988) account which emphasises the lack of informal communication among data-processing staff, even when physically proximate. Thus flexibly working operatives may be impeded in telling and hearing organisational narratives, and therefore possess a limited understanding of their organisations' rationale and their place within that rationale; in other words, their identity at work.

Operatives and the panoptic quality of electronic space

The panopticon was originally conceived as a building, but has now become a metaphor for any system of continual surveillance, or apparent continual surveillance which encourages individuals to police their own activities (Samarajiva 1993; Foucault 1975). Such a system effectively takes identity from those within it by discouraging self-expression and by forcing the individual to internalise the rules of the panopticon, so that they become his or her personal code upon which to act. Thus the identity of each individual within a panopticon is built around the rules associated with that panopticon, rather than individual self-expression or storytelling.

Originally a panopticon was constrained by physical space (Foucault 1975). It is argued here that Communication and Information Technologies (CITs) allow for the creation of panopticons in electronic space; which renders physical space an irrelevant consideration, and which allow for new forms of surveillance. As Samarajiva (1993: 37) states: 'electronic environments tend to allow for easier surveillance'.

In previous forms of industrial panopticon, such as Taylorist production lines, there is evidence that some room existed for self-expression outside surveillance. Hamper (1991) and Beynon (1973) both suggest that illicit expressions of identity were possible without observation on panoptic car production lines. However, as Garson (1975: 151) states: 'business machines control the operator's mind and motions more completely than in almost any factory situation'. A panopticon constructed in electronic space, and occupied by operatives, may be far more pervasive and controlling than any previous form of industrial arrangement, since observation is carried out almost exclusively by technology rather than people. Symbols of surveillance in electronic panopticons include word processors which monitor key-stroke rate and call centres where the number of calls waiting and the average time taken per call are displayed prominently. It is argued here that flexibly working operatives work within electronic panopticons which leave even less room for self-expression than previous panoptic industrial arrangements. Operatives are forced to internalise the rules of the panopticon and are prevented from many forms of self-expression and identity formation via storytelling.

Results and discussion

This section considers the evidence on which we base the assertions in 'Narrative and identity'. First, qualitative evidence on the experience of flexible working operatives is outlined and discussed. Garson (1975) comments on the extreme difficulty of identifying and talking to operatives. The only way she was able to overcome this problem was by taking operative jobs in large organisations for short periods. This was not an option open to us, but it proved to be unnecessary as secondary case study material was available to investigate storytelling and identity construction among flexible working operatives. Having discussed the operative experience, the experience of flexible working knowledge workers is discussed, based on interviews with knowledge workers.

The experience of the operative

The isolation of operatives from organisational storytelling

Machung (1988) compares the experience of secretaries and data entry operatives. She spoke to fifty people and says of operatives, 'the ability to interact socially with a diverse number of people and personalities is not required in these new jobs; in fact the desire to do so can sometimes be counterproductive' (pp. 71–73). Not only are interpersonal abilities *not* constructed as skills necessary for operative work, but the nature of the work also discouraged communication by demanding constant concentration on a computer screen. Machung echoes Garson (1975) in stating that operative work is additionally isolating since there is absolutely no teamwork involved. Meanwhile panoptic devices such as key stroke monitoring further reduce incentives to communicate. Thus it may be argued that operative work is constructed to discourage communication and storytelling. In this way operatives are obstructed in developing workplace identities.

Machung also found that spatial barriers discouraged communication. The operatives in her study generally worked at sites which were separate from other company buildings. Machung found that spatial disconnection isolated operatives from the rest of their organisations. Perhaps teleworking for operatives represents an extension of this process. The nature of work and its location meant that Machung's operatives knew little about the organisations in which they worked or their roles within those organisations. She concludes that, in the case of operatives, 'social mechanisms have been designed which both break down social relations between the clerical and managerial strata as well as eroding ties of dependency, friendliness and mutual support within them' (p. 76).

Turning to work specifically on storytelling among teleworkers, Boris (1994) cites Costello's study of teleworking at the Wisconsin Physicians Services Insurance Corporation (WPS). Teleworkers at WPS were able to create 'informal work networks,…they could use networks to support and aid each other but not to influence the company' (p. 335). Though teleworkers were able to tell stories and construct identity within their own network, they were excluded from the wider organisational storytelling forum and thus were only able to develop a very limited understanding of their role within WPS. At the same time the politicking nature of storytelling in changing organisational perceptions was denied to them.

The above suggests that even operatives working side by side have only very limited opportunities to share narratives. This lack of narrative opportunity leads to an inability to construct identity at work. It may be argued that this is even more true for operatives working alone at home. However, there is evidence that operatives have identity constructed for them, as machines and as independent contractors, and it is to this that we will now turn.

Operatives as machines

In many cases operatives are expected to fulfil quotas in, for example, the number of calls they take or make, or the number of letters they complete. As we have already said CITs contain panoptic devices which enable individual output to be monitored. This method of working helps to create an identity for operatives as 'letter machines' or 'call processing machines'. Indeed Machung (1988: 75) states that 'VDT [Visual Display Terminal] operators complain about feeling like an extension of their terminals'. The testimonies of two such operatives illustrate the view of operatives as machines. A teleworker at WPS said of her work 'once you get it…it's like a factory or assembly line' (Boris 1994: 335); while another operative told Machung (1988: 75):

> When I was a medical transcriber, it was just a sweat shop. We had production levels that we had to meet everyday – 1200 to 1400 lines a day. And that doesn't give you much time for relaxation, or even saying 'hi' to your co-workers.

The marketisation of operatives

There is evidence that the home worker is forced to become both worker and overseer. Allen and Wolkowitz (1987) suggest that, because home workers take responsibility for their own output they are encouraged to see themselves as contractors in a free market where their employer 'buys' their output. The relationship between home worker and employer is thus marketised, with home workers being encouraged to view themselves as free agents within the marketplace rather than as members of their organisations. It may be argued that the teleworking operative is the latest manifestation of this relationship.

Evidence to support the above assertions comes from two American insurance companies, Blue Cross of North Carolina and the California Western States Life Insurance Company (Cal Life). Boris (1994) cites the example of Ann Blackwell, a teleworker or 'cottage coder' (p. 332) at Blue Cross. Ann works 'verging a fifty hour week' (p. 332) and works 'at night when behind her quota' (p. 332). Boris states that 'cottage coders' such as Ann 'sweated themselves' (p. 332). There is an argument that the construction of the cottage coder's work encourages them to 'sweat themselves'. They are paid at piece rates. This encourages them, first, to push themselves in order to earn more money and, second, to see themselves as independent contractors producing 'information widgets' to be sold to their employer. Cottage coders are encouraged further in this belief by the fact that they lease their means of production in the form of computer terminals from Blue Cross, buy their own raw materials such as paper and hold the status of part-time employees, without the benefits of their full-time colleagues (Boris 1994). However, cottage coders remain employees of Blue Cross. They are unable to work for any other clients and thus cannot be classed as truly independent contractors. The argument here is that they are encouraged to take on the roles of independent contractors working outside Blue Cross, even while remaining employees of the company.

A major benefit for organisations of marketising flexibly working operatives is financial (Milne 1995). Blue Cross is able to derive high levels of productivity from piece working cottage coders, without being required to provide the same level of benefits as would be necessary if these workers worked at company sites. The example of Cal Life, cited by both Boris (1994) and DiMartino and Wirth (1990), illustrates very well both the financial motivation for employers in offering teleworking to operatives, and the marketisation experienced by workers as a result of becoming teleworkers. In 1981 Cal Life offered some Claims

Examiners the opportunity to become teleworkers. A number of staff, all women, took up this offer. In order to do so they were required to resign from their permanent positions and become independent contractors. Like the Blue Cross cottage coders, these teleworkers leased equipment from Cal Life; however, in this case they could, in theory, sell their services to other organisations, provided no conflict of interest existed. The scheme offered major financial advantages for Cal Life, since they were not required to make health insurance and social security payments for homeworkers; 'one manager explained, "the average at home claims examiner represents more than $1,000 in reduced costs"' (Boris 1994: 333).

However, in 1985 serious problems arose with the Cal Life teleworking scheme. Eight teleworkers launched a court action to sue the company for '$250,000 in back benefits and at least $1 million in punitive damages' (Boris 1994: 333). The teleworkers charged the organisation with 'fraud, arguing that the independent contractor contract was merely a subterfuge to manoeuvre around benefits' (p. 333). They argued that they were doing the work of company employees and being supervised by company employees and therefore should receive the benefits of company employees. The teleworkers also claimed that they had less freedom as independent contractors than as Cal Life employees, because they needed to work 'fifteen hours a day to cope with company quotas' (p. 333). This situation left them unable to take work from other sources, even if they wanted to. Thus, the teleworkers argued that their work had been constructed in such a way as to make them independent contractors in name only. They found themselves marketised, yet firmly controlled by Cal Life. The legal action of the teleworkers had two results. In January 1988 the company dropped its teleworking programme and in May of the same year an out-of-court settlement was reached.

Even in his darkest days as a production line worker at General Motors, Ben Hamper was certain of his status as a member of the General Motors organisation. The argument of this chapter is that flexibly working operatives do not enjoy that luxury. Unable to construct identity for themselves via storytelling, they find their identity constructed for them by the nature of their work and the technology they use. This identity is that of mechanical processors who exist outside their organisations as free market agents. However, while teleworking operatives may take on the identity of the outsider they often remain firmly within an electronic panopticon of their company's making. Thus they find themselves in an organisational space where they are neither truly inside nor outside their organisations.

The experience of knowledge workers

In order to investigate further the construction of narratives and identity among knowledge workers the authors chose to conduct interviews with four knowledge workers, Peter, Graham, Sarah and Robert, from a single multinational, information-intensive organisation. Interviewees were chosen for their senior positions within the organisation and also for the fact that they either worked from home or from multiple sites. By interviewing individuals from a single organisation the intention was to build a collection of narratives, which could be compared in order to understand how different individuals constructed understandings of the same events (Riessman 1993).

The shifting identities of knowledge workers

In order to better understand the identities taken on by knowledge workers in different projects, interviewees were asked to talk about several projects with which they were highly involved and one where they had a low level of involvement. Until this point our argument has been that knowledge workers construct multiple identities at work and alternate between these identities depending on the projects with which they are involved. However, the results of our interviews point to a different dynamic. Rather than constructing multiple identities for use in different project settings, interviewees appeared to adopt the same basic identity in each project. They did not play many parts at work, but rather the same part on many different stages.

The above is supported by evidence from each interviewee. Peter told stories about three projects with which he was involved. In each he presented himself as a negotiator and a communicator, keen to convince others of the validity of his actions and to act for the common good. In his first narrative he talks about aligning processes via negotiation, in order that a 'common language' can be spoken. In the second narrative he refers to the importance of his staff feeling that they have 'bought into' their working environment; while underlining his altruism by suggesting that his efforts to improve this environment will have little direct benefit for himself due to his home worker status.

The third story Peter tells is about a project of less significance. Here he again casts himself as a facilitator. However, this project offers few opportunities for the type of positive negotiation Peter refers to in the previous narratives. Perhaps this might explain its perceived lack of importance. Expressions of Peter's identity were also found elsewhere in the interview. For example, his two stories about communication skills emphasise his willingness to 'invest the time' in winning others over, both customers and colleagues.

Graham's expressed identity at work appears to be very different. He talked about four projects, three of importance and one of less importance. In the first three narratives he clearly presents himself as a planner and a coordinator. Graham expresses a process-orientated approach to employee morale in these narratives, which may be contrasted with Peter's 'softer' method built around consensus and negotiation. Graham's narratives also point to subtle feelings of exploitation. He presents himself as being put upon, and as often finding himself 'dragged in' to solve the problems of others. Thus, in contrast to Peter, the identity that Graham presents, is that of planner not a talker, someone who is dragged into problems rather than a negotiator of solutions.

Sarah tells three stories about projects with which she is involved. These stories suggest that she adopts the identity of a teacher and a communicator in each project. A good example here is the way that she transforms her role in representing her group on conference calls and in meetings, into an exercise in training and communication. Having told this story she said, 'I guess it's just passing on information and educating the, sort of, [software] patching community'. It may be argued that this is a clear expression of her identity, and illustrates the way in which that identity shapes her approach to the project.

Expressions of identity in Robert's three project narratives are more subtle. It is only as a result of considering the structure of the narratives that similarities become clear. Once each clause of the narratives was classified using Labov's technique (Riessman 1993), the degree of action and the lack of reflection within the stories became noticeable. This impression is enhanced by the way in which the narratives were performed. Robert used his voice very effectively to emphasise the importance of what he was saying. The confident assertiveness of his style of speech may be contrasted to Peter's more reflective and less assertive style. These points in combination lead the author to argue that Bob brought the identity of a man of action to each of his projects. This is illustrated when he talks about 'jumping in the car' in order to visit colleagues, and states that breaking his leg 'crippled' the way in which he worked.

Knowledge workers and the communication skills of electronic space

Davies (1995), among others, emphasises the importance of developing new skills in order to communicate effectively in electronic space (see 'The requirement to learn new methods of storytelling' above). Evidence from knowledge workers as to their progress in doing so is mixed. Peter and Robert both tell stories about how they communicate which are rooted in traditional methods of relationship building. Peter sets great store by informal and semi-social communication; as does Bob who hints at the detrimental effects that isolation from informal communication can have.

By contrast, Graham tells a story about chairing weekly conference calls which does imply that he is learning new methods of communication, albeit reluctantly. In both Graham's stories about how he communicates there appears to be a strong feeling that he is being forced to learn new methods of communication with which he is not entirely happy. Nowhere is there any indication that he is willingly embracing the opportunity to learn new communication strategies.

The above implies that knowledge workers may not be embracing new methods of communication with the zeal suggested by Davies (1995). Interviewees either appear to be working harder and spending more time on traditional methods of relationship building, or finding themselves coerced by the nature of their work into using new methods of communication with which they are not completely happy. Perhaps flexible working is less flexible for knowledge workers than it appears. They may find themselves tied to methods of communication with which they are not comfortable, or spending more hours at the office-building relationships, and consequently more hours working at home making up for lost time.

Towards a conclusion

Evidence from a wide variety of sources appears to support the suggestion that flexible workers are far from being a homogeneous group. The argument of this chapter is that they can be divided into two distinct groups, which we have termed knowledge workers and operatives. Two opposing arguments have been outlined concerning the identity of knowledge workers. The first, supported by most of the academic literature, is that knowledge workers' identity changes with the work in which they are involved. The second, supported by our findings, is that knowledge workers retain a core identity and adapt their work around this identity.

In the case of operatives the picture is somewhat clearer. We have argued that flexibly working operatives are unable to construct identity at work for themselves via storytelling, and find identity constructed for them by the nature of their work and the technology they use. This identity is that of mechanical individuals who exist outside their organisations as free market agents. However, while flexibly working operatives may take on the identity of the outsider, they often remain firmly within an electronic panopticon of their company's design.

Narratives constantly evolve with telling and retelling (Curt 1994; Boje 1995). The story of flexible working is constantly being retold by narrators with differing agendas, and thus it may be expected to change over time. At present flexible working narratives range from the blindingly optimistic (Capowski 1996; Davidow and Malone 1992), to the simply disturbing (Boris 1994). This chapter contributes to the discourse. However, what flexible working will mean in the future, who will be telling the stories and to what ends, is far from clear.

Bibliography

Allen, S. and Wolkowitz, C. (1987) *Homeworking: Myths and Realities*, London: Macmillan.

Atkinson, A. (1989) *Poverty and Social Security*, London: Harvester Wheatsheaf.

Bell, D. (1973) *The Coming of Post Industrial Society*, London: Heinemann.

Barthes, R. (1974) trans. Richard Miller, *S/Z*, New York: Hill & Wang.

Berger, P. and Luckmann, T. (1966) *The Social Construction of Reality*, London: Allen Lane.

Beynon, H. (1973) *Working for Ford*, London: Pelican.

Boje, D. (1991) 'The storytelling organisation', *Administrative Science Quarterly*, 36, 1.

—— (1995) 'Stories of the storytelling organisation: a post modern analysis of Disney as "Tarmara-land"', *The Academy of Management Journal* 38, 4.

Boland, R.J. and Tenkasi, R.V. (1995) 'Perspective making and perspective taking in communities of knowing', *Organisation Science*, 6, 4: 351–72.

Boris, I. (1994) *Home to Work: Motherhood and the Politics of Industrial Homework in the United States*, Cambridge: Cambridge University Press.

Bruner, J. (1990) *Acts of Meaning*, Cambridge, Mass.: Harvard University Press.

Burrell, G. (1997) *Pandemonium*, London: Sage.

Capowski, G. (1996) 'The joy of flex', *Management Review,* January: 3.

Christie, J.R.R. and Orton, F. (1988) 'Writing a text on the life', *Art History*, 11, 4: 543–63.

Cook, S.D.D. and Yanow, D. (1993) 'Culture and organisational learning', *Journal of Management Inquiry*, 2, 4: 373–90.

Costigan Lederman, L. (1986) 'Communication in the workplace: the impact of the information age and high technology on interpersonal communication in organisations', in Gumpert, G. and Cathcart, R. (eds) *Intermedia: Interpersonal Communication in a Media World*, Oxford: Oxford University Press.

Curt, B. (1994) *Textually and Tectonics*, Milton Keynes: Open University.

Davidow, W. and Malone, M. (1992) *The Virtual Corporation*, London: HarperBusiness.

Davies, R. (1995) 'Telecommuting: culture, social roles, and managing telecommuters', a report on a Teleworking Internet Conference held between April and October 1995 at the MCB University Press Virtual Conference Centre.

Di Martino, V. and Wirth, L. (1990) 'Teleworking: a new way of working and living', *International Labour Review*, 129, 5.

Donkin, R. (1997) 'Downsized to the peasantry', *Financial Times*, 12 March.

European Commission (1994) *Business Restructuring and Teleworking: Current Practice*, European Commission.

Finholt, T. (1997) 'The electronic office', *Trends in Organisational Behaviour*, 4.

Foucault, M. (1975) *Discipline and Punishment: The Birth of the Prison*, London: Penguin.

Funkenstein, A. (1993) 'The incomprehensible catastrophe: memory and narrative', in Josselson, R. and Lieblich, A. (eds) *The Narrative Study of Lives*, Vol. 1, London: Sage.

Garson, B. (1975) *All the Livelong Day: The Meaning and Demeaning of Work*, London: Penguin.

Gooding, C. (1993) 'Roses around the door and a fax on the Welsh dresser', *Financial Times* 8 September.

Hamper, B. (1991) *Rivethead: Tales from the Assembly Line*, London: Fourth Estate.

Hardy, B. (1968) 'Towards a poetics of fiction: an approach through narrative', *Novel*, 2: 5–14.

Houlder, V. (1994) 'When the office is the dining room', *Financial Times*, 5 September.

Huws, U., Korte, W. and Robinson, S. (1990) *Teleworking: Towards the Illusive Office*, Chichester: Wiley.

Jackson, P. (1997) 'Changes in work and organisations: new faces and new phenomena?', in Avallone, F., Arnold, J. and de Witte, K. (eds) *Feelings Work in Europe*, Vol. 5, Milan: Guerini Studio.

Johnson, G. (1988) 'Rethinking incrementalism', *Strategic Management Journal*, 9 : 75–91.

Kelly, G. (1955) *A Theory of Personality*, Vols 1 and 2, New York: Norton.

Knights, D. and Morgan, G. (1992) 'Corporate strategy, organisations and subjectivity: a critique', *Organisation Studies* 12, 2.

Machung, A. (1988) 'Who needs a personality to talk to a machine?: Communication in the automated office', in Kramarae, C. (ed.) *Technology and Women's Voice*, London: Routledge & Kegan Paul.

MacIntyre, A. (1981) *After Virtue*, Notre Dame, Indiana: University of Notre Dame Press.

McKinley, M. (1996) 'Teleworking in central and eastern Europe: boundary spanning individuals vs peripheralising nations', paper presented at *New International Perspectives on Teleworking Workshop* at Brunel University, 31 July to 2 August.

Miller, P. (1994) 'Narrative practices: their role in socialisation and self-construction', in Neisser, U. and Fivush, R. (eds) *The Remembering Self: Construction and Accuracy in the Self-Narrative*, Cambridge: Cambridge University Press.

Milne, S. (1995) 'Teleworkers pay as firms make modem savings', *The Guardian*, 1 November.

Neisser, U. (1994) 'Self-narratives: true and false', in Neisser, U. and Fivush, R. (eds) *The Remembering Self: Construction and Accuracy in the Self-Narrative*, Cambridge: Cambridge University Press.

O'Connor, E. (1997) 'Telling decisions: the role of narrative in organisational decision making', in Shapira, Z. (ed.) *Organisational Decision Making*, New York: Cambridge University Press.

Ochberg, R. (1993a) 'Life stories and storied lives', in Josselson, R. and Lieblich, A. (eds) *The Narrative Study of Lives*, Vol. 2: *Exploring Identity and Gender in the Narrative Study of Lives*, London: Sage.

—— (1993b) 'Interpreting life stories', in Josselson, R. and Lieblich, A. (eds) *The Narrative Study of Lives*, Vol. 4: *Ethics and Process in the Narrative Study of Lives*, London: Sage.

Perin, C. (1996) 'The part-week telecommuting option in Telia Research and its organisational and managerial implications', unpublished project report.

Quinn, J.B. (1992) *Intelligent Enterprise*, New York: Free Press.

Reich, R. (1997) 'The menace to prosperity', *Financial Times*, 3 March.

Riessman, C. (1993) *Narrative Analysis*, London: Sage.

Roe, E. (1994) *Narrative Policy Analysis: Theory and Practice*, Durham, NC: Duke University Press.

Samarajiva, R. (1993) 'Consumer protection in the decentralised network: a mapping of the research and policy terrain', in Noam, E. (ed.) *Private Networks and Pubic Objectives*, New York: Columbia Institute for Tele-Information.

Sims, D. (1995) 'A narrative approach to agenda shaping', paper presented to the *Third International Workshop on Managerial and Organisational Cognition*, Strathclyde University, June.

Sims, D., Fineman, S. and Gabriel, Y. (1993) *Organising and Organisations: An Introduction*, London: Sage.

Spence, D. (1984) *Narrative Truth and Historical Truth: Meaning and Interpretation in Psychoanalysis*, New York: Norton.

Sproul, L. and Kiesler, S. (1991) *Connections: New Ways of Working in the Networker Organisation*, London: MIT Press.

Stross, R.E. (1997) *The Microsoft Way: The Real Story of How the Company Outsmarts its Competition*, London: Little Brown.

Wagner, I. and Kompast, M. (1998) 'Telework: managing spatial, temporal and cultural boundaries', in Jackson, P. and van der Wielen, J. (eds) *Teleworking: International Perspectives*, London: Routledge.

Weick, K. (1995) *Sensemaking in Organisations*, Thousand Oaks, CA: Sage.

Wetherell, M. and Potter, J. (1989) 'Narrative characters and accounting for violence', in Shotter, J. and Gergen, K. (eds) *Texts of Identity*, London: Sage.

Widdershoven, G. (1993) 'The story of life: hermeneutic perspectives on the relationship between narrative and life history', in Josselson, R. and Lieblich, A. (eds) *The Narrative Study of Lives*, Vol. 1, London: Sage.

Part III

Management and control in virtual working

In this part of the book we look at the issues involved in the management and control aspects of virtual working. Particular attention in the following three chapters is placed on teleworkers, although the lessons are generalisable to other forms of virtual working.

In Chapter 7, by Astrid Depickere, the relation between control and commitment processes is explored. It is noted here that while traditional Taylorist-bureaucratic organisations emphasised control strategies in managing labour – close supervision and the standardisation of work – new forms of work, such as virtual working, emphasise the importance of commitment strategies and practices. The chapter draws upon empirical work undertaken on skilled, professional workers – or knowledge workers – working for a single employer. The author points out the importance of such empirical work, given that much of what has been written in this area has thus far been largely theoretically-based.

Depickere sets the scene for a discussion of commitment processes by outlining the changes to organisational forms and working practices brought about using the new technology, and their accompanying management processes. It is here that an important choice faces organisations: either to establish intrusive control mechanisms that ensure compliance with operating requirements, or to build commitment among the workforce such that tight material control is no longer required. The author illustrates that in many modern organisations – especially where new technology and knowledge workers are concerned – it is increasingly difficult, if not counterproductive, to assume that management can design and control the work of others in highly prescribed and intrusive ways. Instead, concepts such as empowerment and coaching may provide more helpful guides to managing workers.

Traditional control strategies towards labour, the author points out, often created a downward spiral of distrust, resentment and high levels of surveillance. In moving towards a commitment approach, Depickere shows that control must come from elsewhere. In particular, the creation of a strong organisational culture, through attention to recruitment, socialisation and training, is important – what might be termed 'input' controls. Commitment strategies are thus particularly important in situations where surveillance and monitoring are difficult, if not impossible. However, the author warns us that commitment is not such a straightforward concept and requires careful understanding.

Depickere makes a distinction beween 'affective commitment' – where employees identify with and share the values and interests of the organisation – and 'continuance' or 'calculative commitment'. In the latter form, individuals remain committed to the organisation because of a need to do so: options to go and work elsewhere may be limited or undesirable. As such it is the fear of falling out with the organisation that ensures appropriate and continued participation.

From the empirical work, Depickere notes a movement away from behaviour controls towards input forms of control. These have been accompanied, however, by some increases in output controls, such as variable pay. The author stresses that it is not always easy to determine the extent to which approaches to control and commitment can be tied directly to developments in teleworking. None the less, it is concluded that teleworking has certainly played an important part in the fashioning of new management approaches.

Depickere also points to the differences that exist in the people that constitute a virtual workforce. Whereas some people who begin teleworking may have been socialised into the organisational culture and values, newcomers may not. In addition, even for those who have been part of the organisation for some time, without regular contacts and good communications, teleworking may lessen the bond of commitment between the individual and the organisation.

The author concludes that managers need to recognise the importance of commitment and actively seek to build and maintain it. This will involve a mix of input and output mechanisms – from recruitment and induction, to performance appraisal, economic rewards, training and career opportunities. Such measures will allow organisations to balance autonomy with the necessary control through commitment that is essential to teleworking arrangements, particularly where these involve skilled, professional workers.

In Chapter 8, by Reima Suomi and Juhani Pekkola, the link between management and culture again comes to the fore. This time, however, it is the different cultures associated with levels of management, and the sort of values and norms that go with them, that are addressed. Suomi and Pekkola argue that the main constraints on teleworking developments have been the rationalities (that are seen as elements of culture) held by different levels of management (that are seen as subcultures).

The first of the three rationalities identified by the authors is the 'market' rationality. This, they note, is typically displayed by upper management. Where such a rationality prevails so far as teleworking is concerned, its benefits are judged in terms of the profits and goodwill that are generated. The next rationality they discuss is 'economic', as found in middle management. Here, the benefits of teleworking are viewed in terms of the added value it brings to products and services. Finally, 'resource-based' rationality looks to teleworking for benefits such as a more efficient utilisation of the material and human factors of production.

Suomi and Pekkola's analysis shows us that while culture has a powerful bearing on organisational outcomes, we are not always aware of the extent to which cultural norms and values are bound up with decision making, or in the attitudes that people display. For teleworking to develop, therefore, promoters need to speak the language of all three rationalities outlined above. Few people are in a position to do this, however. For this reason, much of the teleworking that goes on takes place under informal arrangements, where the workers *themselves* have acquired the consent of their immediate managers.

The final chapter in this part, by Louise Adami, focuses on the way control and autonomy have to be balanced when managing newspaper journalists. Journalists can be considered under the ambit of virtual working because of their need for flexibility in space and time in order to cover stories, conduct interviews and dispatch reports. Without flexibility, as the author points out, journalists simply cannot do their job.

Adami draws upon the study of journalists in an Australian newspaper company. In managing journalists, she notes, both direct controls – such as supervision, quality checks, operating procedures, budgetary guidelines – and indirect controls are used. Indirect controls include job descriptions, organisational culture, group pressures, performance appraisals, career opportunities and training. The use and mix of these controls, she notes, depend on the experience and seniority of the journalists involved.

In a similar way to Depickere, Adami points to the importance of social controls gained though socialisation into, and membership of, a work community, and the influence of commitment – particularly towards work groups – in producing work discipline. In the newspaper company concerned, Adami identifies two distinct domains of control – professional and organisational. Whereas the former was applied for more experienced journalists, the more inexperienced and trainee journalists were more likely to be subject to the latter. These included, for instance, financial limits on equipment and travel, strict control of deadlines, specific guidelines on stories (how long they should be, who should be interviewed) and disciplinary consequences (for instance, the removal from a 'round' where performance standards have not been met). Professional controls, on the other hand, were intimately tied to factors influencing an individual's professionalism and image. Through years of experience, such people had a strong sense of what was required of them, and what the 'dos and don'ts' were in the profession.

Adami concludes that organisations considering flexible working need to appreciate the autonomy needs of a particular job, how suitable an individual is for flexible working, and the sort of resources, systems and skills that are needed to support such arrangements. The levels of experience that individuals possess, their degree of socialisation in the organisation, and their level of professional expertise and understanding, are also vital. Such factors will determine the degree of trust and confidence managers will have in allowing individuals to work flexibly, as well as the amount of autonomy they should be allowed.

7 Managing virtual working

Between commitment and control?

Astrid Depickere

Introduction

This chapter will discuss the way virtual working relates to the processes of control and commitment within organisations, as well as the relationship between the two processes. We will consider these issues against the background of new paradigms in organisation theory that present new concepts of organisation, in contrast to the traditional Taylorist-bureaucratic concepts. This shift from traditional models of organisations to new concepts has had an impact on the dimension of *control*, with new concepts like 'empowerment' and 'coaching' being opposed to direct supervision and standardisation of labour. The issue of organisational *commitment* has gained renewed interest here, as it is considered to be an important condition for empowerment and, ultimately, organisational performance and efficiency. At the same time, however, from the point of view of employees, commitment and loyalty to an organisation is no longer self-evident. This seems all the more difficult when organisations start teleworking on a large scale. We will therefore consider how teleworking affects the generation of organisational commitment and point out some measures organisations can take to manage actively for commitment in a teleworking environment. Before considering these issues, we will clarify how virtual working and teleworking are understood in this chapter. We will also situate the research on which this chapter is based.

Conceptual clarification and empirical research

An intra-organisational perspective of teleworking

The chapter draws on the findings of a research project on the organisational and personnel management issues arising from new ways of working that involve the spatial redistribution of work. Because new developments in information and communication technology (ICT) are considered to be an important enabling factor for these changed work configurations, our primary interest is in those forms of working that make use of advanced ICT. In order to describe this dynamic within organisations, concepts like teleworking, virtual working, flexiwork and remote work are used. In this chapter we will mainly use the concept of teleworking, defining it as an activity whereby people work at a distance from an employer (or an instructing organisation), using ICT to overcome that distance. We take virtual working to be synonymous with teleworking.

Our focus will be on the intra-organisational level, as we discuss only forms of teleworking or virtual working that occur within the organisational boundaries. With respect to the dynamics of control and commitment, it is most interesting to consider these issues for more highly skilled employees who belong to the core of the organisation and whose capacities and knowledge are considered to be valuable production factors for the organisation. The commitment of these employees to the organisation is of vital importance for the performance of the organisation as a whole and more specifically for managerial control. New developments in information and communication technology allow for these professionals to work remotely regardless of whether this is necessary for the execution of their jobs (e.g. as with mobile working) or whether they choose to do so because of other advantages (e.g. avoiding commuting, being more productive when working at home).

The need for empirical evidence

The empirical phase of our research consists of two parts. The first part, which was more exploratory, gathered information (mostly by means of interviews but also by reviewing the literature) on examples of teleworking in Belgium and some other European countries. This gave us an idea not only of differences in the way teleworking is done but also of differences in the understanding and the debate around the subject of teleworking. In the second part of the empirical phase we conducted in-depth case studies.

In spite of the abundant literature and research on telework, we believe there is a lack of adequate *empirical* work. Indeed, a large part of the literature on the subject actually focuses on hypothetical situations. These reports are very often written in the future tense, e.g. 'the virtual organisation would be like…' and 'virtual working will…'. The risk here is that arguments about the shape of future work, which are of course very popular arguments, are repeatedly made until they start living a life of their own. Consequently, when looking for possible case studies and gathering information from media, conferences, etc., we often had expectations that were very different from what we encountered when conducting more in-depth research. Not only was it very difficult to find examples of virtual working, we also had to conclude that there was sometimes a large gap between the media hype around certain cases of virtual working or teleworking – or whatever the terminology of the respective companies was – and the actual practices. We almost always found that the company was less virtual and more traditional than had been presented.

Case study: 'Company X'

The arguments in this chapter will be illustrated with a case study we conducted at a large multinational company in the computer industry, to which we will refer as Company X. We think this example is in many ways representative of other companies in the same industry, as well as in other industries such as telecommunications, consultancy and financial services. This is because of the nature of the work in these industries: most are highly skilled mobile jobs. In addition, Company X has, like many companies in the industry, recently gone through a major restructuring. Soon after this restructuring, it started the gradual introduction of a system of office sharing, combined with the possibility of employees to work at home. Today, a considerable portion (60 per cent) of the workforce is working in a shared-office environment.

We gathered data by means of interviews with ten managers from different departments, two persons from the secretariat, and the former as well as the current project manager. We also surveyed the employees who worked in the shared offices.[1] Again, this included some managers. The response ratio for the survey was 40 per cent, which is reasonable since the people in these jobs are very busy (according to the management) and are very often asked to fill in questionnaires.

Most authors discuss different types of teleworking on the basis of certain typical dimensions, of which the most common are the *location* where the remote working is being performed (e.g. at home, multiple locations, a satellite office) and the proportion of the working time that is being spent remotely (e.g. occasional, part time, full time). Other dimensions include the work status (employed versus self-employed), the use of ICT (high or low level) or skill level of the employee (highly skilled versus not highly skilled).

The temporal–spatial work pattern

In order to have a better understanding of the nature of the virtual working at Company X, we present the average temporal–spatial work pattern of the teleworkers in Figure 7.1. We determined this pattern on the basis of a question in the survey that asked how the respondents divide their working time between the different locations they are working at. The figure shows that, on average, one-fifth of the working time is performed at home. Only a little more time (22.7 per cent) is spent at the customer's site and almost 10 per cent of the time is spent at satellite offices of Company X.[2] This means that, on average, the actual time spent at the main office is still 41.6 per cent of the working time. This is much more than we expected in view of the information given in interviews by managers and project leaders and the way in which teleworking is presented in the media.

As this pattern differs strongly depending on the job category, it is more revealing to look at Figure 7.2 where the work pattern is presented for the different job categories. For the purposes of this chapter, it is most interesting to see how much time is spent at the main office. This is highest for managers

(62 per cent). When interviewing managers, most of them said they preferred to be available to their employees and therefore tried to be at the main office during normal working hours.[3] Those in the other job categories, who work in shared offices, also spent a considerable amount of time at the main office, especially salespeople (43.4 per cent) and the software specialists (37.4 per cent).

Changes in the environment and responses of organisations

Environmental turbulence

Contingency theory, as an important perspective in organisation science, states that for an organisation to be successful, it is essential that its nature should fit its environment. This principle is also called Ashby's Law: 'external variety requires internal variety' (Andriessen 1995: 10). As long as environmental conditions were stable and predictable, rigid bureaucratic and Taylorist principles were the basis of successful modes of organisation. Van der Wielen and Taillieu (1995: 4) describe the situation as follows:

> Modern society relied on mass-production industry that was repetition oriented, pursuing efficient reproduction of a limited variety of products or services and enabling increasing returns to scale...Large bureaucracies adopted rigid structures because they perceived the future as stable and certain...These characteristics were optimal in growing but relatively stable markets

The environment of today's organisations is becoming increasingly complex, uncertain, and subject to constant change. Traditional bureaucratic organisations are unable to cope with this if they do not fundamentally alter their structure and function.

> Increasing environmental turbulence has confronted bureaucratic, hierarchical organisations with their inability to adapt to changing circumstances and their failure to reduce uncertainty and enhance stability necessary for production
>
> (van der Wielen and Taillieu 1995: 4)

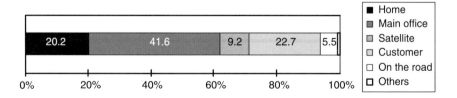

Figure 7.1 Average temporal–spatial work pattern

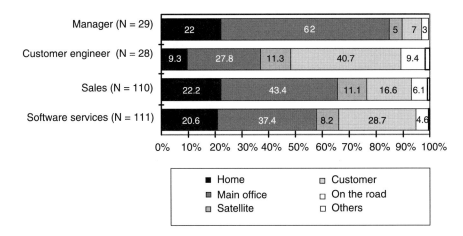

Figure 7.2 Average temporal–spatial work pattern by job category

Another significant change in the structure of the economy is the shift in the employment market from industry to services. Heisig and Littek (1995: 122) state that in most industrialised countries skilled service personnel perform the lion's share of all jobs. Also, Roe *et al.* (1995) found evidence for a growing group of 'Mental Information Workers' who typically work with immaterial objects and frequently make use of information technology.

An industry where this 'environmental turbulence' is most apparent is no doubt the computer industry, the sector of Company X. In the 1960s and 1970s, the market was dominated by a limited choice of large mainframe computers, but the invention of the microprocessor chip drastically cut the cost of computing power and encouraged customers to replace large central processing units with networks or smaller desktop machines. Moreover, the invention of the personal computer created a new market as the computer entered homes, smaller enterprises and schools. It also meant the growth of a new sector in the computer industry: the software sector, which, by the early 1990s, had exceeded the hardware sector as the most important component in the industry. Growing specialisation and diversity in products brought about a new generation of competitors who were smaller and more flexible than the large traditional hardware producers with their rigid structures and high overheads. Furthermore, unlike most typical consumer products like food, cars and clothes, the prices of which increase with inflation, the prices of computer products continue to fall. The enormous price erosion and shrinkage of the profit margins made it difficult for the traditional producers to survive. Another trend in the computer industry that feeds the competition, as well as the complexity of the market, is the growing importance of a whole range of services like training and consultancy for networks, systems integration, and product support. Finally, another interesting thing about this sector is that the information and communication technologies (ICT) also influence the work processes and the functioning of the industry that is producing them.

Organisational change and innovation

The way in which organisations react to this environmental turbulence is described variously within organisation theory. With respect to virtual working, Business Process Redesign (Hammer and Champy 1993; Davenport 1993) is mentioned most frequently because of the role it ascribes to ICT. Sometimes the 'virtual organisation' is even called a new trend itself (Harris 1998). We should also note Socio-technical Design Theory (e.g. de Sitter and van Eijnatten 1995; Christis 1995), Flexible Specialisation (Piore and Sabel 1984), New Production Concepts (Kern and Schuman 1984; Huys *et al.* 1995) and Postmodern Organisations (Clegg 1990). Because of their different geographical origins, these theories are usually seen as representing different developments. Nevertheless they show substantial similarities (Van Hootegem forthcoming) and give evidence of a new paradigm in organisation theory.

The rise of teleworking and the virtual organisation is very often situated within these frameworks, where the virtual organisation is seen as 'the archetypal post-modern organisational form' (Brigham and Corbett 1996: 68; Harris 1998: 78). One thing all these theories have in common is that they oppose the traditional Taylorist-bureacratic organisation. These two concepts of organisation differ in a number respects, such as job integration and job enlargement versus task division in work organisation; a product- or process-oriented versus an operation-oriented production organisation; and coaching and empowerment versus direct control and supervision. Another common feature of these new concepts of organisation is the stress they put on teamwork as an efficient and desirable work configuration.

While management and organisation literature are full of these new organisational paradigms, empirical research shows that organisational practice has not been so quick to adopt these new principles (Kern and Schuman 1984; Appelbaum and Batt 1994; Huys *et al.* 1995; Van Hootegem forthcoming). Instead there is evidence of hybrid forms of organisation, that integrate the newer principles with the more traditional ones. We observed this mixture of new and traditional principles at Company X too.

Organisational change at Company X

Traditionally a producer of office machines, Company X became very successful in the 1970s and 1980s when it shifted to the production of computers. However, in the early 1990s, drastic changes in the computer industry combined with some poor strategic choices ultimately resulted in serious losses. In response to these developments, Company X thoroughly restructured itself to achieve drastic cuts in costs and improvements in the efficiency of work processes.

Two of the measures taken to cut costs are important for our present concern.

First, office space was reduced by selling some buildings and introducing shared offices in the remaining premises. Second, the workforce was reduced dramatically and some activities were outsourced. To improve the efficiency of working processes – which can be seen as an objective in its own right as well as a consequence of the cost reduction measures (the same amount of work had to be done with considerably fewer people) – changes were made in different dimensions of the organisation (e.g. the production organisation, the work organisation, and the managerial dimension). The resulting organisation had several features that are very often attributed to new organisational concepts, such as a flatter hierarchical structure, more customer-oriented work processes, and more responsibility on the lowest level of the organisation. However, while the restructurings at Company X are very often seen as prototypical Business Process Redesign, we also found evidence for tendencies that are typical for traditional organisations, such as a stricter division of labour in the production [4] and stronger, horizontal task division.[5]

Organisational change and the development of teleworking

While changes in the market environment were the most important explanation for the restructurings, developments in ICT played a supportive role and also influenced the functioning of the organisation (and therefore also the development of teleworking). However, like Brigham and Corbett (1996), we want to 'move away from simplistic determinism; the notion that one element drives another', but see 'technological change and organisational structural change as concurrent activities that cannot be separated into universals such as shaper and shaped' (Brigham and Corbett 1996: 69–70).

What role does telework play in this context? Again, we do not want to propound determinism. Work situations – and therefore also teleworking – are always the result of combinations of typical measures on different organisational dimensions, such as work organisation, production and human resources management. Changes in these dimensions are in turn the result of changes in the market environment, with technological developments functioning as a contributing factor. This means that teleworking in the first place results from developments in market conditions and technological changes. Literature on teleworking usually addresses the reverse relationship, namely the effect of teleworking on issues such as work organisation or managerial processes. Although we believe teleworking – and more particularly the specific feature of working temporally and spatially independently – can have a certain effect on several organisational dimensions, many of the changes often accredited to teleworking are in reality the result of broader environmental developments (Figure 7.3). Here again, it is impossible to determine the extent to which the one drives the other.

This can explain why teleworking has not yet achieved its long predicted breakthrough. The same factors that are said to enable teleworking (integrated tasks with a large degree of autonomy; empowerment as a management principle;

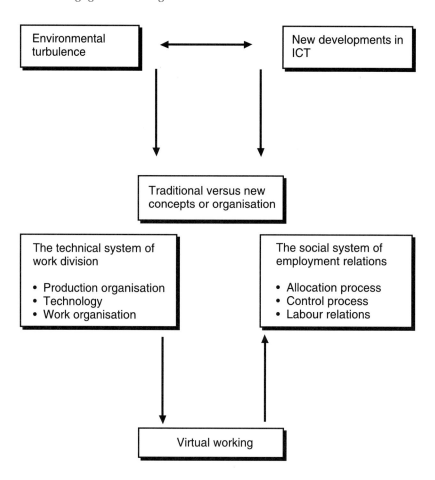

Figure 7.3 The development of teleworking within organisations

use of ICT) are essentially features of the new concepts of organisations cited above. The lack of acceptance of teleworking and virtual working could, therefore, be related to the analogous failure of more integral forms of organisational change and innovation.

Driving factors behind teleworking at Company X

To identify the driving factors behind the teleworking project at Company X, we must first realise that, to a certain extent, teleworking (according to our broad definition of the concept) has always existed at Company X as certain jobs have always been mobile and some overtime has always been done at home. The changes that have occurred are, therefore, not so revolutionary as is sometimes claimed for teleworking but actually have been rather gradual. Perhaps the most obvious change was the reorganisation of the office space. Apart from that, people were given the facilities and – an issue that should not be underestimated – the explicit permission to work at home or at any other place they might consider appropriate. When Company X talks about the introduction of teleworking, it is talking about these changes.[6]

In order to explain these changes, we need to look at the broader context within which they have taken place. Company X had gone through a world-wide restructuring process not long before the introduction of teleworking. This restructuring demanded a drastic cut in costs and an improvement of efficiency. Teleworking can be seen as a development that supports the goals of the restructuring process, and in several ways. Obviously, the introduction of office sharing yields very significant savings. Although companies do not usually stress this as the most important factor but rather as 'something that might as well be done since otherwise offices are too empty', we believe this factor should not be underestimated. It is striking that, when we look at companies that have only recently introduced some form of teleworking, it always seems to be accompanied by some form of office sharing.

Office sharing was, however, not the only way in which teleworking met the goals of the restructuring. Teleworking also contributed to the second goal of the restructuring, which implies enhancement of individual performance. This is, first of all, obtained by an increase in working hours. Figures from the survey showed that the average working time among the respondents was 49 hours a week, which means almost 20 per cent overtime work (a normal working week being 40 hours). Time gained by avoiding traffic jams and redundant travel will usually (at least in the case of Company X) be converted into working time. Another, perhaps the most important, performance increasing factor is the stimulation of overtime work through home-based teleworking on weekends and evenings. Some calculations showed that more than half of the overtime work (which was one-fifth) was being done at home. This means that a large share of the home-based teleworking is actually overtime work. Several managers admitted that teleworking had increased this amount of overtime work. Moreover, as is very often argued by advocates of teleworking, working at home seems to increase individual productivity. The experience of the respondents in the survey was that they were more productive during the hours they worked at home.[7]

Control and the renewed interest in organisational commitment

Situating the control process within organisations

When analysing an organisation, we often follow a model that is inspired by Luhman's Systems Theory and Socio-Technical Design Theory, in which a distinction is made between looking at an organisation as a technical system or looking at it as a social system (Huys *et al.* 1995). When we consider an organisation as a technical system or as a system of division of labour, we are focusing on how the functions of the organisation are grouped within different departments (the production organisation), on what part of the job is done by human actors and what part is automated (the technology dimension), and on how the remaining tasks are poured into different jobs (the work organisation). When we consider an organisation as a social system or a system of memberships, we are focusing on the human actors that occupy the jobs that were formed through the process of the division of labour. As the control issue forms an integral part of the latter analytic dimension, we will discuss it further.

As a system of memberships, the organisation first needs to ensure that the right people occupy the right jobs. For this purpose, it has at its disposal the processes of recruitment and selection, training, promotion, and dismissal (the dimension of the allocation of labour). In these processes, the employee as well as the employer can rely on a structure of negotiation procedures and collective bargaining agreements (the dimension of labour relations). When an organisation has finally hired a new employee, it means that a trade has been made between the employee and the employer whereby the organisation hires the employee's human capacities and knowledge, which can be considered production factors. However, unlike the production factors of capital or raw material, the organisation cannot be sure of the value of the people it has hired, and while it can buy capital or raw material, it can never obtain ownership of human capacities and knowledge. This makes it a relatively uncontrollable factor (Doorewaard and de Nijs 1998). Therefore, the organisation needs to take measures to make sure that the hired capacities will be used to achieve the goals of the organisation (the control dimension).

Old versus new concepts of control

Traditionally, the problem of control and coordination was solved by limiting the employee's alternative ways of acting by means of rigid work division and standardisation. These are the approaches of Scientific Management (Taylor) and Administrative Principles (Fayol, Barnard, Follet), which are typically closed-system approaches that cannot cope with the uncertain and rapid changes confronting companies today (Daft 1998). Traditional organisation structures based on these principles require not only a lot of staff to study and design the best way to organise work processes, but also many middle managers and supervisors to maintain the monitoring and control system (Picken and Dess 1997). As organisations began to confront an increasingly unstable, complex and unpredictable environment (owing to the globalisation of the economy, changed consumption patterns, evolutions in technology, etc.) these traditional control systems became very ineffective and could lead to over-control and a waste of resources (Handy 1995).

Writ large, that sort of attitude creates a paraphernalia of systems, checkers, and checkers checking checkers – expensive and deadening…It exists, they suggest, because we no longer trust people to act for anything but their own short term interest. That attitude becomes a self-fulfilling prophecy. 'If they don't trust me,' employees say to themselves, 'Why should I bother to put their needs before mine?'

(Handy 1995: 44)

Consequently, organisations need to apply different control mechanisms in order to compel the employee to perform in agreement with the goals of the organisation. There are two alternative forms of organisation to turn to. One is to use some form of output control based on market transactional principles. In this case, the rewards are very often linked to performance. The extent to which this type of control is possible largely depends on the nature of the tasks and the extent to which these tasks are measurable or programmable (Ouchi 1979; 1980; Eisenhardt 1985; Daft 1998). An alternative to traditional control principles can be found in the popular new management concepts like empowerment, coaching and entrepreneurship. These principles require the building of a strong commitment on the part of the employee towards the organisation.

This last form of control is similar to what Adami (Chapter 9 in this volume) calls 'input' control. This kind of control needs to be imposed by creating a strong organisational culture through the processes of recruitment, socialisation and training. According to Adami, some combination of the three control principles (behaviour control, input control and output control) is always present in organisations. Whereas empowerment or input control is clearly a feature of the new concepts of organisation, it is rather unclear where output control should be placed, since the principle of linking performance to rewards is essentially a feature of Taylorism (Taylor 1964).

Hope and Hendry (1996) call attention to a critical issue with respect to what we mentioned above about hybrid forms of organisations. More and more companies have started to implement projects of cultural change, aware of the importance of a strong commitment to corporate norms and values. However, paradoxically these changes are very often implemented top down and by means of traditional bureaucratic measures. Obviously, this may well have the opposite effect to what was originally intended. As Hope and Hendry (1996) state, hearing that you will soon be empowered and that you will have to behave that way is something entirely different from actually feeling empowered. This view can also be applied to the way in which teleworking schemes and flexible office concepts are being introduced in organisations. The way in which these projects are implemented can thus cause them to fail.

The role of commitment in organisational control[8]

Because of the role it plays in the strategic control process within organisations, there seems to be a renewed attention in organisation theory to organisational commitment.

> When an organisation finds the means to elicit the commitment of its members, it has at its disposal a very powerful mechanism of control. Indeed the new interest in organisational commitment appears to stem from the realisation that the problem of control in organisations is in large measure solved when the commitment of its members is high.
>
> (Lincoln and Kalleberg 1990: 23)

> Unlike those who say these changes (increased global competition, reengineering, downsizing) make organisational commitment an outdated construct, we believe commitment will be as important or even more important in the future than it was in the past. Admittedly, organisations are likely to employ fewer people, but the employees they retain will be asked to do more and to take more responsibility. Organisations are also likely to invest a great deal in these employees (e.g., through training) and to be in competition with other organisations for their services. Similarly, organisations will want to ensure that those who provide services on a contract basis will be committed to fulfilling their contracts.
>
> (Meyer and Allen 1997: 15)

We need to be aware that commitment is a concept that can assume different forms. Someone can become committed to an organisation because he identifies himself with the organisation (an intrinsic motivation) or because of the resources it offers him (an extrinsic motivation). Meyer and Allen (1991) note that common to the various definitions of organisational commitment is 'the view that commitment is a psychological state that (a) characterises the employee's relationship with the organisation, and (b) has implications for the decision to continue membership in the organisation' (Meyer and Allen 1991: 67). Like several other authors, they acknowledge that commitment can have different natures (Becker 1960; Meyer and Allen 1997).

Research has primarily focused on the following two conceptualisations: 'affective' commitment and 'continuance' or 'calculative' commitment. Affective commitment refers to the employee's emotional attachment to, identification with, and involvement in the organisation. Employees with a strong affective commitment continue employment with the organisation because they *want* to do so. Continuance or calculative commitment refers to an awareness of the costs associated with leaving the organisation. Employees whose primary link to the organisation is based on continuance commitment remain because they *need* to do so (Meyer and Allen 1997: 67). Research has mostly focused on the first component, affective commitment. Meyer and Allen give two reasons for this.

First, only recently have multidimensional models of commitment and appropriate measures been developed. Secondly, affective commitment is arguably the most desirable form of commitment and the one that organisations are most likely to want to instil in their employees (Meyer and Allen 1997).

From an inventory of the research on the consequences of commitment, Meyer and Allen arrive at three groups of consequences, of which the first two, employee retention and productive behaviour, are the most important from the point of view of the organisation. This illuminates again the importance of commitment within the strategic goals of an organisation (Figure 7.4).

While changed market circumstances have brought about a renewed interest in organisational commitment because of the role it plays in control strategies, the same changes in the market environment, and more specifically in the employment market, have changed the attitudes of the employee. The more the durability of organisations is questioned because of the growing instability of the economic and social environment, the less attractive it becomes for qualified employees to develop long-term career perspectives and to enter into a long-lasting commitment to an organisation (Heisig and Littek 1995). The more uncertain an employee's job security becomes, the less that person will be inclined to deliver adequate performance unless it has a clearly beneficial effect. Young employees, for example, will be less inclined to refuse certain job opportunities that provide them more income or more prestige, in favour of a long-term perspective in another company. Given an uncertain future situation, they will try to acquire as much income as possible and the best position as rapidly as possible. Moreover those who have acquired a certain position will cling to that position and to the privileges that accompany it (Heisig and Littek 1995).

During the interviews with younger as well as older managers at Company X, both these tendencies were mentioned. An older manager declared that the personnel dismissals that had accompanied the recent restructurings had come as a shock for several older employees in the organisation. It made them realise that the rights and privileges they had acquired were no longer assured. They had to be regained over and over again. Several managers pointed out a

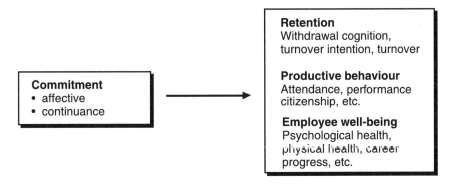

Figure 7.4 Consequences of organisational commitment

completely different attitude on the part of the younger employees, who did not expect Company X to offer them life-long employment but would instead accept another job offer if they could improve themselves financially. We should not forget that the majority of the employees at Company X are highly qualified IT professionals who are very much in demand on the job market. Witness all the headhunting offices for IT specialists that have emerged. As we will discuss below, Company X took measures aimed at enhancing the commitment of this specific group of younger employees.

Teleworking and control

Teleworking is often said to cause changes in employee control, and to encourage empowerment, as well as output control (see e.g. Johnson 1997; Korte and Wynne 1996; COBRA 1994). Later in this chapter, we will illustrate these tendencies with evidence we found at Company X, but we would like to make two critical remarks here. First, we believe that changes in the management system of an organisation that has introduced teleworking should not be attributed to teleworking as such but rather to changes in the environment. Second, in the case of teleworking, it would seem that traditional control principles like direct supervision or behavioural control become increasingly impossible. This, however, is not always the case. In many cases, IT enables work to be done at a distance precisely because IT offers a possibility of control at a distance. In one of the cases we studied, an IT company (other than Company X) used a dispatching system with which it could follow every movement of their field engineers. Management stressed that the system was not being used as a control system. However, following the panopticon principle of Foucault, it is not so much the actual use of the system but 'the awareness of increased visibility – and the possible consequences of this – which instils workers with greater work discipline' (Coombs *et al.* in Jackson 1995). Perhaps new systems such as 360° appraisal can also be seen as increasing visibility and replacing direct management supervision through supervision by colleagues, customers and others.

Control at Company X

We found two clear tendencies in the control mechanism at Company X. First, there was a shift from behaviour control towards empowerment/input control; second, we found an increase of output control and variable pay systems. Most of these changes resulted from the restructuring process but can still be seen as enablers of teleworking. Some indicators of this are summarised in the following developments.

First of all, the formal appraisal system was reconsidered and resulted in a more result- and output-oriented system using more explicitly stated goals. Here, objectives in three different areas (winning, executing and teaming) are defined, first at the highest level of the organisation and next at all the lower levels (department, team, individual) with the restriction that all latter goals need to fall within those already defined. Thus, all employees commit themselves to certain objectives that they have proposed in discussion with their manager.[9] This new system can be interpreted as implying an increase in empowerment as well as in output control.

Second, as the number of management levels has diminished, the professionals at the lowest level have gained a considerable amount of responsibility. This can be linked with the changes in market circumstances, which demand a high degree of flexibility and rapid decision making. Obviously, those in the field are best placed to make such decisions. It can become very ineffective if several hierarchical levels need to be consulted before a decision is made. Managers expect their professionals to be able to work independently and to act as entrepreneurs. From the point of view of the professional, this can have positive as well as negative consequences. It implies a vertical upgrading of tasks but it also means he or she is held responsible for the risks that are taken and the choices he or she makes, which might enhance work pressure.

Finally, we observed a tendency towards a more variable pay system, implying a closer link between rewards and performance on both the team level and the individual level. Overall, a distinction can be made between salespeople, of whom the variable part of their salary amounts to 30 per cent, and jobs like systems engineers or software specialist, who have a variable part of 10 per cent. This shows that the choice of control principle – in this case the amount of output control – depends on the nature of the job. Clearly, the sales objectives, which are mainly based on revenue, are more measurable and quantifiable than those of system engineers, from whom the quality of the output is much more important.

Teleworking and organisational commitment

In this, final, section we will try to link teleworking to the processes of commitment and control we described above. Given the changes in organisations as well as in employee attitudes, the introduction of teleworking at first sight presents a paradox. We could compare this with what is happening in the banking industry: the increased competition requires measures to bind customers to their bank while, for these customers, loyalty towards one bank is less self-evident. When banks start to introduce all kinds of tele-banking, this can have a negative effect on customer commitment.

The question we will now turn to is whether the evolution of teleworking at Company X has influenced employee commitment to the company.[10] We will, therefore, first look at some antecedents for commitment that have possibly been affected by teleworking and see whether we can find evidence for this in our case study. Next, we will discuss how commitment can be managed in order to compensate for the negative effects teleworking has on the development of commitment.

Commitment antecedents

We have stressed the difficulty in determining the extent to which certain changes in organisational processes can be attributed to teleworking. This is equally so with changes in organisational commitment. As the introduction of teleworking at Company X took place in the middle of a broader change process, it is impossible to determine the extent to which teleworking 'as such' affected employee commitment. Nevertheless, we will point out some features of teleworking that seem to have had an impact on organisational commitment. We will do this by considering how teleworking affects certain antecedents for commitment. As noted above, most of the research has focused on affective commitment. In this area, the wide range of variables that have been examined can be categorised in three groups: organisational characteristics, personal characteristics, and work experiences (Meyer and Allen 1997). It is mainly through antecedents of the last category that teleworking will affect commitment.

What we did not find explicitly as an antecedent for commitment, but what we think is considered in most research to be self-evident, is the requirement for physical proximity of the employee and the organisation to which that person is committed. Commitment, as a psychological state, might well be something that is created through perceptions and therefore facilitated by face-to-face contacts. Therefore, the most obvious effect of teleworking seems to come from the simple fact that when people are teleworking, they are not present at the main office. Teleworking implies that, depending on the amount of time spent away from the office, the incidence of these perceptions and interpersonal contacts decreases and along with this the opportunities to become committed to the organisation. To a certain extent, distance communication using ICT can compensate for this. One manager, for instance, stated that he felt more committed to the company since e-mail enabled him to stay in touch with the company in the evening and on weekends and holidays. Still, these forms of distance communication will never equal the richness and efficiency of face-to-face contacts (see e.g. Daft 1998; Nohria and Eccles 1992; McLoughlin and Jackson, Chapter 11 in this volume).

Recalling the temporal–spatial work pattern we mentioned in the first section of this chapter, we can conclude that most of the employees still spend a considerable amount of time at the main office. However, for two job categories (customer engineers and software services), the amount of time spent at the main office does not differ greatly from that spent at customers' sites. Depending on the project they are working on, professionals of those categories sometimes spend several months at the customer's premises, and seldom visit their own company offices. A possible negative effect might be that they begin to feel more committed to the customer's company and ultimately start working for it. This would obviously result in a serious loss for Company X.

From the interviews, we know that a large share of the time spent at the office is for meetings and other formal communication. Furthermore, the survey showed that the amount of informal communication had diminished substantially – a tendency reported by managers, who saw it as a big loss. Informal communication is believed to have a direct effect on organisational performance. This, however, is not what we focus on here, where we are only looking at informal communication as an antecedent for commitment. Further, we will see that the management at Company X is actively trying to stimulate this form of communication.

It is important to note that, according to most managers at Company X, a potential loss in commitment was generally not regarded as a very serious problem at that time. Most employees who work in the shared offices had been with the company for several years before the introduction of the office-sharing environment and had already built up a strong commitment to it. However, several managers foresaw that this issue could become a serious problem in the long term, as more and more new employees start teleworking immediately for a considerable amount of their time. With respect to what will follow, it is, therefore, important to keep a distinction in mind between the younger employees who have only recently come to work for the company and the older ones, who have acquired several years of seniority at the company and, as noted above, have a different mentality.

While we considered the feature of working away from the office as a commitment-decreasing factor, we wondered whether other features can compensate for it. In the introduction, we pointed out one of those features, namely the increased freedom and autonomy employees experience when they are tele-working. The interviews as well as the survey showed that one of the most important reasons for the professionals to devote themselves to the company is the high level of autonomy they perceive in their jobs. This is clearly an issue where teleworking can positively affect commitment. The freedom of arranging one's working hours that is implied with teleworking appears to be especially motivating.

Apart from increased autonomy, other perceived benefits linked with tele-working can increase employee commitment, such as the reduction in travel time, increased productivity when working at home, and the harmonisation of family and working life. The managers mentioned that there was a certain pride among the professionals in working for a company that gives them the opportunity and freedom to work where and when they want. Furthermore, the tools they were offered, such as a portable computer and a possibility to access the company network from home, were seen as prestige factors.

Managing for commitment

As far as management recognises the importance of commitment and realises that teleworking can endanger it, it can actively try to enhance commitment, or in other words, it can 'manage for commitment'. Meyer and Allen indicate several areas of human resources management where commitment-enhancing measures can be taken, such as recruitment and selection, socialisation, training, promotion, compensation and benefits. These processes are part of what we called the 'allocation dimension' within an organisation. Some concrete measures were mentioned during the interviews by managers and project leaders at Company X. It must be noted that not all of these measures were explicitly aimed at enhancing commitment. Furthermore, these measures were not being applied consistently in all the departments. Nevertheless, the following can be of practical use to companies who are aware of the potential for commitment and the risk of losing it when introducing teleworking on a large scale.

Increasing affective commitment
- through the processes of selection and recruitment
- through the process of socialisation: a mentoring system
- offering training and career opportunities

But! Can decrease continuance commitment
- offering challenging jobs
- activities to keep up informal communication
- through compensation and benefits

Increasing continuance commitment
- through compensation and benefits, preferably linked with performance

Managing for commitment can begin even before an employee starts working for the company, namely through the processes of selection and recruitment. When recruiting employees, the company should provide realistic job previews that describe both the positive and the negative aspects of the proposed job (Meyer and Allen 1997). Therefore, through the selection process, the company can actively select on the basis of personal characteristics that are related to high commitment. During the interviews at Company X, we did not discuss this explicitly in the context of commitment, but some managers did mention that, when selecting new employees, they tried to find out whether the person would be able to work in a shared-office environment.

Perhaps the most important area where commitment can be expected is the socialisation of newcomers in the organisation. At Company X, they introduced a mentoring system for this purpose. As the management clearly felt teleworking could in the long run cause problems for the commitment of younger employees, it introduced a formal mentoring system. This system implies that every new employee is appointed a mentor, a colleague who has been working in the company for a longer period of time. This mentor needs to take care of the integration and socialisation of the new employee for 6 months. Although this mentor is also teleworking, he or she makes a commitment to be available. During the critical period of succession, the new employee will spend most of his or her time at the main office. The system has only recently been formally introduced and has, therefore, not yet been put into practice in every department. However, the management as well as the employees were very positive about it.[11]

A third way to enhance commitment is by offering training and career opportunities. This, however, is not always the case as we need to make an important distinction between two components of commitment. Offering training and career possibilities can enhance affective commitment, but it can also decrease continuance commitment. Important antecedents for continuance commitment are the alternatives the employee perceives. Unless this training is specialised for the individual company and has little value outside the company, training will enhance employability and offer an employee more alternatives, which means less continuance commitment. Also, when employees are offered career opportunities, they realise they have other options outside the company. According to the management at Company X, a great deal was being invested in the professionals, and this was considered as having a generally positive effect on their commitment and motivation.

Apart from these measures in the organisational allocation dimension, the organisation can also try to influence commitment by offering challenging jobs with a high degree of autonomy. We already mentioned this as an antecedent of commitment that is affected positively through telework, which means that we were focusing on how telework affected this factor. Here, we see it as a commitment-enhancing measure and focus on how it can enhance commitment given that teleworking has been introduced (and consequently has had an effect).

Similarly, we have already considered how teleworking causes a decrease in informal communication and now turn to measures that can enhance this communication. Managers mentioned certain activities that were organised specifically because of teleworking, such as a monthly happy hour for the entire company. Other activities varied according to the department and the team. Managers considered it their responsibility to ensure that these things took place. Other occasions, such as a team lunch or a weekend, were said to take place more frequently.

Almost all of these measures were aimed at enhancing the affective component of commitment, with the exception of training, which can also have the opposite effect on continuance commitment. The last factor we will consider is much more closely linked to the continuance component of commitment. Recall that, according to Meyer and Allen, this refers to the employee's awareness that costs are associated with leaving the organisation. This component of commitment can, therefore, develop as a result of any action that increases the cost of leaving the organisation. This means that the more compensation and benefits the employees can enjoy, the higher the cost when leaving the organisation. When this compensation and these benefits are linked with performance, which is considered an appropriate control mechanism for most teleworking jobs, continuance commitment can be enhanced even more. As we mentioned earlier, we found evidence for an increase in output and market control at Company X. We can relate this to the fact that, in the context of teleworking, several authors point to a shift from traditional employment relationships towards contractual relationships or pseudo-self-employment based on transactional principles. The more an employment relationship is based on these principles, the more the continuance component of commitment is stressed at the expense of affective commitment.

Conclusion

In this chapter we discussed the relationship between the processes of organisational control and commitment against the background of perspectives in organisational change. Unlike much of the literature in the area of telework and virtual organisations, we tried not to speculate about possible developments but instead to compare theoretical insights with empirical practice. Applying theory on the antecedents and consequences of organisational commitment to a teleworking situation shows where attention should be paid, given that an organisation recognises the importance of commitment for organisational performance. In the last section of the chapter we transferred this into concrete measures whereby organisations can actively manage for commitment.

Notes

1 The survey did not contain only questions that fit into our research objectives. A considerable part of it consisted of a general evaluation of the project at the request of Company X.

2 These satellite offices are not offices that have been established for the purpose of teleworking but are simply the other establishments of Company X and are also organised as shared offices.

3 We note here that, in theory, managers also worked in the shared-office environment, in the sense that they used a private office that, when they were absent, was available as a meeting room. However, when interviewing the managers in their offices, we had the impression that these offices were not much different from traditional managers' offices.

4 Certain secretarial functions were separated from the traditional secretary and put into separate departments. A call centre was established to handle all incoming phone calls and an in-house publishing department to take care of the lay-out of presentations and so on.

5 Whereas salespeople used to have a considerable knowledge of the products they sold and were therefore considered to be product specialists as a result of increasing specialisation their main task now is to sustain the relationship with a limited number of clients. As soon as technical knowledge is required, a project is transferred to another department.

6 This illustrates that every company has its own understanding of the concept depending on its own situation, which makes comparative research in teleworking very difficult. In the following, when we talk about the introduction of teleworking at Company X, we intend the particular changes that have taken place at Company X.

7 We need to note here that, although 78 per cent found themselves to be more productive at home, this percentage shrank to 43 per cent when overall productivity (all locations together) was asked about.

8 In discussing organisational commitment we will rely mainly on Meyer and Allen, whose book *Commitment in the Workplace* (1997) offers an integrated summary of research and conclusions in the area of organisational commitment.

9 Whereas most managers found the new formal appraisal system quite different from the former one, there were at least two managers who stated that in theory employees

now committed themselves to objectives while before they were simply given their objectives. In practice, however, they felt the new system was not so very different from the old.

10 As we have not been able to conduct a longitudinal study on organisational commitment, we will do this mainly on the basis of the information from the interviews. But we would like to note that, even if we would have had the possibility of measuring commitment at different times, it would still be impossible to determine how much of the change in commitment could be attributed to teleworking.

11 An item in the survey showed that 78 per cent of the respondents agreed that 'a mentoring system would be adequate for integrating new employees into a team'.

Bibliography

Andriessen, E.J.H. (1995) 'Telematica en grensoverschrijding, een inleiding', in Andriessen, E.J.H. and ten Horn, L.A. (eds) *Organiseren met Telematica. Een Kwestie van Grensoverschrijding*, Utrecht: Lemma.

Appelbaum, E. and Batt, R. (1994) *The New American Workplace. Transforming Work Systems in the United States*, Ithaca: ILR Press.

Becker, H.S. (1960) 'Notes on the concept of commitment', *American Journal of Sociology*, 66: 32–42.

Brigham, M. and Corbett, M. (1996) 'Trust and the virtual organisation', in Jackson, P.J. and van der Wielen, J.M.M. (eds) *New International Perspectives on Telework*, Tilburg: WORC.

Christis, J. (1995) 'Arbeidsprocesdiscussie en Sociotechniek', in Huijgen, F. and Pot, F.D. (eds) *Verklaren en ontwerpen van produktieprocessen. Het debat over arbeidsprocesbenadering en sociotechniek*, Amsterdam: SISWO.

Clegg, S.R. (1990) *Modern Organisations: Studies in the Postmodern World*, London: Sage.

COBRA (1994) *Business Restructuring and Teleworking: Current Practice*, Brussels: Commision of the European Communities.

Coombs, R., Knights, D. and Willmott, H.C. (1992) 'Culture, control and competition: towards a conceptual framework for the study of information technology in organizations', *Organization Studies*, 13, 1: 51–72.

Daft, R.L. (1998) *Organization Theory and Design*, Cincinnati (Ohio): South-Western Publications.

Davenport, T. (1993) *Process Innovation: Re-engineering Work through Information Technology*, Boston: Harvard Business School Press.

de Sitter, L.U. and van Eijnatten, F.M. (1995) 'Moderne Sociotechniek in Nederland: de benadering van integrale organisatievernieuwing', in Huijgen, F. and Pot, F.D. (eds) *Verklaren en Ontwerpen van Produktieprocessen. Het Debat over Arbeidsprocesbenadering en Sociotechniek*, Amsterdam: SISWO.

Doorewaard, H. and de Nijs, W. (1998) 'Organisatieontwikkeling en human resource management: naar een integraal ordeningsmodel', in Doorewaard, H., de Nijs, W. and Benschop, Y. (eds) *Organisatieontwikkeling en Human Resource Management*, Utrecht: Lemma: 69–91.

Eisenhardt, K.M. (1985) 'Control: organizational and economic approaches', *Management Science*, 31, 2: 134–49.

Hammer, M. and Champy, J. (1993) *Reengineering the Corporation*, New York: HarperCollins.

Handy, C. (1995) 'Trust and the virtual organization', *Harvard Business Review*, May/June: 40–50.

Harris, M. (1998) 'Rethinking the virtual organisation', in Jackson, P.J. and van der Wielen, J.M.M. (eds) *Teleworking: International Perspectives – from Telecommuting to the Virtual Organisation*, London: Routledge: 74–92.

Heisig, U. and Littek, W. (1995) 'Veranderingen in vertrouwensrelaties in het arbeidsproces', in Van Dijck, J., Van Hoof, J. and Henderickx, E. (eds) *Baas over de eigen (loop)baan: veranderende Arbeidsrelaties in België en Nederland. Opgedragen aan Albert Mok ter Gelegenheid van zijn Afscheid als Hoogleraar*, Houten: Educatieve Partners Nederland: 121–44.

Hope, V. and Hendry, J. (1996) 'Corporate cultural change – is it relevant for the organisation of the 1990s?', *Human Resource Management Journal*, 5, 4: 61–73.

Huys, R., Sels, L. and Van Hootegem, G. (1995) *De uitgestelde Transformatie: Technische en Sociaal-organisatorische Herstructureringen in de Chemische, de Automobiel- en de Machinebouwindustrie*, Brussels: DWTC.

Jackson, P.J. (1995) *Organising in Time and Space: A Theoretical Framework for the Study of Worker Dispersal*, London: Brunel University, Dept of Management Studies.

Johnson M. (1997) *Teleworking ... In Brief*, Oxford: Butterworth-Heinemann.

Kern, H. and Schuman, M. (1984) *Das Ende der Arbeitsteilung? Rationalisierung in der industriellen Produktion*, München: Verlag, C.H. Beck.

Korte W.B. and Wynne W. (1996) *Telework: Penetration, Potential and Practice in Europe*, Amsterdam: IOS Press.

Lincoln, J.R. and Kalleberg, A.L. (1990) *Culture, Control and Commitment: A Study of Work Organization and Work*, Cambridge: Cambridge University Press.

Meyer, J.P and Allen N.J. (1991) 'A three component conceptualisation of organisational commitment', *Human Resources Management Review*, 1: 61–89.

—— (1997) *Commitment in the Workplace: Theory, Research and Application*, Thousand Oaks, CA: Sage.

Nohria, N. and Eccles, R.G. (1992) 'Face-to-face: making network organisations work', in Nohria, N. and Eccles, R.G. (eds) *Networks and Organisations*, Harvard Business School Press: 288–308.

Ouchi, W.G. (1979) 'A conceptual framework for the design of organizational control mechanisms', *Management Science*, 25, 9: 833–48.

—— (1980) 'Markets, clans and bureaucracies', *Administrative Science Quarterly*, 25: 129–42.

Picken, J.C. and Dess, G.C. (1997) 'Out of (strategic) control', *Organizational Dynamics*, Summer: 35–48.

Piore, M.J. and Sabel, Ch.F. (1984) *The Second Industrial Divide*, New York: Basic Books.

Roe, R., Schalk, R. and Zijlstra, F. (1995) 'Veranderingen in arbeid: consequenties voor de arbeids- en organisatie-psychologie', *Gedrag en Organisatie*, 8, 4: 209–20.

Taylor, W.F. (1964) *Scientific Management – Comprising Shop Management, the Principles of Scientific Management and Testimony before the Special House Committee*, Harper & Row.

van der Wielen, J.M.M. and Taillieu, T.C.B. (1995) 'Recent conceptual developments in telework research', *Proceedings of the 13th Annual Conference of the Association of Management*, Vo. 13, no. 2: 2–5 August, Vancouver, British Columbia, Canada. Tilburg: WORC.

van Hootegem, G. (forthcoming) *De draaglijke Traagheid van het Management. Productie en Personeelsbeleid in de Industrie*, Leuven: ACCO.

8 Management rationalities and virtual working

Adjusting telework to different organisational cultures and rationalities

Reima Suomi and Juhani Pekkola

Preamble

In our contribution to the First International Workshop on Telework (see Suomi *et al.* 1996), we concluded that management practices and prejudices are a major obstacle for telework. Now we want to tackle this problem more deeply and discuss which kind of basic values managers hold, which kinds of organisational cultures they support, and how these may conflict with the application of telework.

Our theoretical point of reference draws upon two disciplinary backgrounds. First is the literature discussing corporate culture. Unfortunately, telework arrangements are often seen as subcultures within a company, adopting an opposing and disintegrating role. This situation is worsened by the unofficial nature of most telework arrangements.

We argue below that organisational cultures can support three different rationalities. First we have the 'market rationality'. According to this point of view, telework is viewed positively if it expands the position and goodwill of the company in the marketplace. Second, we have 'economic rationality', where everything is measured in economic terms. In this environment, telework might be allowed if it contributes added value to an organisation's products and services. Third, there is a 'resource-based rationality'. According to this view, telework should be adopted where it allows resources, among them staff, to be used more efficiently.

Different rationalities, we argue, are exhibited by different management groups. Upper management, for instance, holds predominantly 'market rationality' values, with middle management more concerned with issues of 'economic rationality', while operational management is more interested in 'resource-based rationality'. When these three rationalities fail to converge over particular subjects of management and decision making, problems are likely to arise. This is found in the case of teleworking, for instance, where because these rationalities are often out of sync, developments may be thwarted, much to the disappointment of certain organisational constituencies.

Introduction

Telework, we could put it, suffers from the 'ketchup phenomenon'. Everyone wants to get a portion of the ketchup; everyone is passing the bottle. The ketchup inside should be in order, but still there is some kind of bottleneck that prevents it from coming out. As we concluded in earlier work about the Finnish situation (Suomi *et al.* 1996):

> To summarise, both according to our theoretical discussion and empirical findings, there should be no major obstacles for successful telework adoption in Finland. The technical facilities are available and especially employees are open for telework arrangements....So, management capabilities and opinions seem to be the critical factor within telework introduction. Small organisations seem to have an advantage in this respect, and larger organisational units should strive to learn from them.

However, when speaking to managers about telework, the situation usually seems more positive. Yet when such managers move towards practical steps, some kind of obstacle rolls in. We can conclude that in spite of the rational benefits, there must be some cultural barrier in organisations to the adoption of telework. In this chapter, we try to find out what that is.

We have two starting points. First, drawing on the rich body of literature on *organisational cultures*. This will allow us to examine whether telework runs against the grain of some basic aspects of organisational culture. Second, we consider whether telework might collide with the *rationalities* held by management. Such rationalities must be considered as a key component of any organisational culture, since it is the management that is the most dominant group affecting it. In what follows, we study these concepts and relate them to telework.

Telework meets organisational culture

Why is organisational culture important?

Culture, by its very nature, is hard to get your arms around. It is caught up in the ebb and flow of living and as such is embodied in the people that populate any organisation (Donnelly 1984: 8). The culture apparent in a business enterprise is often described along the lines of 'company culture' or 'corporate culture'. Even words such as 'management culture' or 'management religion' are used. In this chapter, however, we will speak about *organisational* culture.

Edwin Baker (1980:8) defines corporate culture as: 'an interrelated set of beliefs, shared by most of their members, about how people should behave at work and what tasks and goals are important.'

Henri Broms and Henrik Gahmberg (1983: 482) define the culture of a domain as the collection of values hidden in the shared myths and symbols of that domain. According to Robert Donnelly (1984: 8), corporate culture represents the influence that the leaders, or senior managers – especially the chief executive – have on the organisation, and that permeate the daily work environment, create a climate for the employees and an image for the enterprise.

For Richard Pascale (1984), corporate culture is a set of shared values, norms and beliefs that gets everybody heading in the same direction. Similarly, Ellen Wallach (1983: 29) defines it as the shared understanding of an organisation's employees – 'how we do thing around here'. Vijay Sathe (1983: 6) speaks of culture as a set of important understandings (often unstated) that members of a community share in common. The difficulty of expressing corporate culture explicitly is also noted by Christian Scholz (1987: 80). For him, it is the implicit, invisible, intrinsic and informal consciousness of organisations which guides the behaviour of individuals and which itself is shaped by their behaviour.

W. Brooke Tunstall (1983) defines corporate culture as a general constellation of beliefs, customs, value systems, behavioral norms and ways of doing business that are unique to each corporation. Finally, Alan Wilkins (1983) states – after much consideration – that culture can be viewed as people's customary behaviour and their taken-for-granted ways of seeing the world.

There is considerable agreement, therefore, that cultural orientations have a deep influence on our life (and are things that may be more implicit in our thinking and actions than explicit). For example, William Gorden (1984: 78) has presented four ways in which culture affects organisations:

1   A cultural value that says human nature is basically good will influence organisations to encourage employee autonomy and reliance upon intrinsic motivation.
2   A cultural orientation that holds to the belief that people can master their environment, rather than be its victim, will influence management to be adventurous and proactive.
3   A cultural orientation which values 'being' over 'doing' may be expressed in organisations which emphasise interpersonal sensitivity and a management which is high on consideration and very concerned about morale and climate.
4   A cultural orientation which holds the individual as more important than status will minimise compliance with rules, and will be likely to develop personnel policies which treat people equally.

To summarise, definitions of corporate culture see it as central to the functioning of organisations. Arrangements and initiatives that run against settled company cultures may thus face obstacles if they are to succeed, especially if their business rationality is hard to prove, as is the case in telework. Telework introduction is therefore not merely a technical, process re-engineering task, but also a cultural-bound activity. Here, then, the cultural dimension may have a stabilising effect in that it naturally resists change. However, while the novelties bound up with teleworking may mean that cultural forces act against it, by the same token, were it ever to become an established way of doing things, organisational culture might well support it.

As may seem obvious to state, different stakeholder groups in organisations hold different cultural values. An issue cannot have a perfect fit with every organisational subculture. So far as telework is concerned, for instance, it is relatively easy to see that telework might well be commensurate with the cultural values of upper management. This is reflected, for instance, in strategy speeches and documents (for instance, on flexible working). However, it may not suit the culture values of other managers.

To develop this point we need to dig more deeply into the three sets of cultural values held by management. First, we discuss the rationality of 'the market', as held by upper, strategic management; second, the rationality of 'economy', as held by middle management; and, third, the rationality of 'resources', as held by operational management.

The three management rationalities

The market rationality

According to the market rationality view, telework is a good idea if it expands the position and goodwill of the company in the marketplace. The primary market telework affects, of course, is the *labour* market.

In any market, an organisation can behave either competitively or cooperatively. It is the competition paradigm, though, that has been dominant – a paradigm underpinned by 'the war metaphor', as Mason (1992) shows. According to Mason, the metaphor has the following characteristics:

Issues highlighted

- zero sum game
- winning (losing) in the marketplace
- us/them conflict

Issues hidden

- cooperation
- complexity of relationships
- growth, renewal of social quality of life

Role of competition

- determine a winner

Role of IT/information systems

- develop sustained competitive advantage
- erect barriers to competition

The second option in contrast to competition, is *cooperative* behaviour. According to the same taxonomy, we can define cooperative activity through the following characteristics (Suomi 1994):

Issues highlighted

- not zero sum game
- complexity of relationships
- us/them harmony

Issues hidden

- competition
- winning (losing) in the marketplace

Role of competition

- works at the side of cooperation as a second driving force

Role of IT/information systems

- develop sustained advantage for all parties
- lower barriers for cooperation

A company culture focusing on the market rationality provides implicit normative guidelines for tackling the issues mentioned above. Such kinds of issues are usually found in the sphere of the *upper management*.

In labour markets, competitive behaviour differentiates between the interests of the labour and interests of the organisation. Telework, however, is often seen as some kind of extra privilege for the workers, reflecting, perhaps, their market strength. Within the cooperation paradigm, therefore, telework can be a win–win game both for workers and the organisation.

The economic rationality

As noted above, according to economic rationality, all things should be measured in *economic* terms. This means that telework would be promoted where it contributed added value to products and services.

Economic rationality is most deeply rooted in the systematic planning of financial matters. In general, systematic planning is a cornerstone of economic rationality. As information systems become more complicated, for instance, their building and application demand more systematic and rigorous methods and techniques. Systematic management approaches are now commonly used for both strategic planning and technological change. So far as organisational adaption is concerned, however, the problem is that in addition to 'technology issues', we also have to take into account factors such as 'people' and the 'environment' (such as markets). Both humans and markets are difficult to configure into rigid structures, and resist 'technical fixes' (see also McLoughlin and Jackson, Chapter 11 in this volume).

In general terms, we can say that systematic approaches are needed when we build operative, routine applications. In these systems, technology may have the dominant role. However, with information systems of a more strategic character, where humans and the environmental factors dominate, different management approaches are needed. We strongly believe, here, that teleworking arrangements are not purely operational in nature. As a consequence of this, they are not best served by management approaches that focus solely on systematic, economic rationales.

The economic rationale is most typically adopted by the middle management, the same party (or organisational subculture) that is usually involved in the systematic budgeting processes of the company. It might also be that middle management is actually the strongest opponent of telework in many organisations. This is because of the way such subcultures – being largely driven by economic rationales – will tend to question what kinds of effects telework has on the bottom line of company results.

The resource-based rationality

The kernel of the resource-based thinking on an organisation is described in the classic works of Amit and Schoemaker (1993). For these authors, the challenge for managers is to identify, develop and deploy resources and capabilities in a way that provides the firm with a sustainable competitive advantage and, thereby, a superior return on capital.

According to Hinton and Kaye (1996), operational management is concerned with the efficient and effective application of *existing* organisational resources. This contrasts with strategic management, which governs the total amount of resources, either acquiring or harvesting them. In public administration, strategic management is also concerned with political decision making, and is outside the scope of this chapter. We instead focus more on the operational decision making and managing the resources at hand.

Barney (1994: 3) defines a firm's resources as follows:

> In general, a firm's resources and capabilities include all of the financial, physical, human, and organisational assets used by a firm to develop, manufacture, and deliver products or services to its customers. Financial resources include debt, equity, retained earnings and so forth. Physical resources include the machines, manufacturing facilities, and building firms used in their operations. Human resources include all the experience, knowledge, judgement, risk-taking propensity, and wisdom of individuals associated with a firm. Organisational resources include the history, relationships, trust, and organisational culture that are attributes of groups of individuals associ-

ated with a firm, along with a firm's internal structure, control systems, and dominant management style.

Let us now draw together the insights provided by these three rationalities and apply them to make sense of the link between teleworking issues and organisational cultures.

Telework meets management rationalities

The market rationality and telework

From the above we can deduce that telework is best suited to the market rationality if this occurs in the context of a reorganisation of production processes and staff participation. By nature, telework is better suited to cooperative activity so far as the company's own staff and the external environment are concerned. Humanistic and liberal staff policy guidelines drawn up by the upper management are necessary (yet not always sufficient) conditions for the application of telework (Pekkola 1993). Yet telework is seldom the outcome of a systematic personal policy. In other words, only in certain cases does upper management effect measures that lead directly to the reconfiguration of work, including the application of telework. On the other hand, telework may well form part of broader organisational innovations – especially regarding greater work effectiveness, enhanced customer orientation, and staff and customer commitment – where these are brought about to pursue strategic competitive advantage. The condition for this is, however, a strong humanistic and results-oriented cooperative company culture, permeating all levels of organisational and management practice.

In Finland, most of the potential for telework is still unused. Of those that are teleworking, 80 per cent are doing so unofficially, with the initiative largely coming from the staff themselves. Indeed, in only around 6 per cent of cases has the superior suggested teleworking (Luukinen *et al.* 1996). This evidence also shows that in some cases, teleworking initiatives might well come from (upper) management, i.e. from the direction of market rationality.

Economic rationality and telework

The sceptical attitude of middle management has generally been considered an impediment to telework. Given its principal role in maintaining economic rationality, the limited interest in telework has made middle management appear rather conservative on such matters. To initiate teleworking, middle management needs the support of the upper management, as well as that of the immediate supervisors of work, which naturally complicates negotiations. The negative correlation of company size to telework indicates that perhaps more than one level of management may not be in support of teleworking arrangements. It goes without saying that management based on short-sighted economic rationality, which involves a 'carrot and stick' policy so far as employees are concerned, is unlikely to promote the application of telework.

Several inquiries have shown that company management is aware of the advantages of telework in the production of added value. This illustrates that economic rationality of itself is not sufficient for developments. Yet, systematic reorganisation of work to support telework has seldom been applied as part of a company's personal policy. Such reorganisation would suggest a better integration of business functions. In certain companies, it has been possible, by using IT and work reorganisation, to gain strategic and progressive competitive advantages, which perhaps reflects a more 'mature' stage of progress in teleworking developments.

In most cases, the nature of information provided for this level of management may also be a reason for passivity. The unofficial nature of many telework arrangements, and the general and inadequate evaluation of staff resources in company accounting, may fail to reveal the significance of any work reorganisation so far as economic rationality is concerned. But, then, nor has the significance of telework for market rationality been properly revealed. Where, on the other hand, results-oriented management and process management have been developed, opportunities for telework application have also been created. The issue here is that resource-based management is integrated as an essential part of management relating to economical rationality.

The resource-based rationality and telework

If we interpret telework as an organisational resource, then the *amount* that exists in an organisation becomes a strategic issue, belonging to upper management. However, in the practical daily management of this resource, operational management has a key role. The main question – so far as this cultural orientation is concerned – is whether telework is an organisational resource that brings to the firm a sustainable competitive advantage and, thereby, a superior return on capital.

The informal nature of so many teleworking schemes gives a reason to study the rationality of companies from three management levels, but also from the *employee* level. The spontaneous reorganisations that occur with teleworking, based around autonomy and expertise, is largely brought about by employees *themselves*. Direct employee benefits are therefore of central importance. According to studies in Finland, teleworkers' quality of working life (standardised by staff groups) is better than non-teleworkers. This includes: the meaningfulness of work, equal opportunities, the scope for influencing one's own position, type of management used, upskilling, and obtaining information about business objectives. Teleworkers even considered environmental issues to be in better shape than the average worker (Pekkola 1997)

Telework, of course, is a method of organising work. Such methods are seldom identified as resources. If we take the view that telework is also a means of attaining flexibility, then the flexibility produced might be seen as an important company resource. The main type of resources managers really understand is that of staff. As long as staff can be used without major telework initiatives, organising work along teleworking lines is unlikely to proceed far. Should telework become a key to staff resourcing then initiatives might well proceed more quickly.

Conclusions

If telework is not proceeding in organisations in spite of its clear benefits, it must be confronting fundamental obstacles in organisations, most likely *organisational culture*. Culture sets very powerful limits on what is and what is not acceptable. If telework collides with organisational culture, it is certain to run into difficulties.

We have made a basic distinction between organisational cultures that work either on a cooperation or competition basis. With the cooperation paradigm dominant, conflicts of interests do not surface so easily. In such an environment, telework is also easier to introduce. A second major differentiation we have made is between human- and technology-oriented company cultures. As telework is bound up with the effective organisation of human work, we can conclude that humanistic-oriented company cultures provide a good starting point for it.

But the adoption of telework requires not only a humanistic and cooperative organisational culture but also the integration of functions belonging to different management levels. It is here that the different management rationalities come into play. So far as telework is concerned, the management of staff resources, as well as operational management, are important. Both are in a state of transition, given that in modern, knowledge-based organisations *staff themselves* are able to reorganise their work. This may occur, as we have seen, in an unofficial way, driven by individual as well as production rationalities.

If new management methods, such as the introduction of telework, are to help improve the quality of a company's operations, they must take into account the goals of different management levels. In an information society based on competition, staying in the vanguard of development calls for innovative work organisation which motivates and rewards the employees, satisfies the customers, produces positive economic results and provides opportunities for future progress. The deeper the integration of telework arrangements into business activities at various management levels, the greater the strategic advantages are likely to be.

Telework can be interpreted in the light of all the three management rationalities discussed above: *market*, as used by upper management; *economic*, as displayed by middle-management, and finally, *resource-based*, this being used by operational management. To facilitate faster introduction of telework, its proponents need to speak in the languages of the different management groups involved. According to our empirical research in Finland, telework is relatively easy to integrate with market and economic rationalities. However, understanding it as an important organisational resource might be difficult. As such, the connection between the resource-based rationality (adopted usually by operational management) and telework deserves a closer look.

Bibliography

Amit, R. and Schoemaker, P. (1993) 'Strategic assets and organisational rent', *Strategic Management Journal*, 14: 33–46.

Baker, Edwin, L. (1980) 'Managing organisational culture', *Management Review*, 7: 8–13.

Barney, Jay, B. (1994) 'Bringing managers back in: a resource-based analysis of the role of managers in creating and sustaining competitive advantages for firms', in Barney, Jay, B., Spender, J.C. and Rove, T. (eds) *Does Management Matter – On Competencies and Competitive Advantage*, Institute of Economic Research: Lund University.

Broms, Henri and Gahmberg, Henrik (1983) 'Communications to self in organisations and cultures', *Administrative Science Quarterly*, September: 482–95.

Donnelly, Robert, M. (1984) 'The interrelationship of planning with corporate culture in the creation of shared values', *Managerial Planning*, May/June: 8–12.

Gorden, William, I. (1984) 'Organisational imperatives and cultural modifiers', *Business Horizons*, 3: 76–83.

Hinton, C.M. and Kaye, G.R. (1996) 'The hidden investments in information technology: the role of organisational context and system dependency', *International Journal of Information Management*, 16, 6: 413–27.

Luukinen, A., Pekkola, J., Heikkilä, A. and Zamindar, M. (1996) 'Directions of telework in Finland; Report by the Finnish Expertise with Telework Project', *Publication of Labour Administration 143*, Finnish Ministry of Labour.

Mason, Robert, M. (1992) 'Metaphors in strategic information systems planning', *Journal of Management Information Systems*, 8: 11–30.

Nolan, Richard (1979) 'Managing the crises in data processing', *Harvard Business Review*, 57, 2: 115–26.

Pascale, Richard (1984) 'Fitting new employees into the company culture', *Fortune International*, 11: 62–9.

Pekkola, Juhani (1993) 'Etätyön Soveltaminen Henkilökohtaisella, Tuotanto-Organisaation ja Työmarkkinajärjestelmän Tasolla', *Työpoliittinen Tutkimus, 47*, Työministeriö.

—— (1997) 'Labour market position of teleworkers and employees in information occupations', paper in the *Second European Teleworking Festival*, Serre-Chevalier (Hautes Alpes, France), March: 20–2.

Sathe, Vijay (1983) 'Implications of corporate culture: a manager's guide to action', *Organisational Dynamics*, 2: 5–23.

Scholz, Christian (1987) 'Corporate culture and strategy – the problem of strategic fit', *Long Range Planning*, 4: 78–87.

Suomi, Reima (1994) 'Co-operation in the field of information systems', *Human Systems Management*, 13: 57–64.

Suomi, R., Luukinen, A., Pekkola, J. and Zamindar, M. (1996) 'Narrowing the gap between virtual and actual organisations through management communication-oriented telework adoption', in Jackson, P.J. and van der Wielen, J.M. (eds) *Proceedings of Workshop on New International Perspectives on Telework*, Brunel University, West London,: 468–80.

Tunstall, Brooke, W. (1983) 'Cultural transition at AT&T', *Sloan Management Review*, 1: 15–26.

Wallach, Ellen, J. (1983) 'Individuals and organisations: the cultural match', *Training and Development Journal*, 2: 29–36.

Wilkins, Alan, L. (1983) 'The culture audit: a tool for understanding organisations', *Organisational Dynamics*, 2: 24–38.

9 Autonomy, control and the virtual worker

Louise M. Adami

Introduction

Some form of control is necessary for effective organisational functioning because stakeholders have disparate priorities. Control systems help managers to achieve consistency in actions and activities across employee groups. This is important so that the behaviours and activities of the organisation's members match the organisation's plans and goals. The organisation can identify deviations and make corrections. This issue of control is complicated when workers and supervisors do not work in the same location. Technology, changing attitudes to coordinating work and non-work obligations, the restructuring of work activities (*i.e. organisations seeking to reallocate the costs of rent and utilities; commuting, etc.)*, and the structure of some jobs, are but some of the instigators of a metamorphosis of the traditional ways of managing. For some managers, the strain caused by the relocation of employees is intensified when the nature of the work demands that employees have almost perfect autonomy to achieve their tasks. Lawyers, architects, sales representatives and accountants are a few of the many and varied occupations that can be structured such that the employee works from a decentralised location.

The concept of employee discretion is complex as autonomy is necessary for creativity, but competitive pressures and organisational systems can restrict the domain of this independence. This results in *bounded autonomy*. This is discussed with reference to full-time journalists at a large Australian newspaper. A newspaper is an interesting case because newspaper journalists have an image of requiring flexibility in location and working hours, due to the nature of the news business. Furthermore, controlling journalists is perceived to be obscured because of the unpredictability of news. The fact that news gathering can occur outside the confines of the central office where the work supervisors (for example, the newspaper editor, section editors and chief of staff) are located, means that the supervisors must have trust in the journalists and rely on controls other than direct supervision.

Organisation flexibility and the virtual workplace

Flexibility has been hailed as a panacea to increased uncertainty (Pollert 1988) which is said to be a result of the intense competition characteristic of many sections of the macro and micro environments. At its broadest, 'flexibility' relates to change, adjustment and adaptiveness (De Leeuw and Volberda 1996). It is argued, although this concept has not been clearly defined in the literature, that flexible organisations have the capacity to respond more quickly and appropriately to uncertain environments. So, flexible or dynamic organisations are said to have the internal structures and capabilities to facilitate responsiveness and adaptability to changes in economic and market conditions, changes in government policy and employment legislation, unemployment, developments in technology and methods of production, competitiveness, and removal of skill boundaries. Therefore, in the industries where organisations are urged to be more adaptive than in the past, and if flexible organisations are deemed to be more appropriate 'forms' for uncertainty, then it follows that there should be a focus on implementing 'flexible' components in organisations.

As described by Atkinson (1984, 1987), the workforce broadly is comprised of two layers – the 'periphery' and 'core'. The periphery is made up of a group that is external to the organisation (contractors that provide specialist skills) and another group of employees that is loosely attached to the organisation. This group has low skill levels and can be brought into the organisation in times of peak demand, thus providing numerical flexibility. They have low employment security and have a '*job*' rather than a '*career*' (Atkinson and Meager 1986). The core comprises employees who have specialist skills. The organisation relies on the application of knowledge and expertise of these employees, while the peripheral employees are disposable and more easily replaced. The core employees have job security and provide specialist and functional flexibility for the organisation.

Organisations have several options when considering flexible work practices. These include flexitime, part-time work, job-sharing, and home-based working (Department of Industrial Relations 1996). The notion of the home worker has come a long way from the stereotypical image of the female performing clerical or manufacturing duties to supplement the household's income. Instead, the contemporary homeworker is no longer on the periphery and is performing professional and semi-professional jobs. For these positions, the relocation of the work site to one other than the centralised office represents an extension of the autonomy afforded the employees. The fact that they do their work at another location does not marginalise their role or indicate it as less strategic. This represents a change in the thinking that homeworkers are peripheral employees providing numerical flexibility as described by Pollert (1988).

Organisations are faced with several operational issues in attempting to increase their responsiveness to changes in internal and external environmental contingencies. One of the most important of these issues is determining the extent of control or the amount of autonomy the organisation will impose on organisational members.

Behaviour and output controls

It has been suggested that some organisations are less flexible than others because some organisational activities are tied to rules and controls (Bowman and Kogut 1995). 'Organisation' implies the need for control (Tannenbaum 1962) and control is used as the mechanism to integrate the diverse activities and interests of an organisation's participants. The paradox of flexibility is that an organisation must possess some procedures that enhance its flexibility to avoid the state of rigidity and simultaneously have some stability to avoid chaos (De Leeuw and Volberda 1996).

It is widely agreed in the organisational control literature that a control system is comprised of a standard of performance set and accompanied by a description of the desired action. Performance is appraised against the standard and corrective actions are taken if there are deviations from the standard (Milward 1946; Koontz 1958; Dalton and Lawrence 1971; Storey 1985; Lorange 1993). Thus, control is the process of monitoring activities to ensure they are being accomplished as planned and of correcting significant deviations (Robbins 1994).

The classical concept of control is a strict division of labour characterised by strictly defined tasks governed by explicit rules (Weber 1947). However, this conceptualisation does not pertain to all organisations or all industries. In fact, when considering the control variables of an organisation, one must consider the organisation's structure, people, technology and the external environment (Lorange 1993; Blunsdon 1995). Thus, if there is a change in one or all of these variables, then the control system must change to match the contingent variables.

Pragmatically, control implies something that an individual must do or must not do and it suggests restrictive measures relating to choice or freedom (Tannenbaum 1962). There are several types of control which management can impose on its employees, some of which are overt and others that are covert and may not even be recognised as 'controls' (see Table 9.1). Direct controls include direct supervision over those performing tasks, quality control, designation of authorisation responsibilities, standard operating procedures, rules, and budget and expenditure guidelines. Indirect controls include job descriptions, culture, performance appraisals, career advancement, incentives, compensation and remuneration, training and skill development, and the existence of flexible work arrangements.

Formal behavioural controls are appropriate within a bureaucratic framework. In this case, controls, rules and procedures are imposed top-down and supervisors monitor the performance of employees (Snell 1992). Behavioural controls may be appropriate when the desired behaviours and outcomes are easily defined. For example, in clothing manufacturing by piecework, organisation control extends from controlling the flow of work, to specifying the manner

Table 9.1 Examples of direct and indirect controls

Direct controls	Indirect controls
Procedural	Job description
Quality	Culture
Hierarchical	Performance appraisal
Rules	Career development
Budget	Compensation
Task allocation	Training
Discipline	Flexible work arrangements

and components of the process (fabrics, buttons and so on) and deadlines. Management specifies the sequence of the processes and the quantity of production required, and then it monitors and evaluates the performance of employees to ensure that they comply with the procedures. When behaviour control is imposed in inappropriate circumstances (that is, situations which require flexibility), the organisation faces the danger of being needlessly rigid and thus unresponsive to change (Snell and Youndt 1995).

Ouchi (1977) found that the more complex and unanalysable the task, output control, rather than behaviour control is appropriate. Complex tasks require the employee to apply his or her skills, expertise and professional standards to identify, coordinate and use the resources to accomplish tasks. This is typical for journalists, engineers and physiotherapists. By the nature of their specialised training and socialisation, these employees have the capacity to search, judge and choose directions in the course of problem solving (Tordoir 1995). This passes the onus of the transformation process to the employee and this implies that the employees must be cognisant of the organisation's values and norms.

Agency theorists propose that output control has the potential for providing employees with discretion to exercise judgement and be creative (Snell and Youndt 1995). However, they caution that this might backfire on the organisation as output control passes much responsibility to the employee and the employee may be reluctant to take risky decisions preferring to take safe, satisficing options. This highlights the importance of the role of organisation cultures in guiding behaviours.

Input controls

Input control mechanisms such as recruitment, development and socialisation processes are forms of managerial control. These normative controls are important as strategic-minded organisations choose new members who have the requisite capabilities and values to perform well and *fit in*. Thus, input controls regulate the antecedent conditions of performance (Snell 1992), ensuring that the employees' skills, knowledge, attitudes, values and interests match those of the employing organisation (Etzioni 1964). Behaviour can be learned gradually and unwittingly or the organisation or the profession can demand specific behaviour.

Training programmes are one avenue organisations may take to instil preferred behaviours and attitudes in participants (Robbins 1994). This may be especially important during an employee's orientation and induction period or when the employee starts a new job within the organisation. Typically, the profession, through its association and its members, controls admission to training and requires far more education from its trainees than the community demands (Goode 1957: 195). This association-imposed control serves to address the issue of association membership. It relates to the maintenance of standards and expectations of behaviour and performance. Further, it acts to enhance the reputation of members and means that individuals must satisfy several require-ments before their membership will be recognised. In other cases, there may be no controls of admission into the craft, but instead there are controls on the entry to the organisation. These controls may include experience or networks.

Organisation culture can be viewed as providing a context for the design of control systems and it may itself be a source of control (Berry 1995). 'Culture' communicates the desirable behaviours through rituals and stories which act as messengers. Thus, culture is a variable that can be manipulated to achieve different levels of control and thus flexibility. Culture facilitates control when the control system is consistent with the social norms and values of the organisation and culture can substitute control systems when there is no control. Culture inhibits control when it is incongruent with the shared norms, values and management philosophy.

Social controls are derived from mutual commitments of members of a group to each other and the shared ideals of members (Dalton and Lawrence 1971: 13). Group norms develop from this commitment and are represented as the accepted values and attitudes about standards of performance, relationships and codes of behaviour. Social controls are not usually written, but still can be explicit and powerful (Dalton and Lawrence 1971). One way organisations can encourage the development of this phenomenon is by encouraging group devel-opment activities and tasks. Social controls can also develop through the natural socialisation processes within a team or organisation. Employees who are absent from a centralised office may not be integrated into the cultures of the team or organisation to the same degree as employees who work on-site. Employees who work off-site part time and on-site the other part, and employees who have worked on-site before switching to work off-site, may be integrated sufficiently. However, employees who are absent from a centralised office may not be socialised into the group to the same degree as employees who work on-site and more effort may be required to achieve that integration. A lack of integration can be a problem if performance and behaviour are not clearly defined and refined and if the employee is new to the profession and the organisation.

The structure of the culture defines, regulates and controls the expected modes of achieving goals (Merton 1949). The range of behaviours can be limited and processes become 'tradition bound'. Hall (1968) suggests that formal and informal colleague groupings are the major source of ideas and judgements for the professional. According to Rothlisberger and Dickson (1941), the informal structure is based on personal factors and cliques that form to act as a control. The informal structure introduces a social organisation that develops unconsciously and can be as binding as formal procedures.

Barnard (1940) provides support for Rothlisberger and Dickson (1941) by suggesting that the informal organisation maintains a feeling of personal integrity, of self-respect, of independent choice (pp. 122–3). However, Selznick (1943) suggests that the individual's integrity is protected by the *appearance* of choice and that the individual has to compete with subtle group pressures which control behaviour. Thus, while there are no official controls on behaviour, the group provides control, reducing the liberties of the individual. The concept of social control is most relevant to individuals who work as part of a team, or at least in the company of others. Thus, for employees who work independently and complete all stages of the production themselves, group norms as controls may not be so important. For employees who rely on other organisation members for ideas, inspiration or who work interdependently, social controls are more relevant.

Some combination of behaviour, output and input controls is present in most organisations. Organisational functions that rely on experienced and professional employees to complete novel and complex tasks are most likely to have a balance of output and input controls (and little behaviour controls) as these help to develop the individuals so they behave and work effectively and they encourage workers to use their initiative in selecting and using the most appropriate resources complete the task (presumably socialisation in the culture assists with this, also). When seeking the 'right' balance of control and flexibility, managers must consider the type of work the employee is doing (e.g. complex or simple), the individual doing the work (eg professional or experienced, or cadet or inexperienced), the degree of socialisation into the profession and the organisation, as well as the internal systems of the organisation (e.g. direct or indirect methods of control).

Autonomy and the decentralised workplace

It can be argued that the relocation of some professional and experienced employees to a separate work location (e.g. home) to the supervisor is a natural extension of the autonomy afforded professional or experienced employees. That is to say, professional status and experience legitimates the claim to autonomy. In other words, in some circumstances, autonomy is enhanced when employees work at a decentralised location (Olsen and Primps 1984). Moreover, autonomy is said to be important for creative work (Breaugh 1985) so it stands to reason that employees who are professionals or experienced in their field, socialised in the ways of the profession and the organisation, who are relied upon for their specialised knowledge (functional flexibility), and whose work is self-contained, could be suitable for working at a decentralised location. It would not be practical for research and development scientists who are professionals and are relied upon for their specialised knowledge to work from home as the nature of their tasks is often interdependent and involves the use of cumbersome and expensive equipment that is shared among a group. In many scenarios, the physical presence of the scientist in a laboratory is important (at least part of the time). However, for a newspaper journalist who is socialised, experienced, has expert knowledge and skills, and who works to a large degree independently to pursue stories, work at home may be ideal. In this case, access to information may be a limiting factor, however this may be overcome with technologies.

Wallace (1995) suggests that autonomy is about exercising influence over one's own job-specific tasks. This is to say that people have autonomy if they have considerable freedom, independence and discretion in scheduling their work, in determining the content of their work, and in choosing methods for carrying it out (Wallace 1995: 819). Bailyn (1985) calls this 'operational autonomy' and distinguishes it from 'strategic autonomy' which is the freedom to set one's own work agenda. This is said to be important for satisfying responsibility and recognition needs of employees.

Organisations need to have some control over their employees – this is an important managerial function – but the amount of control (high or low) and types of control vary, particularly, by the type of worker. The literature highlights that professional, core employees are likely to experience different and less direct controls than other employees. To extend this idea, professionals who work off-site are expected to experience different types of management controls than those who work on-site (see Figure 9.1).

In some circumstances the level of autonomy granted to employees is less than optimal as there is a problem balancing the autonomy and control. This means that an employee's liberties may be restricted by managerial prerogative. Thus, while autonomy is necessary for creativity, competitive pressures restrict the domain of the autonomy, and autonomy is bounded.

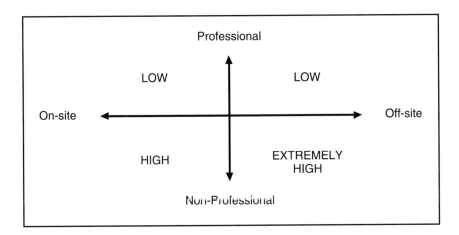

Figure 9.1 Location–status–organisational control strength diagram

Controlling professionals

Professionals feel that they should be able to make their own decisions – without pressure from the organisation. This responsibility and trust is stretched further when professional workers apply their autonomy and discretion to performing their work at alternative sites. Taking extra responsibility for one's work organisation is not new for professionals (Blanc 1989) and is consistent with the general move away from hierarchical patterns of control and narrowly defined tasks. The implication for managers is that they must rethink ways of controlling and evaluating performance. Etzioni (1964) identifies that typically, professionals are not subjected to direct supervision and strict rules.

Child (1972) found that management control is essentially unidimensional, either the decision-making process is a *centralised* or a *structured* activity. As a centralised activity, decision making is confined to senior levels and management instructs employees to implement the strategy decisions (recall the notion of strategic autonomy). In the structured activity, decision making is delegated, with policies and procedures imposed as boundaries on decision-making capacity and used to facilitate decision making at the lower levels. Child found these types of control to be inversely related. Thus, if decision making is decentralised, then policies and procedures are implemented to maintain basic control.

Scott's (1965) typology of professional organisations is similar to Child's typology. Professional organisations are organisations in which members of one or more professional groups play the central role in the achievement of the primary organisational objectives (Scott 1965: 65). As such, organisations are regarded as 'autonomous' if the administration delegates organisation and control to the professionals. In autonomous organisations, the workers are highly skilled and motivated, behaviour is internalised by professional norms and the individual is the dominant source of authority (Hall 1968). An organisation is regarded as 'heteronomous' if administrators retain control over most professional activities (Scott 1965: 66). The workers are clearly subordinated, and there is an elaborate set of rules and a system of routine supervision. In the heteronomous example, the professional function is clearly constrained by the administrative framework. Thus, it could be expected that individuals who deal with non-routine and dynamic problems would be delegated almost absolute control over the achievement of their tasks, rather than establishing bureaucratic mechanisms to maintain control over the decentralised activities.

Control via the traditional hierarchical structure of organisations is deemed to be inappropriate for professionals (Miller 1968). The more professionalised groups have more self-regulation and longer socialisation than non-professionalised groups, so they perhaps have less need for the same types of controls. These professional controls can be equally as constraining as bureaucratic controls and have the same capacity to inhibit flexibility. In the environment where professionals require autonomy and authority to decide the most suitable methods and resources required to solve a problem, the organisation should maximise their skills and functional flexibility by minimising organisational controls. This may mean that flexible work arrangements should be introduced to facilitate the skilled individual's task completion.

People in key positions may be given special considerations by their supervisors and be able to control their work to a greater extent. This implies that employees whose work is perceived to be more important to the organisation or who are more highly respected attract more attention, including more autonomy and self-control (Raelin 1984) and thus, less organisational control.

We have identified an inverse relationship between control and flexibility. This shows that organisations generally choose to be either flexible or controlling or compromise between the two options. Further, it was shown that there are several types of control that organisations can use to affect the behaviours of their employees. The methods of control and the magnitude of the control (as high or low) may be different for employees whose skills are considered to be irreplaceable as compared to workers who perform simple and repetitive tasks. The dilemma of which controls to impose is further complicated by the remote location at which an employee can work. The organisation must overcome space to maintain control and influence over the employee. Thus, organisations may have to reconsider their control methods, changing from direct to indirect controls.

The case of Newsco

Newspaper journalists form an interesting case study in the context of virtual work, as they require flexibility in their work location. Unlike some other occupations, such as nursing and computer programming, the nature of the work of journalists demands that they be not bound to their desks or their work area, but rather, that they have flexibility to be *where the news breaks*. This means that the location where journalists perform the bulk of their work depends on the story and where it is geographically located, and so journalists can be out of the office for an extended period of time.

Some journalists choose to do some preliminary work at home before going into the office. This generally involves telephoning contacts to follow up on story leads. In the instance where a lead comes to fruition, the journalist will often go straight to the scene of the story or the story contact person. The journalist then bypasses the centralised office location, and will go to the office only to write the piece – which is the journalist's final part of the process. In the case where a story breaks close to deadline, then the journalist may dictate by telephone, or alternatively send by electronic mail, the story, and thus bypass the office altogether.

All journalists, regardless of their work location, rely on mobile phones, faxes, electronic mail, and computer access to the newspaper's network of archived stories and library of photos. Section editors coordinate the journalists and while they, too, could theoretically work from a decentralised location, they choose not to do so. This is because they believe that it would be difficult to coordinate their journalists from a remote location.

Newsco is the second largest daily newspaper in Melbourne – Australia's second largest city. Newsco employs 250 full-time journalists. Almost all full-time journalists at Newsco have the opportunity to work from home if they choose and many choose to do some preliminary work at home before they leave for the office or a story location. For our purposes, this does not constitute work at home. We define work at home (or some other decentralised location) for a full-time employee as working at least three days from the decentralised location. As a rule, Newsco does not supply the resources required for a home office. Thus, location flexibility is constrained by the lack of financial support to establish a home office – so journalists who do some work from home use their existing infrastructure, except in the case of the one journalist who works from home. He works on average three days at home and two days at the office. The number of off-site journalists was limited by the nature of the work arrangement the over-whelming majority of reporters have with the organisation.

Unstructured, in-depth interviews were conducted with ten members of the organisation (a small number but the participants were representative of the larger group). The average tenure of the on-site journalists was four and a half years and ranged from six months to ten years. This includes two journalists who were in the first two years of their careers. The tenure of the off-site journalist was 20 years, and he was found to have a wide-ranging breadth of experience in the profession and within the organisation, having previously held the position of section editor. This journalist was perceived to be very important for the news-paper so he had the capacity to negotiate this work-at-home arrangement.

The investigation at Newsco revealed that there was no difference in the controls imposed by location, though there was a difference based on experience. Two distinct domains of control were identified – 'professional' and 'organisa-tional' controls. The research revealed that professional controls were applied for experienced journalists and organisational controls for inexperienced journalists. The study confirms that rule-based control is not appropriate in circumstances where the organisation relies on employees to adapt their creativity.

Methods of control

Some form of control is required to integrate the diverse activities of stake-holders in an organisation, but control can take the form of indirect or direct mechanisms. The methods of control can be separated into organisational controls and professional controls (see Figure 9.2).

Organisational controls

The classical image of *organisational control* is that of direct supervision and the strict division of labour. Rule-based control is difficult to sustain when tasks are dynamic and the organisation is reliant on the application of an individual's specialised knowledge. These can constrain the professionals' capacity to maximise the application of their knowledge. Several types of organisational control were identified at Newsco.

QUALIFICATIONS

This refers to the level of tertiary education that cadets at Newsco must reach. Cadets must be formally educated to at least an undergraduate degree level. Experienced journalists with established reputations are not screened for their education history.

Newsco also requires that, in their first year at the organisation as cadets, reporters must complete a shorthand training course. Cadets are told that if they do not achieve a specified standard in their shorthand skills, they will not be graded as a journalist and will not be promoted. There are no rules regarding the use of shorthand skills in the field.

FINANCIAL

Financial controls are important controls since they can dictate a reporter's entertainment budget, travel and equipment. This can affect the range of stories that the paper has and the depth of information contained in the stories.

Expenditure on entertaining contacts is rebated to the value of A$25. This is said to limit a reporter's capacity to network and make contacts and this may impact upon the breadth of the paper's content. Budgets may also control editorial content when a story is located a long distance away or if it is at a location that is expensive to access. In the event that the section editor perceives a story to be relatively marginal, then *cost* may be the factor that decides whether or not the story is covered.

Financial considerations feature in some reporters' decisions of the location of where their work will be performed – at the office or at the decentralised location. A key reason for some journalists not working at home was the fact that journalists would have to pay for their phone calls and equipment.

DEADLINES

The publishing cycle is a very strict control over reporters. Stories must be completed by a certain time, or they will not be published.

Deadlines can, therefore, affect a reporter's image since a reporter's job is to write stories that will be published. There is no point to finishing a terrific story after the deadline has passed. Thus, this represents one of the most important controls the organisation imposes over its journalists. There can be no wavering on this rule.

GUIDELINES

Section editors and the chief of staff can provide guidelines on story length, the names of people to interview for the story and set questions they want answered in a story. This implies that the reporter simply goes through the mechanics of writing the story, and that the idea and the lines of enquiry are predetermined. This is usually the situation for inexperienced journalists.

For experienced journalists, the section editor spends much less time explaining the task and its requirements. They have the capacity to set their own tasks, and experience helps them to decide the required length of a story. This is also the case for specialist reporters who have the responsibility of setting their own tasks and determining the lengths of stories.

TASK ASSIGNMENT

The responsibility of story assignment usually falls to the section editor. Reporters are assigned to 'a round' like politics, sport, entertainment depending on the experience and, sometimes, technical skills required for the job. Technical skills and contacts can be important in rounds like information technology, health and business. Task assignment depends on who is rostered on and who is available. From that pool, the section editors allocate stories.

Task assignment is a fundamental method of control. In part, the image of a journalist is developed from the stories and the perceived relative importance of the stories (such as 'exclusives' and stories that the competition do not have) that he or she has published. Thus, journalists are governed by their ambition to publish. Journalists who are not published may feel that they are failing in their job. This could affect their confidence and performance.

Senior reporters (the reporters who are experienced and have proved over time that they can complete the task adequately and without supervision) can be treated autonomously. They are expected to set their own tasks and find their own stories. The section editors seldom set tasks for these reporters and instead leave task setting to the reporters' discretion. The section editor may suggest lines of enquiry and then leave the details of the investigation to the discretion of the individual.

For the less experienced reporters and those still learning the craft, section editors assign about half of a reporter's tasks and leave the other half for the reporter to gather. Inexperienced reporters, like cadets and reporters with two or three years' experience, feel that they have to prove themselves to the chief of staff and section editor before they can be assigned more and better stories. Thus, trust is important in task assignment. Responsibilities increase over time as reporters have the opportunity to prove themselves.

The journalist who works from home is experienced in all the aspects of his round – he has been a reporter, a subeditor, a section editor and now reports. Thus, he seeks out a large quantity of his own stories – as was found to be the case for experienced reporters. Typically, the work-at-home journalist and his editor consult with each other at least three times throughout the day.

Missing a story and making factual errors lead to disciplinary consequences and can manifest in removal from the round. Removal from a round for disciplinary reasons acts like a control in two ways. First, it is a symbol of demotion. It indicates that the reporter's standards are not adequate for the tasks. This may be because the reporter has made a mistake or a series of mistakes, or because he or she is missing stories. Second, removal from the round is a public indication of the lowered performance and thus a reporter's image is affected. This can affect reporters' potential for promotion or being assigned tasks that would enhance their image and can affect their prospects if they seek employment at other organisations.

Professional controls

Professional controls refer to the factors affecting an individual's professionalism. The basis of this control is the 'image' of the reporter among his or her work colleagues, supervisor, newspaper editor and the newspaper readers. Interaction and 'mateship' found at the central location were identified as very powerful controls. The limited opportunities for reporters within the industry implies increased pressure for individuals to maintain professionalism and quality, and thus their image, if they expect to be considered for other limited opportunities in the industry.

CODE OF BEHAVIOUR

There are no formalised rules or codes of behaviour for the editorial staff. It is implied that as a reporter 'you know what you should and shouldn't do'. This knowledge is based on personal experience and training over a period of years.

Cadets generally find the process of learning what their job involves and how to perform it as 'very vague'. The induction of a cadet includes four weeks of training. This involves discussions about what a journalist does and how to develop contacts. The organisation relies on the established journalists to impart their knowledge to the cadets, and point out that collegiality is very important.

There are no specific guidelines for the journalist who chooses to work from home. This implies an unwritten code. His job has evolved over a period of years and he seems to have been the instigator of his move to work at home. Thus, the organisation relies on his professionalism rather than rigid rules.

Managers and their supervisors generally do not meet formally during the day; the arrangement is very spontaneous. The spatial distribution of the editorial floor implies a casual and informal work relationship among all employees. The close proximity of reporters to their editors suggests that there is a great capacity for editors to maintain direct supervision over the work produced. For example, the resources writer's desk is separated from his section editor's by a

short partition. They have the capacity to call out to each other over that partition and can easily walk to each other's desk. However, the collegial nature of
the organisation implies that the relationship is impromptu and that the relationship between section editors and their reporters is based on the expected
standards of behaviour rather than official positions.

COLLEGIALITY

Interaction with colleagues is important for journalists and is a subfactor of the
chosen work location. Work colleagues can provide ideas and stimulation.
Discussions with a reporter can yield a line of inquiry for research for a story.
Thus, by virtue of the fact that the majority of reporters work at the central
office, others seek to work there because they like the interaction. This interaction is not necessarily work related, although workmates with different
specialities and contacts can contribute their knowledge or opinion and this can
result in a story. Reporters also go to the office because they have friends there
and like the social aspect of work.

This interaction is a live dynamic. The work-at-home journalist recognises
that he misses this collegiality by working at home and overcomes it by phoning
his workmates through the day and by going into the office for short periods,
about two days per week. Also, he telephones his peers for general conversation
and personal relationship development, rather than story stimulation. He feels
excluded from workmate relationships that flourish in a centralised location and
which he misses by virtue of the fact that he works from home alone.

Journalists of any level of experience can seek assistance from their friends in
the newsroom, and cadets especially are encouraged to seek guidance and help.
Other reporters are keen to help out their junior colleagues. The inexperienced
journalists are more likely than the experienced reporters to ask their workmates
for their opinions about a story idea. Colleagues are often asked by others for
names of contacts. Further, reporters often read each other's stories to check
facts and make suggestions. A reporter's access to this is hampered when the
parties are separated by distance. Thus, distance can serve to affect the completion of a task.

IMAGE

The effects of missing a story can differ, depending on the reason the story was
missed and the perceived importance of the story and the experience of the
journalists. For the inexperienced reporters, missing a story can be devastating to
their professional image. This is because missing a story is perceived as a breach
of the trust the organisation has in its reporters, since their duty is to cover the
range of stories in the round. Furthermore, missing stories reflects badly on the
image of reporters who are perceived as not fulfilling their duties to the organisation. One inexperienced reporter commented that while the section editor and
chief of staff acknowledge that a reporter cannot always cover everything

completely, a reporter should not continuously miss stories. This should be a priority of a reporter and missing a story would encourage that person to work harder next time, since his or her pride would be hurt.

The consequences of making errors in stories are similar to the consequences of missing stories; and making mistakes can be equally damaging to a reporter's reputation. The consequence is a 'black mark against your name'. Thus, when a journalist makes factual errors, their professionalism is questioned and may be considered to be unimportant to them.

Junior reporters generally believe that the best way for them to get a promotion is by impressing the people that assign the jobs and by performing beyond their boss's expectations. This can be achieved by showing enthusiasm, finding new leads and angles, and having many quality stories published.

This discussion highlights that there is no difference in the controls for on-site and off-site journalists at Newsco. However, there are a number of differences in the controls used for experienced and inexperienced journalists. Inexperienced journalists are exposed to more direct controls and monitoring. In contrast, the most experienced journalist was 'rewarded' with a home office and what appears to be a very high level of discretion and autonomy.

Summary of the controls at Newsco

This investigation reveals that there is little rule-based control in the editorial section at Newsco. While in some organisations this might lead to chaos, at Newsco the professional code of conduct and the implied standards of behaviour are powerful enough to elicit the desired actions and behaviours from the reporters. The exception is identified in the junior journalists who need to be socialised in the profession. This implies that there are other forms of control that supplement in the absence of rule-based controls. The controls used at Newsco are summarised in Figure 9.2. The number of stars signifies the magnitude of the controls for each variable – the more stars, the greater the strength.

It was found that some on-site reporters are granted wide-ranging freedom in their choices of tasks and also in the methods they choose to complete the tasks. The investigation revealed this to be true particularly for experienced journalists who have established a reputation for their skills and knowledge. For less experienced journalists it was found to be partly true since the organisation grants them semi-autonomy and retains hierarchical power to delegate stories and suggest guidelines for stories. For experienced journalists, the organisation retains the power to assign stories; however, experienced reporters are expected to find a far greater proportion of their stories than inexperienced reporters.

Qualifications, financial controls and deadlines are pervasive for experienced and inexperienced journalists. Guidelines and task assignments are both high for the inexperienced and low for experienced. The opposite is true for disciplinary consequences. Specifically, the consequences of making a mistake are greater for someone who has been socialised in the organisation and the industry. Inexperienced journalists are more easily 'forgiven' for mistakes. In summary, the

Experienced	Organisational controls	Inexperienced
***	Qualifications	***
***	Financial	***
***	Deadlines	***
*	Guidelines	***
*	Task assignment	***
***	Disciplinary consequences	*

Experienced	Professional controls	Inexperienced
***	Code of behaviour	*
***	Image	**
***	Collegiality	*

Figure 9.2 Salience of controls and experience

professional controls for experienced workers were high, while for inexperienced workers they were all low. Similarly, for inexperienced journalists, professional controls are low, but organisational controls are high.

This can be represented by a negative sloping curve (Figure 9.3). However, there is some discontinuity. Recall qualifications, financial controls and deadlines are strong and pervasive controls regardless of experience. There may be occasions when the organisational and professional controls come into conflict. For example, tight deadlines might mean the professional controls are compromised. So, organisational and professional controls are not necessarily direct substitutes. There may be another case where the organisational controls are low and the employee is inexperienced and has thus not been socialised into the norms of the organisation or the norms of the profession. This scenario may lead to chaos.

Organisations considering implementing workplace flexibility must consider how suitable the *job* is for decentralisation, how suitable the *individual* doing the job is for decentralisation, and ensure that the *organisation* has the resources, systems and skills to manage and support the long-distance relationship. The level of experience of the individual, the degree of socialisation in the organisation and the profession, how expert they are in their field, and whether their work is self-contained are important considerations in evaluating the suitability of the move to flexiplace location. However, all this being well, it would be pointless for the organisation to go to the effort and expense of relocating employees if

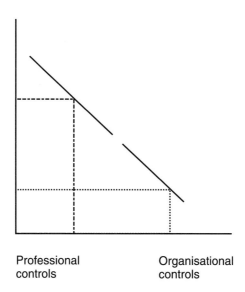

Figure 9.3 Relationship of experience and control

the managers do not have the capabilities to facilitate new ways of communicating, allocating tasks, motivating and controlling employees.

Some organisations encourage their employees to decentralise and in other organisations the employees encourage managers *to let* them decentralise. The freedom of choice that managers offer their staff in making the decision to relocate is very important as some employees have no interest in working from home, just as some other workers have no interest in working from anywhere but the home. The negative effects of working from the non-preferred location may be very costly in terms of productivity, morale and turnover, as well as the expense of establishing the home office.

The finding of organisational control and professional control as substitutes for each other, except in extreme circumstances, can be applied to other organisations where the values of the organisation and the profession become so internalised that the organisational controls are superseded and the need for direct controls is reduced. In that case, and when decentralised workers are trusted to work independently, the role of the manager is modified from tightly controlling the workflow and monitoring task performance, to providing advice and guidance.

Conclusion

Taking extra responsibility for work performance is not new for professional employees and represents a natural extension to the autonomy implied in the task and their work status. In fact, it seems appropriate that the employees should be able to perform their task at a decentralised location because this increases their autonomy. Responsibility and trust are magnified when the employees have the capacity to perform their tasks at a separate location to the supervisor. This was found at Newsco. The ad hoc and unpredictable nature of news, coupled with the journalists' knowledge of the organisation's expectations of their performance and their knowledge of the mechanics of how to perform the task (their professionalism), suggests that it is superfluous to establish strict rules. Developments in telecommunications have increased the capacity for monitoring, and some managers are now more trusting and are encouraging employees' desires to relocate. This may make the work at home scenario now more attractive.

Acknowledgement

The author acknowledges the generous contribution of Betsy J. Blunsdon to the original work.

Bibliography

Atkinson, J. (1984) 'Manpower strategies for flexible organisations', *Personnel Management*, August: 28–31.

Atkinson, J. (1987) 'Flexibility or fragmentation? The United Kingdom labour market in the eighties', *Labour and Society*, 12, 1: 88–105.

Atkinson, J. and Meager, N. (1986) 'Is flexibility just a flash in the pan?', *Personnel Management*, September: 26–9.

Bailyn, L. (1985) 'Autonomy in the industrial R&D lab', *Human Resource Management*, 24: 129–46.

Barnard C.I. (1940) *The Functions of the Executive*, Boston, MA: Harvard University Press.

Berry, A.J. (1995) 'Control of embedded operations spanning traditional operations', in Berry, A.J., Broadbent, J. and Otly, D. (eds) *Management Control – Theories, Issues and Practices*, London: Macmillan.

Blanc, G. (1989) 'Autonomy, telework and emerging cultural values', in Korte, W.B., Robinson, S. and Steinle, W.I. (eds) *Telework – Present Situation, and Future Development of a New Form of Work*, North Holland: Elsevier.

Blunsdon, B.J. (1995) 'The flexible firm model: a multidimensional conceptualisation and measurement model', *Working Paper No. 5*, Monash University, Australia, Department of Management.

Bowman, E. and Kogut, B.M. (1995) *Redesigning the Firm*, New York: Oxford University Press.

Breaugh, J.A. (1985) 'The measurement of work autonomy', *Human Relations*, 28, 6: 551–70.

Child, J. (1972) 'Organisation structure and strategies of control: a replication of the Aston study', *Administrative Science Quarterly*, 17: 163–76.

Dalton, G.W. and Lawrence, P. (1971) *Motivation and Control in Organisations*, Illinois: Richard Irwin.

De Leeuw, A.C.J. and Volberda, H.W. (1996) 'On the concept of flexibility: a dual control perspective', *Omega, International Journal of Management Science*, 24, 2: 121–39.

Department of Industrial Relations (1996) *Success with Flexible Work Practices*, Canberra: Department of Industrial Relations.

Etzioni, A (1964) *Modern Organisations*, New Jersey: Prentice Hall.

Goode, W.J. (1957) 'Community within a community: the professions', *American Sociological Review*, 22: 194–200.

Hall, R.H. (1968) 'Professionalization and bureaucratization', *American Sociological Review*, 32: 92–104.

Koontz, H. (1958) 'A preliminary statement of the principles of planning and control', *Journal of the Academy of Management*, 1: 48–50.

Lorange, P. (1993) *Strategic Planning and Control*, Boston: Blackwell.

Merton, R.C. (1949) *Social Theory and Social Structure*, USA: Free Press.

Miller, G.A. (1968) 'Professionals in bureaucracy: alienation among industrial scientists and engineers', *American Sociological Review*, 32: 755–68.

Milward, G.E. (1946) *An Approach to Management*, London: MacDonald & Evans.

Olson, M. and Primps, S. (1984) 'Working at home with computers: work and nonwork issues', *Journal of Social Issues*, 40, 3: 97–112.

Ouchi, W. (1977) 'The relationship between organisational structure and organisational control', *Administrative Science Quarterly*, 22: 95–112.

Pollert, A. (1988) 'The "flexible firm": fixation or fact?, *Work, Employment and Society*, 2, 3: 281–316.

Quinn, R.E. (1988) *Beyond Rational Management*, California: Jossey-Bass.

Raelin, J.A. (1984) 'An examination of deviant/adaptive behaviours in the organisational careers of professionals', *Academy of Management Review*, 9, 3: 413–27.

Robbins, S.P. (1994) *Management*, 4th edition, New Jersey: Prentice Hall.

Rothlisberger, F.J. and Dickson, W.J. (1941) *Management and the Worker*, Boston: Harvard University Press.

Scott, W.R. (1965) 'Reactions to supervision in a heteronomous professional organisation', *Administrative Science Quarterly*, 10: 65–81.

Selznick, P. (1943) 'An approach to a theory of bureaucracy', *American Sociological Review*, 8: 47–8.

Snell, Scott A. (1992) 'Control theory in strategic human resource management: the mediating effect of administrative information', *Academy of Management Journal*, 35, 2: 292–327.

Snell, S.A. and Youndt, M.A. (1995) 'Human resource management and firm performance: testing a contingency model of executive controls', *Journal of Management*, 21, 4: 711–37.

Storey, J. (1985) 'Management control as a bridging concept', *Journal of Management Studies*, 22, 3: 270–89.

Tannenbaum, A.S. (1962) 'Control in organisations: individual adjustment and organisational performance', *Administrative Science Quarterly*, 7, 2: 236–57.

Tordoir, P.P. (1995) *The Professional Knowledge Economy*, The Netherlands: Kluwer Academic Publishers.

Wallace, J.E. (1995) 'Corporatist control and organizational commitment among professionals: the case of lawyers working in law firms', *Social Forces*, 73, 3: 811–39.

Weber, M. (1947) *The Theory of Social and Economic Organisation*, London: Free Press.

Part IV

Learning and innovation in virtual working

In this final section of the book we are concerned with two broad sets of questions. First, given the structures discussed under the virtual working umbrella, what particular problems and issues are faced in moving towards these new ways of working? How can the process be managed? How does it differ from other types of innovation? Second, given the importance of effective learning and knowledge management to virtual work arrangements, how can the members involved – partnering organisations, team members, teleworkers – make sure that knowledge continues to be transferred across the membership network to ensure it remains agile?

The following three chapters attempt to answer these questions. In the first, by Björkegren and Rapp, the literature on learning and knowledge management is drawn upon to assemble a framework for analysing organisations which exhibit high levels of flexibility in time and space. The authors point out that knowledge, and an ability to manage it effectively, is now seen as a central source of competitive advantage. The management of knowledge is complicated by the fact that while, to some extent at least, it exists in codified and explicit forms (in files and on databases, for example), much of what we know is embedded in social practices, or is only known and expressed tacitly. Identifying and communicating such knowledge to others – especially where they are dispersed in time and space – raises some challenging questions.

Björkegren and Rapp note, so far as learning is concerned, that definitions and interpretations of the subject draw upon three main perspectives and theories. From the 'behaviour' view, learning is understood as a change in behaviour in response to environmental stimuli. According to the 'cognitive' perspective, learning is seen as a change in thinking. Given that organisations – as entities – do not have the cognitive capacity for thinking in their own right, this perspective highlights the importance of *individuals* and how the sum of their learning may contribute to organisational learning overall. For this to happen, learning individuals must be able to interact with others across the organisation and, by making sense of each other's thoughts, assimilate, create and communicate new knowledge.

The third and final set of theories forms the 'situated' perspective. This view posits that learning is largely a product of *context*, since learning is situated in practice, with such practices bounded by time, space and other elements of social structure. This suggests, say the authors, that learning is embedded in cultural and social networks of meanings, relations and activities. Björkegren and Rapp note that although learning and knowledge are highly dependent on context, this may be more important in some cases than others, particularly where the issues and problems involved are more unstructured and unique. This raises important questions, of course, as to whether information technologies can create the necessary social and interpretive contexts for such unique and complex knowledge to be understood and passed on.

Björkegren and Rapp apply this framework to project-based organisations. In so doing they also emphasise that not only are many flexible forms of organisa- tion characterised by rapid change, distance working and IT-facilitated interaction, the *time-limited* nature of certain work arrangements also points to a further dynamic with which learning and knowledge management must contend.

Using their framework, Björkegren and Rapp show the difficulties involved in learning across space due to problems in sharing each other's thoughts, mean- ings and 'lived experiences'. This might be compounded where individuals have different professional backgrounds and skills, thus making the exchange and absorption of knowledge even more difficult. Moreover, say the authors, as learning also involves an ability to explore and share tacit knowledge, and because this is problematic to transmit using technologies, conventional means of communication may sometimes be needed.

From a situated learning perspective, Björkegren and Rapp are able to show that because much of what is learned is rooted in a particular social and cultural context, there may be difficulties in repackaging that knowledge to make it meaningful and useful in other contexts. Moreover, given that the knowledge may be situated by particular projects, the relevance and meaning of that knowl- edge to subsequent projects is uncertain.

To address these problems the authors argue that managers need to become more aware of the complex nature of knowledge, how it is created and passed on, and how and why it may differ in nature and be structured by context. By adopting learning and knowledge management structures that respect these factors (for instance, by holding face-to-face meetings at impor- tant junctures of projects), organisations should be able to ensure that learning does indeed take place and that at least some knowledge is captured and passed on.

In Chapter 11, by Ian McLoughlin and Paul Jackson, the importance of learning in the virtual organisation is considered. The main context for discus- sion here is the innovation process involved in managing to 'go virtual'. Their concern in the chapter is to address the human, social and organisational issues raised by innovations involving virtual organisations. The central question they address revolves around the sort of competencies, expertise and knowledge that organisations need to acquire and manage in bringing about and sustaining virtual organisations.

In setting about this, McLoughlin and Jackson draw together three approaches to innovation. The first focuses on the technologies that support virtual working arrangements, and the issues involved in transferring knowledge to users in order to adopt such technologies in ways that support the work configurations envisaged by ideas of virtual organisation. The second looks at the learning difficulties associated with conventional, bureaucratic organisations, and how these might constrain or frustrate change programmes aimed at going virtual. In particular here, the need to address the learning involved in overcoming the barriers to change is highlighted.

The third and final approach draws upon actor-network theory (e.g. Callon 1987), to examine the way innovations – conceived of as socio-technical networks – are configured and sustained. Attention here is focused on the political skills of the network builders – managers, change agents, vendors – in enrolling supporters and resources to promote the new forms of organisational design.

McLoughlin and Jackson (drawing upon Buchanan) conclude that if we are to understand the issues involved in producing more virtual work innovations, more expertise is required at three different levels. The first involves the 'content' of change itself and the technical knowledge and expertise bound up in designing, installing and debugging the technologies that support the new ways of working. The second addresses the 'control' aspects of change, such as the project management skills involved in setting objectives, managing resources, monitoring progress and meeting deadlines. The third level at which more expertise is needed concerns the 'process' agenda in virtual innovations. These more Machiavellian competencies are important for managing stakeholder interests, neutralising resistance, and otherwise utilising the more manipulative devices needed to bring change about. Learning skills in this area, particularly as they relate to virtual work innovations, may be important for future developments.

In Chapter 12, by Frank Morath and Artur Schmidt, attention is again focused on managing knowledge. This time, though, there is an attempt to go beyond conventional ways of understanding knowledge management and learning, even where this relates to virtual working. The authors argue that a fundamental shift has taken place in capitalist societies. This is more than just a move towards a knowledge-based society, say the authors, but one that can be characterised as a shift from Silicon Valley to 'Cyber Valley'.

The importance of this distinction is brought out by an analogy with the industrial revolution. While it was the railroad companies, among others, that laid the infrastructure for the industrial revolution, those companies that moved in and built factories that exploited this infrastructure were the ones that went on to thrive. The authors compare this situation to what they term today's 'phase 1' companies that are building the technological infrastructure for the knowledge economy, and the 'phase 2' companies that are set to thrive on it in the future. Such companies are built through the networking of participants from all over the world, forging links that mix the physical and virtual, human and non-human and encompass a range of industries and service providers. Such companies need to be more intelligent, say the authors, than even today's knowledge-based companies. Instead of just being thinking organisations, seeking to make sense of the 'real world' and sharing that sense-making between partners, they need to invent their own symbolic, virtual worlds, where they can mingle individuality and collectivity.

Morath and Schmidt argue that contemporary approaches to knowledge-based business reflect a dualism between those that concentrate on intellectual and human capital, and those that concern themselves with the intelligence of the technology. To go beyond this, the authors introduce the notion of 'interface management'. By focusing on interfaces they argue that we can integrate the people-centred approach, as found in most accounts of organisational learning and knowledge management, with the technology approach, that sees organisational intelligence as a more mechanistic network of 'knowledgeable knots' (including individuals and organisations).

Interfaces, say the authors, are temporary, hybrid networks of people and/or computers that integrate human beings as well as intelligent agents and databases. They have open structures, enabling them to adapt rapidly to environmental changes, and they can simulate and extend the properties of the brain by enabling the copying and recording of organisational thinking. Furthermore, interfaces evolve through continuous participation and feedback, in which individuals and interfaces are able to feed on one another, establishing trusting relationships as they do. Such a perspective, the authors acknowledge, challenges a number of principles and ways of understanding the world. In addressing this they introduce the notion of 'endo-worlds' and 'exo-worlds'. Endo, meaning 'inside', refers to the world within an interface – the place at which participants are thus connected to the knowledge of a network and its other participants. Exo-worlds, by contrast, describe the points that are outside of these networks.

Interfaces can also be thought of as virtual communities, according to Morath and Schmidt. This would include, for example, the MUDs (Multi-User Dungeons) that have started to populate 'the Net' in recent years. Such communities are supported by technologies and software that allow individuals to interact across time and space. They are thus informal and brought into being by the actions and interests of their members. In such communities, the authors point out, individuals are able to project new identities and personae into the world. Such new worlds thus bracket out the differences apparent in the exo/'real world', and allow for a new set of inter-personal characteristics and dynamics to be enacted. As the authors point out, this opens up considerable creative space for developing new organisational theories. New peer groups and opportunities for knowledge sharing are produced, and a new set of values and beliefs may be created.

In applying their interface approach to the matter of knowledge management, Morath and Schmidt note that knowledge of reality must be seen as inter-subjective, and defined by participation in interfaces. Here, though, the same barriers to learning can be found as at individual and organisational levels – that one's knowledge is bounded and represents only a limited view of the world. To address this, the authors point to the need to act upon a *range* of inter-faces, and thereby gain alternative ways of constructing reality.

The archaic nature of interfaces, and the need to develop and acquire new knowledge, leads Morath and Schmidt to conclude that effective (endo) manage-ment will be increasingly important in the future. This will require recognition of the complexity involved in interfaces, as well as allowing participants the autonomy they need in order to thrive on it.

10 Learning and knowledge management

A theoretical framework for learning in flexible organisations

Charlotte Björkegren and Birger Rapp

Introduction

In recent years management literature has shown a growing interest in both learning and knowledge (Senge 1990; Huber 1991; Argyris 1993; Leonard-Barton 1992; Nonaka 1994; Nonaka and Takeuchi 1995; Choo 1998, Davenport and Prusack 1998). The reason for this is that knowledge is now seen as a strategic asset and the primary resource for competitive advantage. With the contemporary information and knowledge society (Toffler 1980; Drucker 1993), the picture of organisations' competitive advantage has changed; instead of focusing on physical capital and manual work, the competence and knowledge of the employees have become seen as valuable sources of advantage (Badaracco 1991; Drucker 1993). However, as argued by Grant (1996), consistent with Nonaka and Takeuchi (1995), it is not knowledge *per se* that is of importance, but rather the *knowledge integration* and interaction that help to support the generation of new knowledge in organisations.

Through use of information and communication technology, organisational innovations that provide *flexibility in space and time* are conceivable. In this chapter these kinds of organisations are called *flexible organisations*. As early as the 1980s Toffler wrote in his book *The Third Wave* that flexible work towards the temporary and geographical dimensions was something that was going to become more common. And in 1984, Handy wrote that teamwork was going to be the future organisational form for knowledge-based enterprises. Flexible organisations convey new ways of working and interacting in organisations, thereby posing a challenge for the management of knowledge and learning. Flexible organisations can not only facilitate environmental adaptation and individual work freedom, but also obstruct the generation of new knowledge. This is because members in the organisation no longer interact face-to-face, but communicate largely through information systems.

The purpose of this chapter is *to illuminate learning and knowledge management in flexible organisations*. In so doing, it will discuss how knowledge can be integrated and shared, and how learning can take place when individuals are temporarily and geographically disparate. The chapter begins with a discussion about learning and knowledge, where learning is seen as a process of knowledge creation. Subsequently, learning is addressed from three different perspectives: the behavioural, the cognitive and the situated. Further, an amalgamation with two different organisational forms will be used to illustrate learning in flexible organisations. Finally, some concluding remarks will be made.

The concept of knowledge and its relation to learning

The concept of knowledge

The epistemological question *What is knowledge?* is a highly philosophical question that has followed Man from the pre-Socratic Greek up to today. The discussion of knowledge in this chapter, however, is done more from a pragmatic than from an epistemological point of view, which means that the emphasis will be on the different aspects of knowledge. This will be discussed from an individual as well as from an organisational point of view.

Knowledge can be more or less expressible. Polanyi (1966) discusses this feature by using the expressions *explicit* and *tacit* knowledge. Explicit knowledge is described as knowledge that can be communicated in a formal, systematic language, which means that it can be stored within libraries, databases and archives (Nonaka 1994). Tacit knowledge is described as knowledge that is difficult to formalise and communicate verbally as well as non-verbally, which is illustrated in the following quotation:

> Take an example. We can know a person's face, and can recognize it among thousands, indeed millions. Yet we usually can not tell how we recognize a face we know. So most of this knowledge can not be put into words.
>
> (Polanyi 1966: 4)

As argued by Polanyi (1966: 4) '...*we can know more than we can tell*', i.e. we can know more than we can verbalise and put into words. According to Choo (1998), there is also a third type of knowledge, namely *cultural knowledge*, which can be described as knowledge that is expressed in the assumptions, norms and beliefs used by members to give value and meaning to new knowledge.

To describe more or less expressible knowledge on an organisational level, Badaracco's (1991) concepts *migratory* and *embedded* knowledge can be applied. The concept of migratory (or commercialisable) knowledge tells us that it is knowledge that can easily be transmitted. This knowledge cannot only be transmitted easily within organisations, but also between organisations, as well as nations. Embedded knowledge, on the other hand, can only be transmitted slowly within the organisation despite its highly commercial value. This knowledge cannot be used by particular individuals, but is rather a form of organisational culture and exists in the interaction between individuals and groups.

The relation between learning and knowledge

Bower and Hilgard (1981) illustrate the relation between learning and knowing in the same way as '*a process to its result, as acquiring to a possession, as painting to a picture*' (p. 1). These metaphors give us a picture that learning is a process, whereas knowledge can be described as its result. We would like to amend this illustration by describing learning as an ongoing, never-ending knowledge-creating process (see, for example, Nonaka 1994; Nonaka and Takeuchi 1995), i.e. an iterative process between tacit and explicit knowledge, and individual and shared knowledge. For a further discussion see Nandhakumar (Chapter 4 in this volume). This means that knowledge can never be a result, since the process of creation has no ending and no starting point.

Three perspectives on learning

Hedberg (1981) in agreement with Huber (1991) describe organisational learning as an ambiguous phenomenon, with several definitions and interpretations. One reason for this is that theories about learning have been formulated over a long period of time and within different theoretical fields, e.g. biology, pedagogy, psychology and sociology – see also Morath and Schmidt (Chapter 12 in this volume) for further discussion on this point.

In this chapter learning will be addressed from three different perspectives: the *behavioural* perspective, the *cognitive* perspective and the *situated* perspective.

The behavioural perspective

According to the behavioural perspective learning takes place through *change in behaviour*. Behaviour here, is to be understood as a response to changes in environmental stimulation. Classical behaviourism (e.g. Ivan Pavlov, Bertrand Russell and John B. Watson) was exclusively concerned with measurable and observable data, which means that ideas, emotions and the recognition of inner mental experience, as well as, activity were excluded (Skinner 1938). What Skinner intended when he remarked that all explanation of behaviour resides outside the individual is that change in behaviour (learning) can only take place through external stimulus and that mental activities are denied.

> …behavior is that part of the functioning of an organism which is engaged in acting upon or having commerce with the outside world.
>
> (Skinner 1938: 6)

This notion builds on the basic assumption that learning is better understood from external environmental factors than from internal suitable purposes and that learning is, to a great extent, identical for all living beings (Atkinson *et al.* 1990), i.e. humans as well as animals. The theoretical field of classical behaviourism was characterised by strict determinism and objectivism and based on the belief that behind every response resides a stimulus that evokes it.

From a behavioural perspective, organisations, as well as other systems and organisms, are able to learn. This means that the members of an organisation are understood as instruments, who adapt the organisation's behaviour to the environmental changes over time (Cyert and March 1963; March and Simon 1958). As individuals are exclusively seen as instruments, human behaviour solely involves an adaptation to the social environment, and behaviour that departs from this adaptation is only explained by the individual's incapability to understand how to adapt.

> A man viewed as a behaving system is quite simple. The apparent complexity of his behaviour over time is largely a reflection of the complexity of the environment in which he finds himself.
>
> (Simon 1981: 65)

Cyert and March (1963) saw organisations as adaptive rational systems that learn from experience, i.e. a kind of trial-and-error learning. Organisations thus learn to react to stimuli in the competing environment and to ignore other stimuli. Researchers within the theoretical field of behavioural learning are consequently interested in isolating those specific environmental factors that lead to change, internally as well as externally (Ellström 1996).

> Just as organisations learn what to strive for in their environment, they also learn to attend to some parts of that environment and not to others.
>
> (Cyert and March 1963: 123)

Learning, according to the behavioural perspective described in this chapter, could be related to Argyris and Schön's (1978) theories about single-loop learning, where learning is seen as change in behaviour within the given knowledge structure, which means that the goal of the organisation and its vision are not questioned. This can be described as a more passive adaptive learning, which better suits stable environmental conditions than dynamic ones. Similarly, Senge (1990) describes adaptive learning as adjustments in behaviour within a given feedback structure. The above discussion can be summarised in Figure 10.1.

The cognitive perspective

Cognition was first developed within the field of psychology. The perspective stems from the notion that learning is not exclusively a behavioural process. Edward C. Tolman is one of the early cognitive psychologists who pleads for a more active processing of information in humans and rejects the mechanistic S–R (stimuli–response) psychology. Tolman argued that responses had to do with

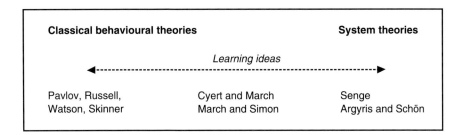

Figure 10.1 Different learning ideas within the behavioural field

internal mental activities (thinking processes) as well as experience. From a cognitive perspective learning is thus seen as *changed thinking*.

According to the cognitive perspective, the source of all learning is human beings (Björkegren 1989). Consequently, this means that even from an organisational point of view, individuals become the focus, and neither organisations nor other social networks can think or learn by themselves. Senge (1990) expresses a similar thought, that organisations learn only through individuals who learn, and that without individual learning no organisational learning will occur.

> It follows both that there is no organisational learning without individual learning, and the individual learning is a necessary but insufficient condition for organisational learning.
>
> (Argyris and Schön 1978: 20)

As argued by Argyris and Schön in the quotation above, individual learning is necessary, but not sufficient for organisational learning. An important condition for organisational learning is, therefore, the interaction between the members in the organisation. Organisational learning is seen as an ongoing interactive process between the members, who continually exchange thoughts, visions and experiences. This point is well made by Björkegren (1989), who sees organisational learning as a process of social construction where similar thoughts and visions arise through the exchange of ideas between individuals. An exchange of ideas can also be seen as an attempt to influence other individuals' thoughts and ways of making sense (Weick 1995).

Weick and Bougon (1986: 102) argue that organisations are socially constructed and exist essentially in the form of cognitive schemas in the head of each individual. What holds an organisation together is therefore what holds together members' thoughts about the organisation. The most important part of reality construction is accordingly cognitive schemata. Gioia and Sims (1986: 55) describe a cognitive schema as follows:

> A schema is a cognitive structure composed of a network of expectations learned from experience and stored in memory. It is a built up repertoire of tacit knowledge that is imposed to structure upon and impact meaning to.

Individuals interpret the world through the recognition of patterns, which are related to the structure of thoughts. Cognitive schemata are thus elements of the individuals' ability to understand and interpret information, i.e. to make sense out of it. It is upon this understanding that individuals are able to act. Considering the cognitive capacity of the individuals, the capacity of the human mind for solving complex problems and possessing information is limited. Simon (1991) describes this as bounded rationality, which means that people are unable to act completely rationally since they cannot acquire all necessary information. However, we do not find bounded rationality to be an appropriate term, since it assumes that if the individuals have complete information, they can act rationally (see also Blomberg 1995 for a discussion on this point). Subjective rationality might therefore be more suitable.

Representations of the organisation exist not only on an individual level. Through interactions, conversations and actions people influence each other and create common understandings and valuations (Berger and Luckmann 1966). This suggests the existence of subjective representations about work, activities and so on, which have been externalised into shared organisational pictures. Accordingly, in every organisation there exists a set of common assumptions, values and norms. It is important to mention, however, that there also exist uncommon ideas and that not all ideas affect the organisation to the same extent (Hellgren and Löwstedt 1997).

Cognitive psychologists believe that individuals have a broad repertoire of alternative responses to a certain stimulus. These alternative responses can lead to many different actions. This is because all individuals have different life experiences and diverse accumulated knowledge. Different individuals will therefore make different interpretations regarding the same incident. Weick (1995) argues that individuals enact and create their own world in which they act. This means that the views of human beings are seen as actively created. As such, the focus shifts from how different stimuli contribute to behaviour, to how actions are affected by cognitive processes such as the creation and recreation of reality. However, these diverse interpretations do not mean that the individuals are not able to perform common actions (Czarniawska-Joergens 1992; Weick 1995; Ericson 1998).

New understanding can only be gained if it can be related to what is already known. What can be learned, therefore, depends on the pre-existing cognitive structures. This point is well made by Feldman (1986), who argues that learning can be seen as an interaction between experience and new information. The above discussion can be summarised in Figure 10.2.

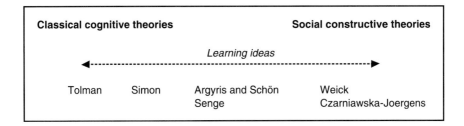

Figure 10.2 Different learning ideas within the cognitive field

The situated perspective

Brown *et al.* (1989) argue that the activity in which knowledge is created and organised cannot be separated from or be ancillary to learning and cognition; rather it is an integral part of what is learned. Situations therefore could be said to co-produce knowledge through activity.

> Situated activity always involves changes in knowledge and action and 'changes in knowledge and action' are central to what we mean about learning.
>
> (Chaklin and Lave 1993: 5)

'All social interaction is situated interaction – situated in time and space...' (Giddens 1986: 86). Chaklin and Lave (1993) make a similar point in arguing that *all learning is situationally bounded* and that the social situation (the context) is a critical but often forgotten component in the process of learning. This means that we have to consider the context (or rather multiple contexts) in which learning occurs. According to the situated perspective, learning is seen as a process of changing understanding in practice through participation in everyday life (Chaklin and Lave 1993). Knowledge is thus not stored in the heads of the individuals, but embedded in a cultural and social network of meanings, relations and activities. Learning, therefore, takes place through individuals actively participating in a 'community of practice' and thereby acquiring the way of thinking, the culture and the behavioural patterns that are specific to a particular community (Lave and Wenger 1991; Chaklin and Lave 1993). It is important to note that communities are *informal*, which means that they are often not recognised by the organisation. Still, they are considered to be of great importance where learning activities are concerned.

Where the interaction takes place, i.e. the physical environment, will determine what the individuals can do, what they know and what they can learn. The context will also determine who can interact with whom and how the interaction can occur. Lave (1988) assumes that individuals will approach a problem in different ways depending on the context. Every context will thus offer suitable forms of thoughts and actions, which means that knowledge is not absolute. It is not only the context, however, that determines how a problem is solved and what can be learned, but also the mutual interaction between activity and the environment, which is created and changed during the process of problem solving (Rogoff and Lave 1984). The principal concern about the context involves learning being seen as rather limited, situational-bounded and therefore difficult to generalise and use in new, unknown situations.

> In our view, learning is not merely situated in practice – as if it were some independent reifiable process that just happened to be located somewhere; learning is an integral part of generative social practice in the lived-in world.
>
> (Lave and Wenger 1991: 35)

When problems are more structured and of a known nature, the physical location is of less significance (Tyre and von Hippel 1997). This is because some problems can be solved with tacit knowledge, whereas the rest are solved through the individuals understanding what information must be acquired, how it can be acquired and how it can be interpreted depending on where it is found. This perspective emphasises the importance of informal, experience-based learning through active participation in a community of action or through apprenticeship. Participation does not mean just observing and imitating, but both absorbing and being absorbed in the community of practice.

Learning from a situated perspective means that the individuals will not learn abstract, objective knowledge but rather learn to function in a community and learn to speak its language (Brown and Duguid 1991). Transfer models, which isolate knowledge from practice are, according to the situated perspective, therefore rejected; instead knowledge is put back into the context in which it has meaning (Lave and Wenger 1991; Brown and Duguid 1991). Knowledge needs to be presented in an authentic context, a setting that would normally involve this knowledge, since it is the embedding circumstances that efficiently provide essential parts of its structure and meaning. Brown *et al.* (1989) illustrate this with the learning that comes from dictionaries. Here, they argue, it is quite possible to acquire a tool without being able to use it. Learning requires social interaction and collaboration. This is because it is within the group that social interaction and conversation take place. Further, Brown and Duguid (1991) argue that organisational members do not configure themselves as individuals. People work and learn collaboratively, which means that invisible communities are continually being formed and reformed.

If we want to understand learning and knowledge transfer, Lave and Wenger (1991) argue that 'legitimate peripheral participation' is an important concept. It describes the relation between newcomers and old-timers, where newcomers become a part of a practice, i.e. the process of becoming a full participant in a sociocultural practice (see also Campbell, Chapter 2 in this volume). The organisation therefore must reconceive of itself as a community-of-communities (Brown and Duguid 1991). The organisation is thus seen as a collective of communities, not simply of individuals, where separate community perspectives can be amplified by interchanges among these communities.

Conclusion

In this section we have tried to illuminate learning by describing the phenomenon from three different perspectives. Depending on the perspective taken, different aspects of learning will be emphasised. As illustrated in Figure 10.3, the perspectives are neither mutually exclusive nor completely cover the concept of learning.

The literature gives us a pastiche of different interpretations of organisational learning. Some authors argue that learning is exclusively cognitive (e.g. Argyris and Schön 1978), others that it is both cognitive and behavioural (e.g. Hedberg 1981; Senge 1990), and others that it is exclusively behavioural (Cyert and March 1963). (For an overview, see Rapp and Björkegren 1998.) Another way to describe the differences is through adaptation and learning. Fiol and Lyles (1985) argue that adaptation is nothing but an incremental adjustment and has nothing to do with learning, whereas Senge (1990) sees adaptation as lower level learning.

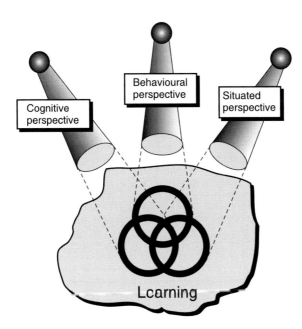

Figure 10.3 The learning phenomenon from different perspectives

Learning: The development of insights, knowledge, and associations between past actions, the effectiveness of those actions, and future action.

Adaptation: The ability to make incremental adjustments as a result of environmental changes, goal structure changes, or other changes.

(Fiol and Lyles 1985: 811; emphasis added.)

Flexible organisations

In this section two different forms of flexible organisations will be described – namely, teleworking and project-based organisations. The section concludes by the illustration of important dimensions in flexible organisations.

Teleworking organisations

There are many different concepts that can be related to different forms of virtual working – or as we call it in this chapter, *teleworking* – e.g. multiflex, flexiplace, mobile work, work at home, satellite offices, virtual organisations and outsourcing. What is common to these different forms, however, is a movement away from traditionally permanent office spaces to more distant workplaces.

Our aim in this section is not to define teleworking *per se* or different forms of virtual working; rather, we wish but to explore the concept and illustrate the different dimensions and aspects that we find worthy of consideration in seeking to understand learning and knowledge management in flexible organisations. Accordingly, we do not believe that there exists any universal definition of teleworking, or that there is one best way to work at a distance. This point is also made by Lamond *et al.* (1997: 138; see also Lindström *et al.* 1997) who see teleworking as an ongoing process with a number of participating actors. Lamond *et al.* further imply that teleworking is better thought of as a multidimensional phenomenon, varying along the following five dimensions: use of information and communications technology, knowledge intensity, inter-organisational contact, external-organisational contact, and localisation.

The extent and use of information and communication technology is not explicitly expressed in all forms of telework (for an overview, see Lindström *et al.* 1997). It is important, however, that by using advanced information systems, telework serves as a possibility for employees to work from wherever they want, as long as they have access to a computer terminal (Raghuram 1996). This means that they can get important information, as well as contact with people, from inside and outside the organisation.

Inter-organisational contacts can be related to the question: Is just one individual working at a distance, or is a whole department decentralised? This has to do with social contacts and touches the problem of loneliness (e.g. Ramsower 1985; Huws *et al.* 1990; Sproull and Kiesler 1991; Dowell 1992; Wikström *et al.* 1997). Many researchers argue that young people especially need a workplace that includes colleagues for socialisation (Kugelmass 1995; Rapp and Rapp

1995; Raghuram 1996) and to learn the organisation culture. It also has to do with the possibility of exchanging experiences with colleagues, since individuals who are working at a distance are not able to share daily informal occasions and participate in informal corridor discussions. Learning at a distance (see Rapp and Björkegren 1998) is accordingly a challenge to management.

> Telecommuters are invisible employees, working in corporate cultures that value visibility.
>
> (Christensen 1992: 133)

As mentioned in the quotation above, people who are working remotely are in some sense experienced as invisible, both by co-workers and management. This situation has been investigated by Bergum and Rapp (1998), who found that managers experience more difficulties in managing employees working from home, for example, than people working in the traditional permanent office. Teleworking will accordingly demand new ways of managing employees (for a discussion on telemanagement, see Forsebäck 1995). An important issue is, of course, how long the individuals are distance working, for how many days per week, etc.

Regarding knowledge intensity, a matter for discussion, of course, concerns the kind of work tasks that could be performed when distance working. Some authors argue that work tasks ought to be simple, since these are easier to measure, while others argue that independent work tasks are better suited, since those can be performed without ongoing communication with colleagues. However, distance working is increasing, in different personal categories as well as on different organisational levels. Olsson Lagg (1994), Huws (1993) and Engström and Johansson (1997), for example, describe contemporary distance workers as professional, well-educated key persons within companies. Forsebäck (1995) argues, however, that what is common for distance working has to do with data, information or knowledge.

Project-based organisations

Projects are not a new organisational invention, but can even be traced back to the Viking tours and the building of the Egyptian pyramids (Packendorff 1993; Engwall 1995; Lundin 1998). During the last decade, projects have enjoyed a renaissance and Lundin (1998) argues that this organisational form will have an even greater impact in the future. Many reasons can be found in the literature for why projects are becoming more popular. Partington (1996) and Kreiner (1992) mention the organisations' need for continual renewal and innovation, with Engwall (1995) arguing that projects are essential in an environment characterised by uncertainty.

One of the main differences between projects and organisations depends on the *temporal* dimension. Projects are time-limited, whereas organisations are said to be going concerns (even if they are not). A new theoretical wave in the field of project management, which emphasises projects as temporary organisations, has occurred. According to Lundin (1998), this temporal dimension can have implications for learning. Since a project no longer exists after the project's objective (task) is fulfilled (Packendorff 1995), Lundin argues that temporary organisations have few possibilities to reach anything beyond individual learning. The conventional organisation is more appropriate for this, of course, since it can store knowledge for future use. Ayas (1996), on the other hand, argues that when a project is completed, the project members are re-absorbed into new projects or into the organisation, which means that knowledge can be shared with individuals who did not participate in the project.

A project group consists of a group of individuals with different knowledge, experiences and skills. The purpose of a project is to integrate competence and experiences from different parts, from inside as well as outside the organisation. This means that the project group has requisite knowledge areas, although not necessarily people who work well together. Projects can thus be seen as arenas for knowledge meetings (Allen 1999, forthcoming). The main duty of the project leader, here, is to lead this knowledge-wise heterogeneous group so that the competence of the members is utilised. Working together on a project means that the individuals not only have to understand each other but also have to create a shared vision and work towards a common goal.

The distance dimension, i.e. that the project members may be geographically separate, is not explicitly expressed in project literature. However, since it is not always the case that all knowledge needed in a certain project is found within an organisation, this is an important issue. Furthermore, many organisations are active in several countries, which means that a project can involve geographical boundaries where the use of information systems is essential – see also Nandhakumar (Chapter 4) and Harris *et al.* (Chapter 3) for a discussion on this point.

Important dimensions in flexible organisations

The two cases described above can be characterised along a number of dimensions, which must be taken into account for learning and knowledge management in flexible organisations. Teleworking, or virtual working, is mainly characterised by distance and the use of information technology. In this respect, management is also an important dimension – something that has only recently been considered. What has almost not been considered at all is knowledge transfer and learning. Neither has the temporal dimension been considered to any great extent.

The temporal dimension can actually be said to form the main characteristic of project working. Management, too, is something that is important to consider in projects. Through internationalisation, the number of teams with a geographical spread has increased. When geographical distance becomes the norm among team members, the use of ICT is likely to increase. Finally here, learning and knowledge transfer are also central dimensions, with knowledge integration not only important within the project itself, but also between the project and the organisation.

This can be summarised in Table 10.1, where ++ means very important today, + important today and (+) of growing importance.

Table 10.1 Important dimensions in flexible organisations

	Distance	Temporal	Learning	Knowledge	Management	ICT
Telework	++	(+)	(+)	(+)	++	+
Projects	(+)	++	+	+	++	(+)

Learning and knowledge management in flexible organisations

In this section we use the concept of flexible organisations to describe organisations where individuals are geographically and/or temporally disparate. In the section below some important dimensions, mentioned in the previous section about flexible organisations, will be analysed. The dimensions are related to the three perspectives on learning discussed above and illustrated in Figure 10.3.

The behavioural perspective

The distance dimension means that the members of the organisation do not mainly interact face-to-face, but exchange information through various information systems. When analysing the distance dimension from a behavioural perspective, learning can lead to certain problems. Since this perspective sees learning as a response to stimuli, learning will occur as long as the organisation changes behaviour due to environmental stimulation. In summary: as long as the organisation ensures that those who are geographically and temporarily disparate receive the right external stimuli, learning will take place.

As the behavioural perspective does not take the interaction between individuals into consideration, what happens inside the organisation is of less interest. Organisations can be illustrated as black boxes, where input and output are the significant factors. Individual, subjective knowledge does not exist. Thus knowledge can be stored in a database and shared within the organisation. Using information and communication systems means that decisions can be made both faster and more rationally, since top management can use all the organisation's knowledge in its decision-making process.

For management, it is of great importance to understand how the organisation responds to different stimuli and how this leads to change in behaviour and getting the organisation to react quickly to changing conditions in the environment.

The cognitive perspective

Analysing flexible work from a cognitive perspective means that knowledge integration and learning in organisations poses a challenge for management. Whereas teleworking distances people from their organisation as well as co-workers, projects isolate people from their organisation as well as home departments. When analysing the distance dimension from a cognitive perspective, learning can become a problem.

Huber (1991) argues that learning is stimulated when people share each other's thoughts. Because of the distance, thoughts and meanings cannot interact in the same way as when individuals meet each other in an impromptu way in the traditional office building. This also applies to individuals who are not able to share daily informal events at the office or home department. Weick (1995) in a way contradicts Huber by arguing that common understanding both stimulates and limits learning. If people do not understand each other at all, they will not be able to create new knowledge. But partly common understandings can still provide advantage, by individuals gaining insights into other's comprehension and thereby increasing their knowledge – something expressed by Fiol (1994: 404): 'To learn as a community, organisational members must simultaneous agree and disagree.'

Offering a different interpretation and at the same time challenging the existing knowledge structure can lead to new knowledge. Since project members might come from different departments and therefore have different skills and experience, learning might be problematic. People with completely disparate understandings might not, because of time limits, bother to absorb (Cohen and Levinthal 1990) members' knowledge, or even try to understand others' thinking processes. It might even be impossible to exchange or absorb knowledge, since the members cannot relate this new knowledge to what they already know (see Feldman 1986; Weick 1995). However, working in projects can also provide arenas for knowledge creation since partly common understanding and cognitive schemas can provide occasions for sensemaking and learning (Weick 1995). The knowledge that the individuals acquire during the project can then be taken back to the workplace or carried forward to the next project.

When the members of an organisation are teleworking, various interpretations of an event can arise. If these interpretations are exchanged and integrated into the organisation, new knowledge can be created. Problems arise, here, as those who distance work may not integrate to the same extent as those working in the office, which means that knowledge continues to be individual. According to Czarniawska-Joergens (1992), the central part is not common or uncommon understanding, but rather lived experience. If lived experiences can freely be exchanged, even between individuals at a distance, learning in teleworking organisations will take place. However, if shared lived-experience is important, learning at a distance will be problematic since individuals who are working remotely are not able to share the whole interaction in the formal as well as informal daily work. Further, the sharability of the cognitive schemata depends on the sharability of experience (formal as well as informal) upon which expectations are built, and the possibility to communicate tacit knowledge. Limited cognitive abilities, according to Raghuram (1996), can thus lead individuals to simplify complexity, which means that they may not take time trying to understand ambiguous statements.

To learn, individuals must be able to explore and share their tacit knowledge with each other, as well as combine their explicit knowledge in the form of new conceptualisations (Nonaka 1994). Explicit knowledge can, according to Grant (1996), be transmitted without problem because of its communicability, and advanced information technology can even facilitate this transmission. In addition, information technology offers the possibility to codify, store and retrieve explicit knowledge. Baskeville and Smithson (1995) argue that it is of importance to have access to a collective memory, i.e. a database, which can help knowledge (here explicit) to be spread in the organisation. This gives the individuals who are working at a distance the possibility to access important knowledge and add new knowledge. It can also be an important vehicle for project groups to share and exchange their knowledge with others.

If we consider learning between projects, or between projects and organisations, learning might be more problematic than learning within projects. What is gained within the project is not easily documented. First, we cannot presume that project members know what they have learned, and even if they do, it might be complicated to write down. Second, even if they do write it down, it cannot be assumed that someone will read it or understand it. Lundin (1998) argues that similar mistakes in projects tend to be made again and again. Information technology systems can surely facilitate some form of knowledge transfer between projects; however, as mentioned above, it is not certain that this knowledge can be related to something that others already know, which means that they might not be able to use it.

It is complicated to transmit tacit knowledge, in comparison with explicit knowledge, between the individuals within the organisation without some kind of shared experience. Accordingly, tacit knowledge cannot be transferred using today's information systems, but still, we cannot say anything about those of tomorrow. It is important that the individuals who are working temporarily or geographically disparately continue to interact face-to-face with the other individuals. Not just to *get* new knowledge but also to *give* it. Regarding the management dimension, it is therefore important to create conditions for knowledge interactions within the organisation, i.e. to create arenas for knowledge meetings, both in teleworking and project-based organisations. It is thus important that management understands the difficulties regarding distance – the temporal and ICT dimension mentioned above.

The situated perspective

When analysing flexible organisations from a situated perspective, learning might face problems. As argued above, the distance dimension means that people in the organisation do not mainly communicate face-to-face, but exchange information through various systems. Baskeville and Smithson (1995) argue that these systems can be used to enrich internal communication. Tyre and von Hippel (1997) propose that it might not be the togetherness of the members that is of greatest importance, but rather the social situation in which learning takes place, i.e. the context. This implies that a large set of information and indefinable influences, which are bound to the context, will be inaccessible for those who interact solely through information systems.

> Existing electronic media can provide excellent vehicles for sharing ideas, documents or design; however, they are limited because they are decontextualised.
>
> (Tyre and von Hippel 1997: 81)

Since knowledge is embedded in a social context it is thus difficult to communicate through poor media (Brown and Duguid 1991). Further, decontextualised knowledge is not as rich as contextual knowledge and can therefore lose value, as described by Chaklin and Lave (1993: 23):

> To decontextualise knowledge is to form-alise it (to contain it, pour it into forms) at a more inclusive level. To formalise it to contain more forms it follows that abstraction from and generalization across 'contexts' are mechanisms that are supposed to produce decontextualised (valuable, general) knowledge.

Because of limited physical cues, telework has a potential for weakening the link between experience-based knowledge and the acquisition of tacit knowledge (Raghuram 1996). Brown and Duguid (1991) argue that information systems can support the distribution of stories, i.e. shared representation. However, since stories are embedded in a social and cultural context, they cannot simply be uprooted and repacked for circulation (cf. Galpin and Sims, Chapter 6 in this volume). This means that people who are distance working will not feel part of a community or may even never become part of one. Finally, the distance dimension means that there are fewer opportunities to interact with the community and less field experience will therefore be shared; added to this is the contextual difference (Raghuram 1996).

> Becoming a full participant certainly includes engaging with the technologies of everyday practice, as well as participating in the social relations, production process, and other activities in the communities of practice.
>
> (Lave and Wenger 1991: 101)

As argued by Brown and Duguid (1991; see also Lave and Wenger 1991) organisational members are parts of informal communities. It is therefore the communities and not the individuals that are central units of analysis. To share a community of practice is to share a special work culture and a common language. A common language can facilitate understanding and participation even if the individuals are geographically or temporally separate from the head office. Physical proximity and a cultural community can contribute to knowledge transfer within an organisation.

By creating a temporary, formal organisation (a project) we cannot create a community. It arises by itself. Accordingly, the project members are most probably already participants in different kinds of communities. If a project touches many communities, this implies that when the project is due, the individual knowledge gained in the project can be transferred over to the different communities. However, as the knowledge gained in the first project is *situationally* dependent, this means that we might not be able to use it in other projects. Thus, consideration of the situational perspective on learning between projects does not take place (Packendorff 1993).

Regarding the management dimension, it is important for management to understand the situated nature of knowledge in order to facilitate knowledge transfer and learning. Further, it is important to promote informal communities and see them as flourishing knowledge transfers.

Conclusion

The need for knowledge transfer and sharing within organisations has created a vast interest in systems for managing learning and knowledge. Organisational innovations, with flexibility in time and space, are continually being created – see, for example, Nandhakumar (Chapter 4) and Morath and Schmidt (Chapter 12) in this volume. Since knowledge is exchanged and created when people interact with each other, these flexible organisations will pose a challenge for management.

In this chapter we have tried to highlight learning and knowledge management in flexible organisations. By discussing three different perspectives we have shown three different views on learning: the behavioural, the cognitive and the situated. None of the perspectives gives us a complete picture of the learning phenomenon, but rather they can all be seen as complementary and overlapping. Criticism can be levelled at each of the perspectives. The behavioural perspective, for example, can be criticised for just taking into consideration the external world around us and seeing this as the creator of change and learning. The cognitive perspective views knowledge as universal, which means that it can be used everywhere. The situational perspective implies that *all* knowledge is context-dependent, which means that experience-based learning is rather limited and hard to apply in unknown or new situations.

In order to manage knowledge and learning within an organisation it is vital for management to understand the concept of knowledge, its creation and how it can be shared and used within the organisation. The analysis of flexible organisations provides us with some important dimensions that have to be taken into account in order to understand learning and knowledge management in such organisations, i.e. in those where the members are temporarily or geographically disparate.

As has been shown in this chapter, it is a challenge for management to organise learning in an efficient way in order that the different needs regarding different aspects of knowledge can be considered. The character of knowledge is of importance when discussing learning and knowledge management. Explicit knowledge can, with little difficulty, be transferred, even if the members are geographically and/or temporally disparate. This is because explicit knowledge is possible to communicate in formal language. Tacit knowledge is not easily integrated and shared between members, because it is difficult to communicate tacit knowledge verbally. Since tacit knowledge is central for organisational learning, it is important that this knowledge is not lost. Considering the work of information system designers, it is important to understand that databases and on-line communication do not seem to be sufficient for sharing and integrating all kinds of knowledge. Some knowledge can be transferred or stored in databases, whereas other knowledge requires face-to-face contact.

Since not all knowledge can be communicated through information systems, it is important for management to organise forums where knowledge can be integrated and shared, and where new knowledge is created. Members cannot work virtually all the time, but have to meet face-to-face from time to time. It is also important to remember that not all people want to work at a distance. Regarding project-based organisations, it is vital to build bridges between people and projects and make it easy for them to meet. Furthermore, it is important to create a culture that encourages knowledge sharing.

Acknowledgement

This work has been supported partly by the KFB (Swedish Transport and Communication Research Board) and the IMIE (International Graduate School of Management and Industrial Engineering). The IMIE is supported by the Swedish Foundation for Strategic Research.

Bibliography

Allen, T.J. (1999, forthcoming) *Organizational Architecture*, Cambridge: Oxford University Press.

Argyris, C. and Schön, D. (1978) *Organizational Learning: A Theory of Action Perspective*, Reading, Mass.: Addison-Wesley.

Argyris, C. (1993) *Knowledge for Action*, San Francisco: Jossey-Bass.

Atkinson, R.L., Atkinson, R.C., Smith, E.E., Bem, E.R. and Hilgard, E.R. (1990) *Introduction to Psychology*, San Diego: Harcourt Brace Jovanovich.

Ayas, K. (1996) 'Professional project management: a shift toward learning and a knowledge creating structure', *International Journal of Project Management*, 14, 3: 131–6.

Berger, P. and Luckmann, T. (1966) *The Social Construction of Reality: A Treatise in the Sociology of Knowledge*, London: Penguin Books. (Reprinted: 1991.)

Badaracco, J.L. (1991) *The Knowledge Link: How Firms Compete through Strategic Alliances*, Boston: Harvard Business School Press.

Baskeville, R. and Smithson, S. (1995) 'Information technology and new organizational forms: choosing chaos over panacea', *European Journal of Information Systems*, 4: 66–73.

Bergum, S. and Rapp, B. (1998) 'Challenges of managing remote workers: some empirical results from interviews in Sweden and Norway', *ITS-98 Conference*, 21–4 June, Stockholm.

Björkegren, D. (1989) *Hur organisationer lär*, Lund: Studentlitteratur. (*How Organizations Learn*, in Swedish.)

Blomberg, J. (1995) *Ordning och chaos i projektsamarbete: En socialfenomenologisk upplösning av en organisationsteoretisk paradox*, Stockholm: EFI, Handels. (*Order and Chaos in Project Collaboration*, in Swedish.)

Bower, G.H. and Hilgard, E.R. (1981) *Theories of Learning*, 5th edition, Englewood Cliffs: Prentice Hall.

Brown, J.S. and Duguid, S. (1991) 'Organizational learning and communities of practice: toward a unified view of working, learning, and innovation', *Organization Science*, 2, 1: 40–57.

Brown, J.S., Collins, A. and Duguid, S. (1989) 'Situated cognition and the culture of learning', *Educational Researcher*, 18, 1: 32–42.

Chaklin, S. and Lave, J. (1993) *Understanding Practice – Perspectives on Activity and Context*, Cambridge: Cambridge University Press.

Choo, C.W. (1998) *The Knowing Organization: How Organizations use Information to Construct Meaning, Create Knowledge, and Make Decisions*, Oxford: Oxford University Press.

Christensen, K. (1992) 'Managing invisible employees: how to meet the telecommuting challenge', *Employment Relations Today*, summer: 133–43.

Cohen, W.M. and Levinthal, D.A. (1990) 'Absorptive capacity: a new perspective on learning and innovation', *Administrative Science Quarterly*, 35: 128–52.

Czarniawska-Joergens, B. (1992) *Exploring Complex Organisations – a Cultural Perspective*, Newbury Park: Sage.

Cyert, R.M. and March, J.G. (1963) *A Behavioural Theory of the Firm*, 2nd edition, Cambridge: Blackwell. (Reprinted: 1992.)

Davenport, T.H. and Prusack, L. (1998) *Working Knowledge: How Organizations Manage What They Know*, Boston: Harvard Business School Press.

Dowell, A. (1992) 'Home alone? – Teleworking', *Management Science*, October: 18–21.

Drucker, P.F. (1993) *Post-Capitalist Society*, Oxford: Butterworth Heinemann.

Ellström, P.-E. (1996) 'Rutiner och reflektion', in Ellström, P.-E., Gustavsson, B. and Larsson, S. (eds) *Livslångt lärande*, Lund: Studentlitteratur. (*Lifelong Learning*, in Swedish.)

Engström, M.-G. and Johansson, R. (1997) *Med IT mot nya organisationsformer: Flexibilitet i tid, rum och organisation*, KFB-Rapport 1997: 28. (*With IT towards new Organisational Forms.*)

Engwall, M. (1995) *Jakten på det effektiva projektet*, Stockholm: Nerenius and Santérus Förlag. (*The Pursuit of the Efficient Project*, in Swedish.)

Ericson, T. (1998) *Förändringsidéer och meningsskapande – En studie av strategisk förändring*, Linköping University: Dept. of Management and Economics. (*Ideas of Change and Sensemaking*, in Swedish.)

Feldman, J. (1986) 'On the difficulty of learning from experience', in Sims, H.P. and Gioia, D.A. (eds) *The Thinking Organization*, San Francisco: Jossey-Bass.

Fiol, C. (1994) 'Consensus, diversity and learning in organizations', *Organization Science*, 5, 3: 403–20.

Fiol, C. and Lyles, M. (1985) 'Organizational learning', *Academy of Management Review*, 10, 4: 803–13.

Forsebäck, L. (1995) *20 Seconds to Work: Home-based Telework*, Swedish experiences from a European perspective, Farsta: Teledok Rapport 101.

Giddens, A. (1986) *The Constitution of Society*, Cambridge: Polity Press.

Gioia, D.A. and Sims, H.P. (1986) 'Introductions: dynamics of organizational social cognition', in Sims, H.P. and Gioia, D.A. (eds) *The Thinking Organization*, San Francisco: Jossey-Bass.

Grant, R.M. (1996) 'Prospering in dynamically competitive environments: organizational capability as knowledge integration', *Organization Science*, 7, 4, July/August: 375–87.

Handy, C. (1984) *The Future of Work: A Guide to a Changing Society*, Oxford: Blackwell.

Hedberg, B. (1981) 'How organizations learn and unlearn', in Nyström, P.C. and Starbuck, W.H. (eds) *Handbook in Organizational Design*, Oxford: Oxford University Press.

Hellgren, B. and Löwstedt, J. (1997) *Tankens företag*, Stockholm: Nerenius and Santérus Förlag. (*The Organisation of Thoughts*, in Swedish.)

Huber, G.P. (1991) 'Organizational learning: the contribution process and the literature', *Organization Science*, 2, 1: 88–115.

Huws, U. (1993) 'Teleworking: facing up to the future', *Health and Safety Information Bulletin*, 223: 9–11.

Huws, U., Korte, W.B. and Robinson, S. (1990) *Telework: Towards the Elusive Office*, Chichester: Wiley.

Kreiner, K. (1992) 'The postmodern epoch of organization theory', *International Studies of Management*, 22, 2: 37–52.

Kugelmass, J. (1995) *Telecommuting: A Manager's Guide to Flexible Work Arrangements*, New York: Lexington Books.

Lamond, D., Daniels, K. and Standen, P. (1997) 'Defining telework: What is it exactly?', paper at the *Second International Workshop on Telework*, Amsterdam.

Lave, J. (1988) *Cognition in Practice – Mind, Mathematics and Culture in Everyday Life*, Cambridge: Cambridge University Press.

Lave, J. and Wenger, E. (1991) *Situated Learning – Legitimate Peripheral Participation*, Cambridge: Cambridge University Press.

Leonard-Barton, D. (1992) 'The factory as a learning laboratory', *Sloan Management Review*, Fall: 23–38.

Lindström, J., Moberg, A. and Rapp, B. (1997) 'On the classification of telework', *European Journal of Information System*, 6, 4: 243–55.

Lundin, R.A. (1998) 'Temporära organisationer – några perspektivbyten', in Charniawsk-Joergens, B. (ed.) *Organisationsteori på svenska*, Malmö: Liber Ekonomi. (*Organisational Theory*, in Swedish.)

March, J.G. and Simon, H.A. (1958) *Organizations*, New York: Wiley.

Nonaka, I. (1994) 'Dynamic theory of organizational knowledge creation', *Organizational Science*, 5, 1: 14–39.

Nonaka, I. and Takeuchi, H. (1995) *The Knowledge Creating Company: How Japanese Companies Create the Dynamics of Innovation*, New York: Oxford University Press.

Olsson Lagg, A. (1994) *Med distans till jobbet – distansarbete i USA*, Stockholm: Utlandsrapport från Sveriges Tekniska Attachéer. (*With Distance to Work*, in Swedish.)

Packendorff, J. (1993) *Projektorganisationer och projektorganisering*, Umeå University: Handelshögskolan i Umeå, Inst för Företagsekonomi. (*Project Organisations and Project Organising*, in Swedish.)

—— (1995) 'Inquiring into the temporary organization: new directions for project management research', *Scandinavian Journal of Management*, 11, 7/8: 859–70.

Partington, D. (1996) 'The project management of organizational change', *International Journal of Project Management*, 14, 1: 13–21.

Polanyi, M. (1966) *The tacit dimension*, Gloucester: Peter Smith. (Reprinted: 1983.)

Raghuram, S. (1996) 'Knowledge creation in telework context', *International Journal of Technology Management* (Special Publication on Unlearning and Learning), 11, 4: 319–35.

Ramsower, R.M. (1985) *Telecommuting – The Organizational and Behavioural Effects of Working at Home*, Michigan: UMI Research Press.

Rapp, B. and Björkegren, C. (1998) *Arbete på distans och lärande*, KFB report No. 1996–182. (*Working at Distance and Learning*, in Swedish.)

Rapp, B. and Rapp, B. (1995) *Skärgårdskontoret: En framtida resurs för skärgården*, Mariehamn: Nordiska Ministerrådets Skärgårdssamarbete, Rapport 1995:2. (*The Archipelago Office*, in Swedish.)

Rogoff, B. and Lave, J. (eds) (1984) *Everyday Cognition: Its Development in Social Context*, Cambridge: Harvard University Press.

Senge, P. (1990) *The Fifth Discipline: The Art and Practice of the Learning Organization*, New York: Doubleday.

Simon, H.A. (1981) *Science of Artificial*, Cambridge: MIT Press.

—— (1991) 'Bounded rationality and organisational learning', *Organization Science*, 2, 1, February: 125–34.

Skinner, B.F. (1938) *The Behaviour of Organisms: An Experimental Analysis*, New York: Meredith Publishing Company. (Reprinted: 1966.)

Sproull, L. and Kiesler, S. (1991) *Connections: New Ways of Working in the Networked Organization*, Cambridge: MIT Press.

Toffler, A (1980) *The Third Wave*, New York: Morrow.

Tyre, M.J. and von Hippel, E. (1997) 'The situated nature of adaptive learning organizations', *Organization Science*, 8, 1: 71–83.

Weick, K. (1995) *Sensemaking in Organizations*, Thousand Oaks, CA: Sage.

Weick, K. and Bougon, M.G. (1986) 'Organizations as cognitive maps: charting ways to success and failure', in Sims, H.P. and Gioia, D.A. (eds) *The Thinking Organization*, San Francisco: Jossey-Bass.

Wikström, T., Palm Lindén, K. and Michaelson, W. (1997) *Hub of Events or Splendid Isolation. The Home as a Context for Teleworking*, Lund University: School of Architecture.

11 Organisational learning and the virtual organisation

Ian McLoughlin and Paul J. Jackson

Introduction

One of the most commonly repeated findings from research on the organisational consequences of technological change is that new technical systems fail to achieve their goals because of an inadequate consideration of the 'human', 'social' and 'organisational' dimensions of change (Benders *et al.* 1995). It is already apparent that promoters of virtual forms of work, such as teleworking have, also underestimated or inadequately understood the social basis of such innovations (Jackson this volume). It is also increasingly common for such observations to be linked to failures in, or barriers to, learning that prevent in some way the questioning of prevailing socio-technical design assumptions. For many, it is increasingly necessary to challenge such assumptions in order to enable, in Zuboff's phrase, a 'new division of learning' to replace the classical bureaucratic 'division of labour' (Zuboff 1988). The significance of this point is more than adequately brought home by the apparent revelation that until recently only two of the 30,000 personal computers within Microsoft were formally authorised to be connected to the Internet (Wallace 1997).

We begin this chapter with a discussion of the emergent concept of the 'virtual organisation' and some of the 'virtual technologies' said to underpin it. In so doing, attention is drawn to the danger of viewing the technical capabilities and characteristics of virtual technologies as *synonymous with* 'virtual organisation' itself and the need to develop an understanding of the social basis of such innovations. We then go on to consider three models of innovation and learning. Our central concern is the question: 'What competencies, expertise and knowledge might be required in bringing about and sustaining "virtual organisations"?' As we will see, each of these models suggests rather different things about the nature of the process of learning required to 'go virtual'.

In search of the virtual organisation

The idea of 'virtual organisation' has gained increasing currency in the wake of a spate of popular management books published in the early 1990s, of which Grenier and Metes (1995) *Going Virtual: Moving Your Organisation into the 21st*

Century, is a typical example (see also Nohria 1992; Davidow and Malone 1992; Barnatt 1995). For most of these authors, 'virtual organisation' represents the coming together of two contemporary trends.

First, advances in the capabilities of computing and telecommunications technologies that have enhanced the technical capacity to capture, process, display and distribute information while at the same time have allowed new levels of 'immersion' of human actors in these processes. Such technologies have given new impetus to the possibilities of redefining both the spatial/temporal location and the nature of work itself (see, for discussion, Appel and Behr 1996). The second involves the restructuring of organisations to make them more flexible and responsive to rapidly changing and unpredictable global market, customer and technological conditions. For many, organisational survival in the context of such perceived imperatives requires a move away from conventional 'modern' hierarchical bureaucracies to 'networked' forms of organisation (Handy 1995).

Moreover, in many renditions, these trends are seen as increasingly making the distinction between the 'organisation' and the 'technology' which it deploys seemingly irrelevant:

> it is possible to see organisations becoming synonymous with their information systems, since microprocessing facilities create the possibility of organising without having an organisation in physical terms....Many organisations of the future may have no fixed location, with members interacting through personal computers and audio-visual devices to create a network of exchange and interrelated activity.
>
> (Morgan 1997: 4)

For an increasing number of commentators, therefore, 'virtual organisations' represent a way in which virtual technologies can be harnessed to bring about radically new ways of working which are perceived as necessary for organisations to survive in the new competitive conditions of the late twentieth century. Barnatt (1995: 82–3) suggests that virtual organisations have three defining characteristics:

- a reliance on cyberspace in order to function and survive;
- no identifiable physical form;
- employer–employee relationships are transient and their boundaries defined and limited by the availability of virtual technology rather than bureaucratic rules or contracts.

Other proponents place less stress on cyber-mediation but rather see 'virtuality' as embedded in the transient and bespoke character of organisational networks created to perform particular knowledge-based tasks (e.g. new product development) and the fluidity and lack of definition of organisational boundaries both within and in relation to the network itself (see also Jackson, Chapter 1 in this volume). According to Davidow and Malone (1992: 5–6), for example:

To the outside observer it [the virtual corporation] will appear almost edge-less, with permeable and continuously changing interfaces between company, supplier and customers. From inside the firm the view will be no less amorphous, with traditional offices, departments and operating divisions constantly reforming according to need.

Jackson (1996 and this volume) summarises some essential characteristics of 'virtual organisation', as represented in this 'popular' literature. These include:

- a collapse of hierarchy and an erosion of boundaries, both within and between organisations;
- transient, project-based work organisation involving collaboration between co-workers, suppliers and other associated organisations;
- increased mediation through cyberspace, with reduced use of 'centres', buildings and offices.

Recent academically informed treatments of 'virtual organisation' seek to link the concept to broader analytical trends. Brigham and Corbett (1996), for example, see virtual organisation as an archetypical postmodern form of organi-sation which they suggest (quoting Reed 1992: 229) 'celebrates, even luxuriates in, the dissolution and demise of normative regimes and disciplinary practices associated with rational bureaucracy'. In place of the routinisation and alien-ation characteristic of bureaucracy, virtual organisation promises, in the view of its proponents, a new world of high trust and empowered work relationships embodied in the characteristics and capabilities of virtual technologies.

Cambell (1996) drawing upon Snow *et al.* (1992), usefully identifies different types of 'virtual organisation' which starts to draw out a more contingent and variable model of virtual organisational forms (see also Campbell, Chapter 2 in this volume). Campbell (1996: 83) distinguishes between:

- *Internal networks*, where relatively autonomous 'enterprise' or 'business' units are formed within a large conventional bureaucracy to provide operational synergies and tailor responses to specific customer demands;
- *stable networks*, where conventional bureaucratic organisations outsource non-core activities to a small network of key suppliers whose activities become highly interdependent and integrated with those of the mother firm (for example, as in the 'lean production' model);
- *dynamic networks*, where organisations concentrate on core competencies but introduce external partners in co-operative ventures throughout their opera-tions;
- *Web enterprises*, a new type of organisational form, with temporary networks rapidly formed 'to exploit new market opportunities through the mutual exchange of skills and resources'.

Unlike the other types, the Web enterprise is not a variation on existing bureaucratic organisational forms. Rather, Web enterprises represent virtual organisation in its 'purest form'. They are manifested not as spatially and temporally fixed sets of systems and structures, but rather as a spatially dispersed and temporally flexible cultural community, the reproduction of which is dependent upon the learning and innovation of its constituents. 'Going virtual', therefore, can mean a variety of things. In most instances it involves innovation within the context of existing conventional organisational arrangements. Only in the case of 'Web enterprise' forms does 'virtual organisation' suggest the end of conventional organisation as we know it. More important, as Campbell (this volume) argues, it is in this type of organisational form in which the need for learning is greatest.

This approach also indicates the dangers of assuming virtual organisation to be synonymous with virtual technology. While each of these forms of virtual organisation might be seen to be enabled by virtual technologies in some way, the degree and manner in which this is so is likely to be variable.

All this suggests is that, even at a generic level, the concept of virtual organisation embraces a broad range of different socio-technical configurations. This point is well made by Nohria and Eccles (1992: 289) who make it clear that *'network organisations are not the same as electronic networks, nor can they be built entirely on them'* (original emphasis). They argue that electronically mediated exchange cannot completely replace face-to-face interaction. This is especially the case in networked organisations, where tasks are likely to be characterised by high levels of uncertainty, ambiguity and risk. It is precisely this kind of task environment where electronically mediated forms of interaction are likely to be least effective. Electronically mediated interaction requires, almost by definition, no co-presence of the participants. Such encounters are stripped of the multiplicity of social clues that contextualise face-to-face encounters; involve none of the physical and psycho-emotional dimensions of interaction (the impressions 'given off' as well as those 'given' are lost); and the sequential nature of interaction means that the capacity in conventional encounters for interruption, repair, feedback and learning are absent. All this means that electronically mediated exchange offers only limited impressions upon which to construct meaningful identities. For example, in the context of team formation, it places limits on the capacity of actors to resolve uncertainties and ambiguities, makes it more difficult for collective action to be mobilised in order to seize new opportunities or deflect threats, and is likely to constitute a set of relationships that are less than robust in a context where strength and adaptability are at a premium.

This results in a rather nice paradox. The enabling capabilities and characteristics of virtual technologies are least likely to result in effective organisational outcomes precisely in the 'agile' circumstances that many proponents see as the purest form of 'virtual organisation'. As Nohria and Eccles (1992: 299) put it:

> electronically mediated exchange can substitute for face-to-face interaction only when the identities of the interactants are not very important, when

the circumstances at hand are certain and unambiguous, when the actions necessary are standard and routine, and when ongoing interaction does not depend on a robust structure of relationships.

And thus (1992: 300)

this leads to the somewhat ironic conclusion that the best circumstances for using electronically mediated exchange to replace face-to-face interaction are those in which the more traditional market or hierarchical organisation is quite effective

and the hypothesis that in at least the 'purest' forms of virtual organisation (1992: 300),

in order to derive the benefits of the increasing capability of electronically mediated exchange, the amount of face-to-face interaction will actually have to increase.

A hypothesis that seems to be borne out by anecdotal and other evidence shows that the use of video-conferencing or e-mail is accompanied by increases in executive travel and meetings rather than a reduction.

All this should caution us from viewing the learning issues facing organisations seeking to 'go virtual' as wholly or even mainly technical ones. Quite clearly much learning must also concern the social dimensions of such innovation. Given this, we can now consider models of the *process* of learning that might be involved.

Innovation, learning and virtual organisation

How can conventional organisations transform themselves into 'virtual organisations'? What kind of learning process is required? What types of knowledge and expertise are needed to build and sustain virtual forms of work and organisation? In this section we consider three 'perspectives' which might give us some purchase on these issues. The first of these constructs the problem in terms of the issues raised by the adoption of virtual technologies themselves and focuses on the problem of transferring knowledge to users. The second focuses on the 'learning difficulties' associated with conventional bureaucratic organisations, how these might act to constrain or frustrate attempts to 'go virtual', and what learning processes might help to overcome these barriers. The last approach examines the way socio-technical networks are configured and stabilised as a *political* process. In particular, it is concerned with the active role played by 'change agents' in configuring and representing new technologies and organisational forms.

Learning as knowledge transfer

Virtual technologies are a classic case of technology that is difficult to adopt because the transfer of knowledge about how to use it – from supplier to user – is problematic. Like other advanced computing and information technologies, virtual technologies are technically complex and abstract, inconsistent in their operation, generate requirements for after-sale 'hand holding' of users by suppliers, pervasive in their influence across user organisations, and are difficult to configure as 'off the shelf' products (Eveland and Tornatzky 1990 cited by Attewell 1996: 207–8). Thus, while adopters can readily acquire technologies and systems which embody the innovation, the knowledge required to use them is much more difficult to come by quickly.

In part this is because the mobility of technical know-how from suppliers to users in such cases is relatively low (Attewell 1996: 208). However, it is also because such systems require a lengthy period of 'post-adoption innovation' (Fleck 1993) and 'learning by doing' within adopting organisations. During these, as Attewell points out, previous innovations may be substantially modified by users while often unanticipated changes in organisational practices and procedures are likely to be required as learning takes place by 'using'. At the individual level, experiences are distilled into new personal skills and knowledge which must then be embodied in organisational routines, practices and beliefs. Therefore, much of the new knowledge concerning the use of the technology is actually generated within the adopting firm and cannot be the product of transfers from outside, or, if it can, is only transferred with great difficulty (Attewell 1996: 210).

Given this, it can be predicted that the relative low mobility of technical know-how and the premium attached to post-adoption innovation will be perceived as major barriers to the adoption of virtual technologies and the development of virtual organisational forms. In response it might be anticipated that relations between suppliers and users will be structured by the task of reducing these barriers through mechanisms which lower them or allow them to be circumvented. To this end, supply side institutions can be expected to emerge that act as mediators between the user and complex technology (Attewell 1996: 224). These mediating institutions will 'capture economies of scale' in 'rare event learning' (e.g. dealing with non-routine system breakdowns), and provide the option to the user of consuming the new technology as a 'bureau service' from them as a precursor or even alternative to 'in-house' adoption. In the long term, however, as learning and economic barriers fall, adoption is more likely to be undertaken 'in-house'. At the same time the consumption of an innovation via an external supplier will not obviate the need for post-adoption innovation within the user firm. Issues of how best to apply the technology in a given organisational and business context will remain, such as developing 'work arounds' to circumvent bugs and other technical constraints in the system, 'bending the system' to conform to formal and informal organisational practices, and using the technology as a trigger to change how the organisation operates (Attewell 1996: 222–3).

This focus on 'post adoption' organisational learning is clearly an improvement on the conventional stance in innovation studies. This has normally viewed adoption as a function of the proximity of organisations to pre-existing users and the judgements made by potential users as to the cost–benefit of adoption. Here, organisational learning essentially refers to the 'innovative capacity' of firms to become aware of and assess the cost–benefit of adoption at a particular point in time (Attewell 1996: 208). The focus on post-adoption learning, on the other hand, recognises that the adoption of advanced systems is not a 'one off' decision-event but rather a complex organisational process where the transfer of technical know-how is problematic and possibly incomplete (Attewell 1996: 211).

In this approach organisational learning clearly becomes a central feature of the innovation process and a key factor in determining the success of adoption and the diffusion of new technologies. Significantly, however, such learning is frequently seen as above, or even beyond, the political and power systems of the organisations in which it is to occur while the social shaping and cultural dimensions of technology are downplayed (see, for example, the recent treatment in Tidd *et al.* 1997 and Pavitt's commentary 1987). As a result, 'technical know-how' tends to be portrayed as an unproblematic entity determined by the characteristics and capabilities of the technical system concerned. Further, the problem of innovation is constructed in terms of 'barriers' to communicating what the suppliers clearly and unambiguously know, to the users who have to work out ways to absorb and apply it. This betrays a strong linearity in the characterisation of the process of innovation. Finally, organisational learning is presented as a necessary response to the stimulus provided by external competitive and technological imperatives.

Organisational learning to become virtual

From an organisational behaviour perspective, the more virtual organisations are manifested in agile form, the more they will need to be self-regulating and reliant for their continuation on the capacity to change. Organisational learning will therefore be a key characteristic/requirement in order to create and sustain such organisational forms. Moreover, virtual organisations might also be expected to be highly conducive contexts for the development of what has been termed 'double' or even 'triple' loop learning (Argyris and Schön 1978; Swieringa and Wierdsma 1994). That is, an ability to question the validity of operating norms or even the strategic principles which form the basis of such norms.

This suggests that conventional organisations seeking to 'go virtual' will need to go beyond single loop learning – the highest form of learning achieved by most conventional bureaucratic organisations. However, this transition faces significant barriers. Bureaucratic organisational forms can become proficient at scanning environments, setting objectives and monitoring the performance of organisational sub-systems in relation to planned objectives; and advances in information technology further enhance the capabilities and effectiveness of the organisational information systems which embody these abilities (Morgan 1997: 88). But conventional organisations have problems with double loop learning (Morgan 1997: 88–9). Bureaucracy creates fragmented patterns of thought and activity. Different functions, departments and hierarchical levels operate on the basis of their own sectional interests, goals and views of organisational reality. Organisational complexity demands that action is based on a 'bounded rationality' and employees are encouraged and rewarded for acting and thinking within these constraints, not for challenging them. Similarly, punishment and accountability systems encourage 'defensive routines' such as 'rigging figures', impression management, the dilution of bad news for consumption by senior management and so on. All this serves to conceal the scale of problems and difficulties that are faced. Deep-seated flaws in the basic way the organisation operates are avoided and concealed by 'burying the problem'.

Virtual organisations, especially Web enterprises, appear to be the epitome of the 'learning organisation' (Morgan 1997: 89–94). Here, environmental change is the norm and organisations must develop skills and competence in scanning this environment and recognising/anticipating changes and new possibilities must be developed. Going virtual requires boundaries between organisation and environment (customers, suppliers, collaborators) to be continuously challenged. New operating norms and assumptions and their underlying metaphors, paradigms and mind-sets need to be understood by organisation members but at the same time the strategic reframing of norms and assumptions must not get 'out of synch' with operating realities. Cultures which support change and risk-taking need to be encouraged at the operating level, as well as emergent forms of organisation (e.g. through continuous improvement philosophies). At the same time 'going virtual' requires the development of capacities to manage the tensions created by learning which follow from the constant challenging of existing organisational arrangements.

From this perspective, 'going virtual' is likely to prove problematic for many organisations. For example, it is possible that perceived problems of managing employees who are spatially and temporally dispersed are likely to be confronted by seeking corrective actions based on a series of technological 'fixes'. This may include, for example, seeking to ensure alignment between employee behaviour in a high-trust work situation with operating norms based on low-trust assumptions. Most obviously this might occur by using virtual technologies as monitoring, surveillance and 'panoptic' devices (Zuboff 1988) (the infamous example of BT's surveillance of its home-based directory enquiry operators is the classic illustration of this, and the negative reports of working conditions in call centres provide more recent examples). In many instances, therefore, 'virtual' organisational outcomes are likely to result in both a failure fully to exploit technical capabilities, and exhibit the usual range of human and organisational problems associated with poor socio-technical design.

As with approaches that are concerned with knowledge transfer, a focus on internal processes of organisational learning gives us considerable purchase on many of the difficulties that might be involved in 'going virtual'. However, a number of problems remain. It seems that most concepts of organisational learning betray their origins by being derived from psychological stimulus–response theory (Hatch 1997: 374). 'Learning', therefore, is defined as an individual, a team of individuals or an organisation responding *differently* to a situation (stimulus) that has been confronted before. However, the more common observation is that the same individual/organisational responses are made to *different* situations. In this sense organisations do not learn but instead suppress learning (Weick cited by Hatch 1997: 374–75) – a point echoed in Sims and McAulay's view that 'people learn wherever they are. Learning is a universal part of the human condition, and people do not suspend their capacity for learning when they come to work' (Sims and McAulay 1995: 5). As Hatch notes, the 'jolt to our senses' provided by such observations suggests that:

> perhaps the study of organisational learning would benefit from a non-traditional approach that runs counter to the stimulus–response model of traditional psychology which emphasises action and its outcomes. If learning is a process – and nearly everyone agrees that it is – then perhaps this process isn't located in action, but rather in the domains of knowledge, language and interpretation.
>
> (Hatch 1997: 375)

A further necessary 'jolt' to our senses is also provided by the criticism that learning in organisations is a *political* process. While, as noted above, some models of innovation and learning seek to deny or downplay this, organisational politics and prevailing distributions of power are an inevitable factor. As Clausen and Neilsen (1997) point out, what constitutes a problem and an appropriate solution within an organisation are politically informed preconditions for learning. As such, organisational learning is all part of the organisational 'political game' and to date many discussions have remained staunchly managerialist and Anglo-American in their assumptions and orientations (Borttrup 1997).

Building and sustaining networks: the learning of politics and the politics of learning

Elsewhere one of the current authors has made the case for considering the development of virtual working, such as teleworking, through ideas espoused by 'actor network theory' (see Callon 1987). As Jackson and van der Wielen (1998) note, these ideas are concerned with the way technological innovations are shaped and stabilised into particular socio-technical configurations. They can provide a means by which the multiple actors, agendas and complicated web of relationships involved in 'going virtual' might be more adequately understood (*ibid.*). They also point to the overtly political character of network building and the political actions of change agents/agencies in promoting, enrolling, alliance-building, negotiating and stabilising the socio-technical configurations that constitute an actor network (Koch 1997: 130). Finally, the actor network concept – by focusing on *actors* rather than on institutions, and viewing technology as a social construct rather than an exogenous variable – breathes necessary life into the concept of 'networks' (*ibid.*).

For actor network theory, innovation is understood as a process of changing networks of social relations – identities, expectations, beliefs, values etc. In this perspective technology is a form of congealed social relations which 'just happens to take a material form' (Woolgar 1997). The formation of new social relationships – virtual forms of organisation, for example – involves the alignment of an initially diverse set of actors and interests. Actor network theorists also make the counter-intuitive suggestion that the 'actors' concerned are both human and non-human. The process of alignment, if successful, therefore results in a new *socio-technical* configuration – for example, a 'virtual organisation' or virtual team – which comprises a stabilised set of relationships between both human/organisational and technical elements.

The aligning of actor networks involves the following processes (see Jackson and van der Wielen 1998: 9–10):

*   *Translation*: Actor networks are the consequence of an alignment of otherwise diverse interests. Alignment is dependent upon the enrolment of different actors into the network. This is accomplished through a process of translation, where the interests of actors are changed to accord with those prescribed by key actors (individuals, groups, organisations, technology) which are seeking to bring about innovation.
*   *Problematisation*: These key actors seek to construct scenarios (by defining problems and their solutions) that demonstrate to potential members that their interests would be best served by enrolment into the network.
*   *Displacements*: Once actors have been enrolled through the problematisation process a range of entities is mobilised to ensure the stabilisation of the network.

Stabilisation is threatened by:

*   *Juxtaposition*: Actors are members of juxtaposed networks (e.g. families as well as organisations) and membership of other networks may be a stronger influence in the definition of interests and perceived 'problems' and 'solutions'.
*   *Simplification*: Enrolment in a network is thus dependent upon an actor's willingness to accept the simplification of their interests in the process of enrolment to new networks.

In this view, 'going virtual' may involve organisational decision makers accepting the images promoted in the marketing strategies of Telecom and other virtual technology supplier companies (such as the current 'Work where you want' marketing campaign being run by Canon). These images seek to present new (and some not so new, such as '0800' numbers!) 'virtual' products and services as solutions to corporate problems of communicating and competing in a globalised marketplace; as a means of resolving the dysfunctional corporate, social and environmental costs of employee commuting; or as a means of achieving increased workforce flexibility.

The success of such attempts at 'problematisation' will rely on a translation of employer, employee and other stakeholder interests into a series of complex socio-technical alignments. This may occur, for example, in relation to managerial attitudes towards the use of such technology as means of empowerment, and employee willingness to embrace the home as a workplace and a new relationship between work and domestic life. A key element in the stabilisation of networks will be the alignment of such social constructs with an effectively implemented and operational technical system. This raises issues that can undermine network formation. For example, employees may reject home-based work as a solution to the need for flexible working because, in their eyes, teleworking addresses issues of commuting and work location when the real problem – defined in terms of their membership of family networks – is the employer's long hours and inflexible work times. By the same token, suppliers of virtual technologies may find it difficult to develop an adequate understanding of user needs and requirements or seek merely to provide 'technological fixes' that downplay or ignore the human and organisational dimensions of socio-technical systems. The more radical the concepts involved – as indeed those embraced by 'virtual working' are – the more likely it might be anticipated that such problems will manifest themselves.

While offering considerable analytical purchase, ideas derived from actor-network theory also pose a number of problems. Three noted by Koch (1997: 130–3) are of relevance here. First, the treatment of technology as if it were a subjective actor with interests and capable of negotiating with other members of the network. The second is the weak or non-existent conceptualisation of the context in which actor networks form, other than in the sense that this context is one made up of other juxtaposed actor networks. Third, and related to this, a reluctance to focus on the organisation as a unit of analysis. Put at its simplest, the bias towards action in the actor network approach seems to exclude any intrusions by the structural properties of the situation in which action occurs.

Some of these issues have been better addressed within organisational sociology in recent years where the outcomes of technological change have been seen as bound by both internal and external context but at the same time uniquely shaped by local social choice and political negotiation within adopting organisations (see, for example, Wilkinson 1983; Buchanan and Boddy 1983; Clark *et al.* 1988; Dawson 1994). In this view, the crucial features of both the social *and* technical outcomes of change are the result of incremental local/internal customisation and adaptation of generic systems and models – albeit shaped and constrained by broader conditions and influences. This process has been described by Badham (see, for example, Badham 1995; Badham *et al.* 1997) as a *configurational process* carried out in the context of existing *configurations* of technological, organisational and human resources bounded by broader internal and external environmental contexts. Configurational processes have the effect of transforming the manner in which material resources are transformed into outputs and in so doing re-define the configuration of existing technological, organisational and human resources.

Such configurational processes can be construed as 'situated' learning processes, in the sense that what comes to be considered as 'knowledge' is a product of a particular interpretation and politically negotiated context – a 'community of practice' (see Björkegren and Rapp, Chapter 10 in this volume). But they are also inherently political processes. For example, key to this approach is the notion of *configurational 'intrapreneurs'* – translators or 'heterogeneous engineers' in the parlance of actor network theory. These actors might include, among others, relevant IT managers, systems engineers, human resource managers and senior executives, but also 'external' actors such as suppliers, government agencies and consultants. Such actors play a key role as organisational 'champions', establishing and operating new configurations, managing their boundaries, as well as ensuring their survival and guiding their development. This role is active, uncertain and risky. Such actors seek to manipulate both technical and social elements, and overcome obstacles in both areas in order to design and implement working technical systems (Badham 1995). These actors are agents of learning in a practical context where their action is highly political.

One consequence of this line of thinking occurs in relation to the expertise and competence of change agents engaged in configuring new socio-technical systems – in particular those of a radical and vulnerable nature such as 'virtual organisations' (what follows draws strongly on Buchanan and Boddy 1991). At one level the expertise required might be seen as defined by the *content* of change itself – the technical knowledge and expertise required to design, install, program, debug virtual technologies themselves. At another level, expertise might also be required in the form of generic skills and competencies associated with the *control* of complex technical and organisational change programmes such as project management skills concerned with bench marking, objective setting, planning, monitoring and so on. These may be highly specialised where virtual organisational forms mean the adoption of new and novel relationships with suppliers, customers and empowered teams of employees (the interfaces between the 'endo' and 'exo' worlds, as stated by Morath and Schmidt in Chapter 12 of this volume). Third, expertise in the human relations and organisational development aspects of change will also be important – particularly if tendencies towards constructing and resolving problems in terms of a series of 'technological fixes' are to be avoided. However, the argument to be made here stresses the centrality of a further strand of expertise – what might be seen as Machiavellian competencies, where the devices of manipulation and threat are used to enrol and re-enrol key stakeholder interests and to overcome or neutralise sources of resistance. As Child and Faulkner (1998) note, to ensure that learning is effective requires both the setting of limits to the actions of network participants and an assessment of learning outcomes. At the same time possibilities of learning being misdirected to serve sectional stakeholder interests have to be confronted (p. 307). Not for nothing has the role of change agents in bringing about new organisational forms been described as that of the 'new princes and princesses of socio-technical change' (Buchanan and Badham 1999)! Thus, if organisational learning is to be effective it seems a much sharper perspective is required of both the political context of learning *and* the role of those promoting or seeking to bring it about. The kinds of radical organisational transformation suggested by, at least some, virtual working concepts would indicate that this political dimension to the learning process will be particularly marked.

Conclusion

The discussion in this chapter is necessarily tentative, exploratory and subject to revision and reformulation. An attempt has been made to explore how we might conceptualise the organisational learning issues involved in 'going virtual'. We have considered three perspectives, each of which offers a degree of analytical purchase on the issue. The innovation approach usefully focuses our attention on the problem of knowledge transfer, relationships between suppliers, users and mediating institutions, and the role of post-adoption learning as a key, possibly crucial factor in innovation. The organisational learning literature provides useful conceptualisations of the problems bureaucratic organisations 'learning to learn' face, and usefully fleshes out some key issues in post-adoption learning. However, the sentiment is that the third approach, based on an ongoing attempt to synthesise new developments in the sociology of technology with a burgeoning interest within organisational sociology with the micro-politics and representation of innovation and change, offers the promise of generating the kind of new perspective required to confront the learning challenges inherent in concepts of virtual working.

Bibliography

Appel, W. and Behr, R. (1996) 'The importance of modern information and communication technologies for the formation of virtual organisations', in Jackson, P.J. and van der Wielen, J. (eds) *Proceedings of Workshop on New International Perspectives on Telework*, Tilburg: WORC.

Argyris, C. and Schön, D.A. (1978) *Organisational Learning: A Theory of Action Perspective*, London: Addison-Wesley.

Attewell, P. (1996) 'Technology diffusion and organisational learning', in Moingeon, B. and Edmonson, A. (eds) *Organisational learning and competitive advantage*, London: Sage.

Badham, R. (1995) 'Managing socio-technical change: a configuration approach to technology implementation', in Benders, J., de Haan, J. and Bennett, D. (eds) *The Symbiosis of Work and Technology*, London: Taylor & Francis.

Badham, R. and Buchanan, D. (1995) 'Power assisted steering: the new princes of socio-technical change', *Leicester Business School Working Paper No. 33*, De Montforte University.

Badham, R., Couchman, P. and McLoughlin, I.P. (1997) 'Implementing vulnerable socio-technical change projects', in McLoughlin, I.P. and Harris, M. (eds) *Innovation, Organisational Change and Technology*, London: ITB Press.

Barnatt, C. (1995) *Cyberbusiness: Mindsets for a Wired Age*, Chichester: Wiley.

Benders, J., de Haan, J. and Bennett, D. (1995) 'Symbiotic approaches: contents and issues', in Benders, J., de Haan, J. and Bennett, D. (eds) *The Symbiosis of Work and Technology*, London: Taylor & Francis.

Borttrup, P. (1997) 'A learning process approach to discussions of working conditions', in Neilsen, T. and Clausen, C. (eds) *Working Environment and Technological Development – Positions and Perspectives*, Working Paper No 3, Roskilde University/Aalborg University/DTU.

Brigham, M. and Corbett, M. (1996) 'Trust and the virtual organisation: handy cyberias', in Jackson, P.J. and van der Wielen, J. (eds) *Proceedings of Workshop on New International Perspectives on Telework*, Tilburg: WORC.

Buchanan, D. and Badham, R. (1999) *Politics, Power and Organisational Change: Winning the Turf Game*, London: Sage.

Buchanan, D. and Boddy, D. (1983) *Organisations in the Computer Age: Technological Imperatives and Strategic Choice*, Aldershot: Gower.

—— (1991) *The Expertise of the Change Agent*, London: Prentice-Hall.

Callon, M. (1987) 'Society in the making', in Bijker, W.E., Hughes, T.P. and Pinch, T.J. (eds) *The Social Construction of Technological Systems: New Directions in the Sociology of History and Technology*, Cambridge, Mass.: MIT Press.

Clark, J., McLoughlin, I.P., Rose, H. and King, J. (1988) *The Process of Technological Change: New Technology and Social Choice in the Workplace*, Cambridge: Cambridge University Press.

Cambell, A. (1996) 'Creating the virtual organisation and managing the distributed workforce', in Jackson, P.J. and van der Wielen, J. (eds) *Proceedings of Workshop on New International Perspectives on Telework*, Tilburg: WORC.

Child, J. and Faulkner, D. (1998) *Strategies of Cooperation: Managing Alliances, Networks and Joint Ventures*, Oxford: Oxford University Press.

Clausen, C. and Neilsen, T. (1997) 'Working environment and technological change', in Neilsen, T. and Clausen, C. (eds) *Working Environment and Technological Development Positions and Perspectives*, Working Paper No. 3, Roskilde University/Aalborg University/DTU.

Davidow, W.H. and Malone, M.S. (1992) *The Virtual Corporation*, London: HarperBusiness.

Dawson, P. (1994) *Organizational Change: A Processual Perspective*, London: Paul Chapman Publishers.

Eveland, J.D. and Tornatzky, L. (1990) 'The deployment of technology', in Eveland, J.D. and Tornatzky, L. (eds) *The Process of Technological Innovation*, London: Lexington Books.

Fleck, J. (1993) 'Configurations: crystallising contingency,' *International Journal of Human Factors in Manufacturing*, 3, 1: 15–36.

Grenier, R. and Metes, G. (1995) *Going Virtual: Moving Your Organisation into the 21st Century*, New York: Prentice-Hall

Handy, C. (1995) 'Trust and the virtual organisation,' *Harvard Business Review*, May/June: 40–50.

Hatch, M.J. (1997) *Organisation Theory: Modern Symbolic and Post Modern Perspective*, Oxford: Oxford University Press.

Jackson, P. (1996) 'The virtual society and the end of organisation', *Department of Management Studies Working Paper*, Uxbridge: Brunel University.

—— (1997) 'Information systems as metaphor: innovation and the 3 Rs of representation', in McLoughlin, I.P. and Harris, M. (eds) *Innovation, Organisational Change and Technology*, London: ITB Press.

Jackson, P.J. and van der Weilen, J. (1998) 'From telecommuting to the virtual organisation', in Jackson, P.J. and van der Weilen, J. (eds) *Teleworking: International Perspectives – from Telecommuting to the Virtual Organisation*, London: Routledge.

Koch, C. (1997) 'Social and technological development in context', in Neilsen, T. and Clausen, C. (eds) *Working Environment and Technological Development – Positions and Perspectives*, Working Paper No. 3, Roskilde University/Aalborg University/DTU.

Kohn, M. (1997) 'Technofile', *Independent on Sunday*, 5 January.

McLoughlin, I.P. and Clark, J. (1994) *Technological Change at Work*, 2nd edition, London: Open University Press.

Morgan, G. (1997) *Images of Organisation*, 2nd edition, London: Sage.

Nohria, N. (1992) 'Is a network perspective a useful way of studying organisations', in Nohria, N. and Eccles, R.G. (eds) *Networks and Organisations*, Cambridge, MA: Harvard Business School Press.

Nohria, N. and Eccles, R.G. (1992) 'Face-to-face: making network organisations work', in Nohria, N. and Eccles, R.G. (eds) *Networks and Organisations*, Cambridge, MA: Harvard Business School Press.

Pavitt, K (1987) 'Commentary' on Chapter 3 in Pettigrew, A. (ed.) *The Management of Strategic Change*, Oxford: Blackwell.

Reed, M. (1992) *The Sociology of Organisations*, Brighton: Harvester Wheatsheaf.

Sims, D. and McAulay, L. (1995) 'Management learning as a learning process: an invitation'. *Management Learning* 26, 1: 5–20.

Snow, C.C. *et al.* (1992) 'Managing 21st century network organisations', *Organisational Dynamics*, Winter: 5–20.

Swieringa, J. and Wierdsma, A. (1994) *Becoming a Learning Organisation: Beyond the Learning Curve*, London: Addison-Wesley.

Tidd, J., Bessant, J. and Pavitt, K. (1997) *Managing Innovation: Integrating Technological, Market and Organisational Change*, Chichester: Wiley.

Wallace, J. (1997) *Overdrive: Bill Gates and the Race to Control Cyberspace*, Chichester: Wiley.

Weick, K. (1991) 'The non-traditional quality of organisational learning', *Organisational Science*, 2: 116–24.

Wilkinson, B. (1983) *The Shop Floor Politics of New Technology*, London: Heinemann.

Woolgar, S. (1997) 'A new theory of innovation?', Third Annual 3M Innovation Lecture, Brunel University, 11 June.

Zuboff, S. (1988) *In the Age of the Smart Machine*, Cambridge, MA: Harvard University Press.

12 Management of knowledge as interface management

From exo-worlds to endo-worlds

Frank A. Morath and Artur P. Schmidt

Introduction

We head towards a knowledge-driven society. A society in which the management of organisational intelligence becomes the essential resource of any organisation. Yet the most prominent approaches focused on organisational intelligence, namely 'learning organisations' and 'virtual organisations', only view knowledge from a limited perspective. They focus either on people *or* on technology. To meet the challenge of knowledge management in a cyberspaced future, a broader view is necessary. We believe that the concept of 'interfaces' provides such a perspective, as it allows us to blend people *and* technology, as well as endo-worlds and exo-worlds. However, this is not without risk. An interface approach will not only change fundamentally the way we do (knowledge) management but also the way we do business. But that is *Zukunftsmusik*. Let's first start with the future's promises.

The knowledge economy: from Silicon Valley to Cyber Valley

There is broad consensus that we are in the midst of a fundamental global transformation of society comparable to the first (steam engine, railway) and second (computers) industrial revolutions. It is a transformation towards a 'post-capitalist society', in which 'it is certain that knowledge will be the primary resource' (Drucker 1994: 4) – and no longer money (Toffler 1981: 394). In terms of the economy, the changes are obvious. In an industrial and service-based economy, the value of a product is based on the integration of work and material. In a knowledge-based society, the value depends much more on the 'embedded intelligence' of products and services (as is the case with software, computers, microchips, etc.). Consequently, the importance of traditional productive factors (land, capital, work) will diminish while the importance of expertise and knowledge will increase (Drucker 1994: 64–5).

In the hub of this transformation lies the development of a technical infrastructure that is known as 'information-superhighway', or 'telecosmos' (Morath 1998). This evolving telecosmos contains modern information technologies with their hard components (e.g. computers, fax machines, cellular phones), hard/soft components (e.g. network and video-conferencing systems, virtual reality) and soft components (e.g. groupware, edi programs). It is wrapping up the globe like a new electronic atmosphere, enabling new individual, social and economical 'forms of life' on earth. At the leading edge of this knowledge (r)evolution is a striving group of high-tech businesses. Within this group one can distinguish two types of companies. Phase 1 companies (those building 'telecosmos') and phase 2 companies (those inhabiting 'telecosmos'). You might compare this situation to the beginning of the Industrial Revolution: the railroad companies (phase 1) spread the infrastructure, while the first factories (phase 2) were 'driving on' the infrastructure. The history of economy since these early days has revealed a simple principle: phase 2 companies move on and prosper, while phase 1 companies eventually stop developing and diminish. We believe that this principle is valid for our modern information infrastructure, too. Phase 1 companies build the future; phase 2 companies *are* the future. Hence it seems reasonable to look to phase 2 companies for innovational impetus – companies such as *ID-Mediengruppe* in Germany, constructing the *cycosmos*, a virtual communication platform for bringing together people who share common interests. Similarly, *ID* also created the virtual figure *E-CYAS* (Endo-Cybernetic Artificial Superstar), the counterpart to the virtual Japanese popstar *Kyoko Date*. In Table 12.1 we can see some of the characteristics that distinguish Cyber Valley companies (phase 2) from Silicon Valley companies (phase 1).

Moving on from Silicon Valley to Cyber Valley, one major change is obvious: companies and products are becoming more virtual and more intelligent. In the virtual Cyber Valley you do not find a production site at a physical location, with physical borders and a physical product. In Cyber Valley companies and products are built on a virtual logic, only to be seen when activated. They are formed through the networking of participants from all over the world – the local and global, physical and virtual, human and non-human – encompassing virtual industries, service centres and software producers around the globe (Schmidt 1998: 639).

To follow this virtual logic, they have to be more intelligent, i.e. built on knowledge rather than on physical components. This development will change

Table 12.1 Silicon Valley versus Cyber Valley

	Silicon Valley	*Cyber Valley*
Phase	Phase 1: Build Telecosmos	Phase 2: Inhabit Telecosmos
Typical products	Microchips	User-software, community server, intelligent agents, games, cryptography, data-mining
Key markets	Hardware and software	Software and brainware
Spatial and product logic	Physicality	Virtuality

the rules of the game fundamentally. Companies in Cyber Valley take social constructivism one step further. They are more than 'thinking organisations' (Sims and Gioia 1986) that function as collective interpretation systems to make sense of the 'real' world (Berger and Luckmann 1966; Daft and Weick 1984; Weick 1979, 1995). Instead of relying on a questionable physical and social reality, they invent their own symbolic virtual worlds (cyberspaces) constituting their own (business) reality. This is a reality or technosphere with completely different rules: a complete immersion of individuality and collectivity; of global interaction and new forms of synergy between human and artificial intelligence (Barnatt 1996).

If this reality invention were an individual phenomenon, one might call such a company 'schizophrenic' or simply 'crazy'. However, the construction of this new reality is inter-subjectively shared and appreciated. Hence it seems more appropriate to term these companies 'innovative' or 'creative'. If they are indeed the future, the art and practice of innovation and creativity in cyberspace obviously becomes essential for a company's survival; 'organisational intelligence', as the 'complete system of knowledge which permits people to coordinate their activity together' (McDaniel Johnson 1977: 6), has to become the focus of managerial activity.

In the current literature on organisational intelligence, two conceptual approaches can be distinguished. One approach focuses on the human intellectual capital of organisations (where organisational intelligence is pushed by people). The second approach emphasises the importance of intelligent technology (where organisational intelligence is pulled by technology). By looking more closely at these approaches, we show that both are somewhat limited in their future reach. By ignoring the situation and reality of phase 2 companies, a lot of possible learning about knowledge gets lost. As we shall show, by transforming the two into a third concept (interface management) one can overcome these limitations.

The need for intelligent organisations

Learning organisations: the people approach

Since the influential work of Argyris and Schön (1978), the concept of learning organisations (LOs) has been a popular theme in the management literature (Klimecki and Thomae 1995, 1997; see Björkegren and Rapp, Chapter 10 in this volume for a good overview). A LO is an organisation 'that facilitates the learning of all its members and continuously transforms itself' (Pedler *et al.* 1991: 1). Depending on the theoretical provenience of the author(s), this transformation reflects an adaptation to the environment (March and Olsen 1975), a change of the culturally embedded organisational theories (Argyris and Schön 1978), an expansion of the knowledge base of the organisation (Blackler 1993), or the perfect systemic tuning of individual abilities, culture and communication (Senge 1990). In general, this learning process is described as a continuous cycle of balancing individual and organisational learning (Kim 1993) – a process that Nonaka and Takeuchi (1995) call 'knowledge conversion'. However, many authors stress that 'OL draws upon the integration of the sum of individuals' learning to create a whole that is greater than the sum of its parts' (Starkey 1996: 2; Kim 1993: 40). Two major obstacles may impair organisational learning. One is the existence of defensive routines (Argyris 1990). These routines are a result of processes which typically take place in organisations: micro-politics, power games or group thinking. Defensive routines result in 'skilled incompetence' in dealing with new insights, leading to organisational inertia, as expressed by idea killers like 'the boss won't like it', 'I do not have the authority', 'it's never been tried'. If one looks closer, most of these organisational learning disabilities are rooted in a clash of different realities: owing to their dominant 'mental models' (Senge 1990: 174), organisations or individuals can only see what they can see – strange, new or 'just other' ideas that do not fit with their own concept of reality are not taken into account (Senge 1990: 174–205; Dörner 1989: 288–94; Watzlawick 1976).

The second obstacle is rooted in the fact that learning is fundamentally a self-organising process (Klimecki *et al.* 1995). Management can try to establish learn-promoting structures and processes and work towards an open learning culture, but it cannot force people to learn and take part in collective learning efforts. Owing to both obstacles, organisational learning sometimes just does not take place.

In terms of their organisational understanding, LO authors are still inclined to a very traditional idea of organisations with stable boundaries and a relatively clear distinction between inside and outside. Concepts such as virtuality or cyberspace do not play an independent role in their approach. Computer technology, if mentioned at all, is seen instrumentally as a possible learning tool – as a 'microworld' – including computer simulations and scenarios of real business processes (Senge 1990: 313–38). In other words, the cyberspace, in which phase 2 companies work and prosper, is *terra incognita* in the LO literature.

Virtual organisations: the technology approach

In contrast to the people approach, regarding organisations as virtual organisations (VOs) is a very technical perspective (for a detailed description of VOs, see Campbell, Chapter 2 in this volume). The term 'virtuality' was first coined in the field of information technology where it was used to describe memory that could be activated ('put into being') only for a specific purpose. With such a task specificity it is possible to make computer memory appear bigger than it is in reality. It was applied to organisations to preserve a similar phenomenon; this being organisational structures and processes that only exist when activated. Thus, VOs appear big on the outside, while being small on the inside. This is possible with the extensive use of computer-mediated networks. VOs have been described as 'dynamic networks of knots (individuals, organisational sub-units, organisations) whose (computer-mediated) links are configured dynamically and only for specific problems' (Picot *et al.* 1996: 396). Hence, VOs are characterised by a constant process of shaping and reshaping (Barnatt 1996; Davidow and Malone 1992).

Organisational intelligence, here, is treated in a somewhat mechanistic and rationalistic way. Each knot is said to have a specific set of core competencies which makes it the most competent provider of services or goods within the value chain. The specific know-how of each knot of the network then add up to the overall knowledge (Wüthrich *et al.* 1997; Harris 1998: 76–77). The role of information technology is to push the production of knowledge by enabling direct and instant connections between knots. In this view, a perfect information technology environment logically leads to a perfect knowledge accumulation.

In such a perspective, human aspects of knowledge generation are not taken into account. Questions such as 'Are people willing to share their knowledge (electronically)?', 'What personal benefits do people have from participating in VOs?', 'Can they trust other participants they have never seen or met in reality?' (Handy 1995; Nohria and Eccles 1992) are ignored.

Hence, the VO approach only exploits the very technical surface of cyberspace. It does not explore the inner workings and possibilities of cyberspace (as indicated by Cyber Valley companies). Nor does it consider its human side.

Table 12.2 summarises the main feature of both approaches.

Interfaces: synthesis of people and technology

To integrate both people and technology, and to accommodate the intellectual possibilities of cyberspace and Cyber Valley companies, a broader perspective is necessary. The concept of interfaces opens up such a perspective. In our under- standing, interfaces have a number of distinct features:

1   Interfaces are temporary networks of people and/or computers, integrating human beings as well as intelligent agents and databases. They only exist by means of inter-subjective construction and maintenance. Interfaces are, in other words, socio-technological actor networks (Callon 1986: 28–34).

2   In contrast to closed system concepts (e.g. organisations), interfaces have open structures, thereby enabling constant bifurcations that can lead to new solutions. Hence, interfaces are very flexible in their adaptation to new realities.

Table 12.2 Characteristics of learning organisations versus virtual organisations

	Learning organisation	*Virtual organisation*
Link parameter	Personal links	Computer links
Organisational focus	People	Technology
Knowledge acquisition	Knowledge generation	Knowledge accumulation
Space and time	Within boundaries – permanent	Beyond boundaries – temporary

3   The construction of interfaces does not follow a simple human or techno-
     logical logic. Instead, in interfaces computer and human logic are
     intertwined: interfaces expand the human thinking electronically by
     'copying' the functional principles of the human brain, allowing human-
     based computer thinking. And interfaces provide a digital coding and
     decoding of cyberspace and (virtual) realities, providing for a computer-
     based human thinking.
4   Interfaces evolve through a continuous process of participation and feed-
     back. Bi-directional feedback loops between interface and participant secure
     a two-fold responsibility for both individual and interface activity, thereby
     enabling a trustful environment in which individuals are willing to partici-
     pate.
5   Interfaces form parallel worlds. With their capacity of simulation, evolution
     in interfaces can be reversible in contrast to the irreversible evolution of
     physical worlds. With the advance of interface technologies (nanotech-
     nology, quantum computers, biotechnology) this permits new human life
     configurations and the formation of a global brain with a possible meta-
     consciousness.

With such an interface perspective, it is possible to address both human as well as
technical questions of collective intelligence. Such a perspective will also change
some of the paradigmatic principles guiding our epistemological and managerial
understanding (see Table 12.3).

Interfaces as endo-worlds

Endo (Greek for 'from inside') means that we are inside an interface – a
constructed borderline of our knowledge. Interfaces, as a lens for construction of
reality, allow us to make an endo-/exo-cut (Schmidt 1999: 236) between the
knowledge of a network or a participant and the outside world. Exo (Greek
'outside') means that we are outside of this interface. For example, if you have a
submarine team, the people who are in the submarine are 'endo', and the rest of
the world is 'exo'. Cyberspace is virtual and endo to the physical world. So we
can say that any virtual world is endo to a physical world, but not every endo-
world has to be virtual. With this endo/exo distinction one can (analytically) cut
through the fluidity of interfaces.

Take, for example, the largest electronic endo-world existing today: the

Table 12.3 Paradigm shift

'Organisational' paradigm	Interface paradigm
Objectivity	Intersubjectivity
Individuality	Collectivity
Reality	Hyper-reality
Linearity	Parallelity

Internet. What most newcomers do not understand is that the main issue in the Internet is not to sell an exo-product or an exo-service, but to connect people to communicate. They mistakenly believe that the Internet is constructed as digital copy of the physical exo-world. Yet, it is a living electronic endo-world with its own rationale: it has no owner (if at all, the Global Brain is the 'owner'). And it is still a non-regulative world. So, the most important rule in the Internet is to minimise the number of rules to provide enough space for different interfaces to connect. The main currency is attention. Hence, a constant effort has to be put in to maintain it and attract participation. In addition, the Internet does not follow the same causal logic as some of the exo-worlds do, which leads to non-linear dynamics and chaotic patterns of events (Schmidt 1999: 130). Yet one thing should be kept in mind: endo-worlds and exo-worlds are not clearly distinguishable; they are more like a seamless meta-interface.

Interfaces as virtual communities

In the past few years, virtual communities have evolved on 'the Net' (Turkle 1995; Rheingold 1993). These MUDs (Multi-User Dungeons) are social virtual realities displaying many of the interface features. Technically speaking they are nothing more than computer programs allowing distant people to communicate instantly. Virtually, they are much more. In contrast to other similar technologies – e.g. video-conferencing, e-mail, bulletin boards – MUDs have a life of their own. They exist because people want them to exist, and because people want to build their personal world and realise their vision within it. They log-in and become their virtual character, their *personae*; and with it they and their virtual friends build their virtual community.

So let us see how such a virtual community – InterfaceMUD – (hypothetically) works.

People log-in to InterfaceMUD, changing their identity to whatever they want to be and possibly are best at, thereby leaving reality and its limitations behind. A virtual personae is thus not bound by one's gender, societal position, sexual orientation or handicap in real life. In InterfaceMUD there is no glass ceiling – as a matter of fact, there is no ceiling at all. People in InterfaceMUD are judged by what they say and not by what the sign says on their door, turning the world from a bureaucracy, where floor level and size of your bureau determine your position, to a meritocracy, where your social position is based on what you are capable of.

In InterfaceMUD people get together who have not met in reality. Life is culturally rich, benefiting from a broad background of lifestyles, experiences and a lot of different individual interface links. Without immediate real world consequences, this opens up a lot of creative space for experiencing and creating new organisational theories.

The technical possibilities of InterfaceMUD are immense. People discuss problems not only with their immediate peers, but with peers from all over the world. Discussion groups on all kind of topics are installed in InterfaceMUD.

Virtual Libraries, the InterfaceMUD Open University and real world databases are accessible, enlargeable and changeable for everybody. The keyword is 'free' – free information for everybody who enters InterfaceMUD. Free information that is free to be used, free to be passed on and free to be modified according to individual needs. Have a technical problem with a software program? Put it on a virtual discussion group. Need an idea for a new project? Look it up in the virtual database of former projects. Want to study 'intercultural management'? Join the programme at the virtual Open University. You are not satisfied with the way the real organisations work? Find some equally dissatisfied and interested people to play around with new ideas. This newly generated knowledge can easily be transferred to reality via individuals and electronic links, enabling both quick solutions and ongoing learning processes in 'real' interfaces. In terms of boundaries and membership, InterfaceMUD is open. It equals any real community or organisation as much as the inhabitants want it to. In InterfaceMUD people develop a sense of belonging because they actually build a world they can oversee within self-determined boundaries. They also trust people they have never seen. This is because it is a world that is pseudonymous but not anonymous: each persona stands for a set of values, beliefs and words. Furthermore, each member is participating in InterfaceMUD for similar reasons: to have fun, learn and build bridges.

Interface management as knowledge management

Knowledge generation in interfaces

According to constructivist thinking, our knowledge of reality depends on our individual cognition. Owing to individual differences in perception and cognition, there is no absolute truth but only relative certainty (Schmidt 1998: 7). Hence, knowledge – in the sense of finding and defining truth – can only be described in subjective and not in objective terms.

From an interface perspective, knowledge of reality becomes an inter-subjective concept, defined by participation in interfaces. On this inter-subjective level you find the same learning barriers as on an individual or organisational level. As the research of limitologists has shown, it is impossible to see the full picture of a universe from inside. Everyone who sees the world through interfaces has only a limited view of the world. It is therefore necessary to have the ability to realise the existence of other interfaces and to understand their constructions of reality. Knowledge can then be generated by differentiation between interfaces and by producing interferences (superpositions) of different interfaces.

The construction of these intelligent interfaces through individuals, computers, communities and companies in cyberspace will change the micro interface between man and machine dramatically. The human brain is not fast enough to handle huge data amounts efficiently. By expanding into interfaces, individuals are able to overcome some of the biological and social restrictions: each human brain can more easily contribute to the overall knowledge, thus generating new knowledge in a more productive way. However, for inter-subjective knowledge generation, intensive communication will obviously be necessary. Knowledge management in this sense is communication management, making the navigation, construction, communication and use of knowledge more efficient. Thus, the increasing use of electronic media allows a new transfer of complex content through the parallel use of text, voice and pictures. Agents and Knowbots can freely move in the parallel navigation in n-dimensional knowledge spaces. Routine processes can be performed through programs which are able to learn by themselves and self-organise their evolution.

Endo-management: tapping the global brain

The evolution of knowledge cannot be left to itself: it has to be managed in a new, creative way. Interfaces tend to be anarchic and chaotic without effective management. Therefore, interface management or endo-management requires us to understand the complexity of interfaces to be able to influence them. It is not through reducing the complexity, but by understanding the complexity, that we will have a chance to make a difference. To do so, four features are impor-tant:

Interactive feedback loops

The management of interfaces is strongly dependent on interactive feedback loops which can either lead to self-organisation or *creative destruction* (J.A. Schumpeter). As described, interfaces have the tendency to self-destruct. So, existing management principles directed towards sustenance and status quo cannot be applied adequately.

Positive feedback is essential for the complexity of self-organised processes and deterministic chaos. In interfaces it influences phenomena like innovations, virtual organisations and group-dynamic processes. For example, small and medium-sized firms have new chances to reach huge numbers of network knots through positive feedback. Therefore, economy of scale is not the important factor in an interface economy, but economy of simulation – the efficiency of software and the flexible use of hyperlinks. In interfaces power is broadly distributed: because of the intensive feedback loops from and to the interface, every person can be the reason for massive change and transformation.

Blurred boundaries

Interfaces can be both exo and endo. So depending on where you are, you will be able to see either from inside out or from outside in. With more people devel-oping an endo perspective, not only the endo-world, but also the exo-world will change. This is because it makes a difference from where you look at the world. When you look at the world from an endo perspective, you develop other tech-nologies that transform our exo-worlds, too. The central theorem of Rössler's endophysics is that 'the endo-world can change the exo-world' (Rössler 1992: 131). This theorem is the key to the future economy. For example, if we use the technology of virtual prototyping, we can simulate a complete aeroplane before we manufacture a prototype. This knowledge production by simulation can lead to a more profound understanding and a better exo-product.

Respect for a greater individual independence

Interfaces provide greater autonomy for participants, allowing us to decouple from actual power structures. This makes them a driving force for liberty and freedom in cyberspace. With the emergence of new interfaces, developing countries, whose economies have always been dependent on developed nations, have new chances for independence. They can overcome economic barriers and be integrated into the new endo-worlds. They are no longer observers and recipients, but interactive participants in a new world order. This order is not based on the accumulation of money but on the sharing of knowledge. This can be equally said for other individuals, who have also been excluded from or deprived of successful participation in economic processes. Endo-management consequently can only convince but not command.

Interface design

Because every product, service and process has to be integrated into interfaces, interface design 'is everything' (Bonsiepe 1996: 74). Hence, to be successful they have to be designed in accordance with certain design principles: (a) adaptability, i.e. is a service flexible enough to accommodate for different needs?; (b) reversibility, i.e. can a process be reversed within a different context?; (c) replicability, i.e. can a product be easily replicated to be used in other interfaces?

The new endo-economy: simulation of a simulation

How could economies look, functioning according to interface principles and not market and hierarchy principles? Endo-economies, based on interfaces of virtual reality and simulations, undermine the principles that organise the production and distribution of goods in a capitalistic market economy. The market system is focused on an exo-perspective, where money determines who is inside or outside a market. It is based on competition of participants and on self-interest. However, in cyber economies 'markets' will be more dependent on an endo-perspective. Instead of exclusion, inclusion of participants will be the driving force. In the endo-economy, the owner of a commodity will have difficulties in excluding others from using a commodity. This is because a virtual commodity can easily be copied, with the transaction costs for using a commodity becoming increasingly cheaper.

In an endo-perspective the economy of producers and consumers will be much more of a gift-economy than a purchase-and-sale economy. In an endo-economy the use of a commodity will no longer necessarily involve competition. If goods are non-competitive, charging a price per unit does not make sense because it restricts the distribution of a product. If the marginal cost of reproduction of a virtual good is near zero, everyone can have it for almost free. The problem is that a producer who cannot make profit similar to the market system will go bankrupt. Competition has been the standard way of controlling buyers through sellers. But with non-competitive goods appearing in endo-economies, the whole market system can be challenged. The shift of power from producers to clients and to non-rivalry products and services will lead to a new way of thinking about markets.

In a world of increasing data and complexity the elementary characteristic will be a lack of transparency. The market for virtual and complex products and services is anything but transparent. Therefore the most important growing market of the future will not be products and services but interfaces which make the endo-economy more transparent, like intelligent agents and knowledge-navigators. Consumers' failure to acquire full information about the software they need led to the shareware market – to beta-versions free to public and free browsers.

The rise of CommodityBots such as *DataWarehousing* of *Living Systems* offers an opportunity for consumers to aggregate their preferences on a worldwide scale. As it becomes increasingly easy for consumers to communicate their individualised preferences to participants, *DataWarehousing* allows us not only to bring products nearer to buyers, it also brings together customers who want to sell or exchange second-hand goods. The potential of these second-hand markets is tremendous because not everything has to be recycled but can be in use in other places on the planet, turning the global village into a global marketplace.

Summary

In conclusion, one might maintain that the future world is an interface, where it is a matter of success or even survival to be included or to be excluded – to be endo as well as exo. Yet this interface has different rules than the world of hierarchy and rationality we have known so far. The history of success is therefore no good guiding light. Instead of relying on the proved facts, management has to look for new and challenging 'science fiction', as displayed by phase 2 companies of virtuality or the new virtual communities. Knowledge in interface, then, constitutes a fluid moment of connection rather than a solid commodity that can be stored, labelled and moved around. Consequently, knowledge management in the future becomes a management of the moment – the "now". Not more, but also not less.

Bibliography

Argyris, C. (1990) *Overcoming Organisational Defenses*, Boston: Allyn & Bacon.
Argyris, C. and Schön, D. (1978) *Organisational Learning – A Theory of Action Perspective*, Reading, MA: Addison-Wesley.

Barnatt, C. (1996) *Cyber Business – Mindsets for a Wired Age*, Chichester: Wiley.

Berger, P. and Luckmann, T. (1966) *The Social Construction of Reality*, Garden City, NY: Doubleday.

Blackler, F. (1993) 'Knowledge and the theory of organisations: organisations as activity systems and the reframing of management', *Journal of Management Studies*, 30, November: 863–84.

Bonsiepe, G. (1996) *Interface*, Mannheim: Bollmann.

Callon, M. (1986) 'The sociology of an actor-network: the case of the electric vehicle', in Callon, M., Law, J. and Rip, A. (eds) *Mapping the Dynamics of Science and Technology*, London: Macmillan: 19–34.

Daft, R. and Weick, K. (1984) 'Toward a model of organisations as interpretation systems', *Academy of Management Review*, 9, 2: 284–95.

Davidow, W. and Malone, M. (1992) *The Virtual Corporation, Structuring and Revitalizing the Corporation for the 21st Century*, New York: HarperBusiness.

Dörner, D. (1989) *Die Logik des Mißlingens: Strategisches Denken in komplexen Situationen*, Hamburg: Rowohlt.

Drucker, P. (1994) *Postcapitalistic Society*, New York: HarperBusiness.

Handy, C. (1995) 'Trust and the virtual organisation', *Harvard Business Review*, May/June: 41–50.

Harris, M. (1998) 'Rethinking the virtual organisation', in Jackson, P. and van der Wielen, J. (eds) *Teleworking: International Perspectives – from Telecommuting to the Virtual Organisation*, London: Routledge: 74–92.

Kim, D. (1993) 'The link between individual and organisational learning', *Sloan Management Review*, Fall: 37–50.

Klimecki, R., Laßleben, H. and Altehage, M. (1995) 'Zur empirischen Analyse organisationaler Lernprozesse im öffentlichen Sektor – Teil 2: Methoden und Ergebnisse', in *Management Forschung und Praxis*, University of Konstanz, Dept. of Management, Diskussionsbeitrag Nr. 13.

Klimecki, R. and Thomae, M. (1995) 'Zwischen Differenzierung und Internationalisierung: Neuere Trends in der Erforschung organisationalen Lernen', in *Management Forschung und Praxis*, University of Konstanz, Dept. of Management, Diskussionsbeitrag Nr. 11.

—— (1997) 'Organisationales Lernen: Eine Bestandsaufnahme der Forschung', in *Management Forschung und Praxis*, University of Konstanz, Dept. of Management, Diskussionsbeitrag Nr. 18.

March, J.G. and Olsen, J.P. (1976) 'Organisational learning and the ambiguity of the past', in March, J.G. and Olsen, J.P. (eds) *Ambiguity and Choice in Organisations*, Bergen: 54–67.

McDaniel Johnson, B. (1977) *Communication: the Process of Organizing*, Boston: Allyn & Bacon.

Morath, F. (1998) 'Virtuelle Organisationen: Szenarien an der Schnittstelle Mensch-Maschine' ('Virtual organisations: scenarios of human-machine interfaces'), in *Documentation of the 19th Alcatel Symposium on Virtual Enterprises*, Zürich.

Nohria, N. and Eccles, R. (1992) 'Face-to-face: making network organisations work', in Nohria, N. and Eccles, R. (eds) *Networks and Organisations*, Boston, MA: Harvard Business School Press: 288–308.

Nonaka, I. and Takeuchi, H. (1995) *The Knowledge-Creating Company*, New York: Oxford University Press.

Pedler, M., Burgoyne, J. and Boydell, T. (1991) *The Learning Company*, London: McGraw-Hill.

Picot, A., Reichwald, R. and Wigand, R.T. (1996) *Die grenzenlose Unternehmung*, 2nd edition, Wiesbaden: Gabler.

Rheingold, H. (1993) *The Virtual Community*, Reading, MA: Addison-Wesley.

Rössler, O. (1992) *Endophysik*, Berlin: Merve-Verlag.

Schmidt, A.P. (1998) *Endo-Management*, Bern: Haupt.

—— (1999) *Der Wissensnavigator*, Stuttgart: DVA-Verlag.

Senge, P. (1990) *The Fifth Discipline – The Art and Practice of Learning Organisations*, New York: Doubleday.

Sims, H. and Gioia, D. (eds) (1986) *The Thinking Organisation: Dynamics of Organisational Social Cognition*, San Francisco: Jossey-Bass.

Starkey, K. (ed.) (1996) *How Organisations Learn*, London: ITP.

Toffler, A. (1981) *The Third Wave*, Toronto: Bantam.

Turkle, S. (1995) *Life on the Screen*, New York: Simon & Schuster.

Watzlawick, P. (1976) *How Real is Real?*, New York: Random House.

Weick, K. (1979) *The Social Psychology of Organizing*, Reading, MA: Addison-Wesley.

—— (1995) *Sensemaking in Organisations*, Thousand Oaks, CA: Sage.

Wüthrich, H., Philipp, A. and Frentz, M. (1997) *Vorsprung durch Virtualisierung: Lernen von virtuellen Pionierunternehmen*, Wiesbaden: Gabler.

13 Conclusion

Paul J. Jackson

In a book such as this a variety of phenomena have been discussed. Many theories and perspectives have been brought to bear, highlighting some important issues and lines of analysis on virtual working dynamics. Drawing together all the threads would, of course, be impossible. As the chapters can stand alone as important contributions to the virtual working debate, I will only attempt here a personal exercise in drawing out the more important points of connection and suggest the sort of direction research and practice should be headed in the future. We will begin with a brief summary of the book's four main parts.

The inter- and intra-organisational issues

In the first part of the book we looked at virtual working issues at the inter- and intra-organisational levels. This highlighted the element of 'boundary erosion' – where functional, organisational and even spatial divides are transcended by new organisational designs and networks, often with IT support.

Where inter-organisational relations were discussed, the issues of learning and knowledge management, and networking/relationship-building, came to the fore. In his discussion of the Web enterprise, Campbell noted the importance of learning and knowledge sharing in environments subject to uncertainty and change. As with several later authors, Campbell introduced the notion of 'communities of practice' to illustrate how this might be achieved across organisational boundaries. Particular emphasis was placed on the informal arrangements by which partners learn together, building on and reinforcing shared sets of beliefs and values. Because of the need to produce mutual strategies, and pool risks and rewards with other network partners, Campbell pointed to the importance of building trust in such work arrangements, particularly where knowledge sharing was concerned.

For Harris *et al.*, the process of building and sustaining collaborative networks was the subject of discussion. Because of the focus on the need to enrol resources and support, and to sustain high-trust relationships among partners, network building was viewed here as not simply a 'technical' process but as a political and relationship-building exercise. The ability to create a sense of shared goals and culture was thus seen as vital, together with the creation of a climate of trustworthiness, openness and fairness. This approach urged us to recognise the political sophistication demanded for building and managing successful networks, as well as the interpersonal skills needed to produce open and trusting relationships.

In the chapter by Nandhakumar, it was the transcending of spatial rather than organisational boundaries that formed the topic for discussion. While the new communications technologies were seen as central for doing this, Nandhakumar reminded us that social and hierarchical constraints may not be as easy to overcome as those of geography. In a similar way to both Harris *et al.* and Campbell, Nandhakumar pointed to the importance of trust between team members as an antecedent to open and effective collaborations. Where team relationships were intended to be enduring, it was noted that trust may need to be developed through personal relationships (and thus occasional, or initial face-to-face encounters). Indeed, a fear of isolation and a desire for 'warmer' forms of engagement – particularly where greater openness and knowledge sharing was required – meant that the technology alone was not seen as sufficient for supporting the operations of virtual teams.

Individual level issues

In exploring virtual working issues from the level of the individual, we saw that many attitudes among management may act against developments such as tele-working. In looking at teleworking cost-benefits, for instance, it was noted that both economic and non-economic aspects need to be considered. One problem, however, may be managing expectations such that organisations do not expect to see benefits before they incur costs. A willingness to manage the uncertainty and risk involved in teleworking, rather than avoiding it, may therefore be needed. As Mirchandani showed, this may be a function of management style and culture, with certain managers being less conservative. Such factors were also prevalent in the way teleworking arrangements are managed, with many younger managers more willing to engage in the trust relationships demanded for tele-working. It was also highlighted here that trusting styles of management could even lead to a greater sense of worker commitment and individual motivation. In addition, having their working mode valued and seen as legitimate may also be important for many teleworkers.

As well as issues of motivation, we also saw the importance of matters of 'identity' in virtual working. In looking at the way identity is constituted, maintained and expressed through narratives and storytelling, Galpin and Sims demonstrated the contrasts between groups of operatives and knowledge workers. By focusing on the capacity of each group to assemble narratives about themselves, they showed that while knowledge workers were able to construct a strong sense of identity, operatives were more isolated and found it hard to construct a coherent identity.

Access to stories and opportunities for storytelling also has implications for organisational culture, and whether certain individuals will have the learning opportunities needed to fit into such cultures. While operatives may find difficulty in seeing how they fit into wider organisational processes, as well as exchanging stories and conversations about the organisation, knowledge workers have few such problems. This is because the nature of their roles and relation-ships allows them to connect their experiences, roles and identities to the broader organisational picture.

Management and control issues

In the third part of the book we looked at the management and control aspects of virtual working. Here, the relation between control and commitment processes was explored. In virtual working, it was noted, it is difficult if not impossible to design and control the work of others in a highly prescribed way. Instead, approaches that emphasise empowerment and coaching may be needed. In moving towards a commitment approach, Depickere showed that control could be derived, for instance, from creating a strong organisational culture, or through attention to recruitment, socialisation and training – the issues that were termed 'input' controls. It was noted, however, that commitment is not such a straightforward concept. For instance, Depickere illustrated the distinction between 'affective commitment' (based on shared values and interest) and 'continuance' or 'calculative commitment' (commitment due to a lack of attractive options for working elsewhere). Depickere concluded that managers not only need to recognise the importance of commitment, they must also actively build and maintain it.

   The link between management and culture also came to the fore when discussing the sort of values and norms associated with different levels of management. Suomi and Pekkola argued that the main constraints on tele-working developments have been the rationalities associated with different management levels (or corporate subcultures). It was noted that while culture has a powerful influence on organisational outcomes, it is not always obvious as to how cultural norms and values affect decision making and other management predispositions. For forms of teleworking to develop, therefore, promoters need to identify such norms and values and be able to speak the language of the ratio-nalities associated with the different levels of management.

   The need to balance control and autonomy was the item of concern for Adami. This focused on newspaper journalists – people that require high levels of flexibility in space and time in order to do their jobs. In managing such workers, we saw two types of control – 'direct', as found in face-to-face supervi-sion, quality checks and operating procedures – and 'indirect', such as organisational culture, career opportunities and training. The mix of these controls is likely to vary, depending on the experience and seniority of those being managed. For established journalists, for instance, 'professional' controls may be used, drawing upon the individual's sense of what the 'dos and don'ts' are in the job. More junior journalists, however, are likely to be subject to 'organ-isational' controls, such as strict deadlines and specific story guidelines. The conclusion reached by Adami was that organisations considering virtual working must appreciate the autonomy needs of a particular job, how suitable an individual is for a given form of virtual working, and the sort of resources, systems and skills that may be needed to support such changes.

Learning and innovation issues

In the last part of the book we looked at the learning and innovation issues involved when introducing virtual working. We saw in particular that the technologies and work arrangements involved demand new ways of thinking about learning and knowledge management issues. While the management of knowledge is now seen as crucial for competitive advantage, because much of it is either embedded in social practices or only known tacitly, problems may exist in learning from or communicating knowledge to those who are absent in time and/or space.

Björkegren and Rapp showed that, from the 'cognitive' perspective, learning can be viewed as a 'change in thinking'. This emphasised the fact that since organisations don't have cognitive capacities themselves, *individuals*, and the sum of their learning, were at the root of *organisational* learning. Enabling individuals to interact was thus seen as the basis for assimilating, creating and communicating new knowledge. A further perspective discussed by the authors was the 'situated' approach, where learning is viewed as a product of *context*, bounded by time, space and social structure. According to this view, learning and knowledge are particularly dependent on context where the issues involved are unstructured and unique. This raises important questions, of course, for learning and knowledge management across time and space. Björkegren and Rapp showed, for instance, that because what is learned may be rooted in a particular social and cultural context, difficulties may arise in repackaging it for use in other situations, such as subsequent projects. The authors concluded that managers must become more aware of the complex nature of knowledge, how it is created and communicated, and how various aspects of context may structure it.

The approach by Ian McLoughlin and Paul Jackson concentrated on the virtual organisation. It highlighted, for a start, that there may be various problems in simply transferring the knowledge needed for users to work with the technologies that support virtual working. The authors also pointed to the learning difficulties faced by conventional, bureaucratic organisations attempting to 'go virtual'. Their third approach used actor-network theory to focus on the political skills of network builders, such as managers and change agents, in building the new forms of organisation. This suggested that more Machiavellian competencies may be important for managing stakeholder interests, neutralising resistance, and otherwise utilising manipulative devices for bringing about virtual working changes.

The final chapter by Morath and Schmidt sought to develop a new way of thinking about knowledge management issues in virtual working. The companies that are set to thrive on cyberspace, they noted, need to invent their own symbolic, virtual worlds, as well as to transcend the dualism between intellectual and human capital. To explain how this could be done the authors introduced the notion of 'interface management' – where virtual communities, supported by technologies and software, are developed. This allows individuals to interact across time and space, in a similar way to the ideas that underpin 'communities of practice'. Such arrangements are thus informal and brought into being by the actions and interests of their members.

Summary

Table 13.1 provides a summary of the key issues raised by the book's chapters according to the different levels of analysis. Let us now turn to some areas of connection illustrated by these chapters and suggest the directions in which they may lead us in developing new ideas about virtual working dynamics. The key connections we will explore are: the management of risks and uncertainty; trust, fairness and equity; time and investment in virtual working; control and commitment; learning and community building; relationship-building; and contexts, places and knowledge management.

Table 13.1 Management and control, and learning and innovation issues

	Management and control	*Learning and innovation*
Inter-organisational level	The development of formal and informal networking agreements; building a climate of openness and trustworthiness between partners; creating a sense of fairness; neutralising resistance	Building networks and relationships as a basis for collaboration; creating communities of practice in which members learn together; transferring knowledge from vendors of virtual technologies
Intra-organisational/team level	Establishing trust between team members; use of project management techniques to coordinate and schedule team outputs	Creating opportunities for face-to-face encounters; creating contexts where knowledge can be transferred and understood
Individual worker/teleworker level	Ensuring appropriate input controls through careful recruitment procedures; attention to induction and socialisation into corporate culture; building commitment among workers – both calculative and moral	Allowing individuals the opportunity to engage in story-telling with others; providing learning opportunities for developing cultural and professional norms and values

Managing risk and uncertainty

The chapters illustrate a variety of risks and uncertainties associated with virtual working. As Mirchandani notes in the case of teleworking, there are many 'what-if'-ers that those wishing to promote teleworking must confront. She also found, however, that many younger bosses are quite willing to take these risks. There is also an issue here as to whether the arrangements involved receive formal backing in the form of organisational policies. Suomi and Pekkola, like Mirchandani, note that many teleworking arrangements are informal. While this may allow managers to avoid the problems of developing corporate policies, there may be a downside for the workers themselves. Mirchandani showed that teleworkers often want their organisations to believe in and be committed to their work arrangements in order to feel secure and valued.

Related dynamics are also illustrated by Harris *et al.* in the context of inter-firm networking. These authors noted a paradox here: while networking often takes place to spread risks and handle uncertainty, the collaborations that result may bring their own risks and uncertainties. These may be seen as greater where networking takes place without formal agreements. However, where formal agreements to network do exist, they often produce the basis for trust to develop. Social encounters are likely to follow, with personal networks and personalised trust created over time. In this sense, formal agreements (which appear to speak of distrust) may set a climate or context for trust to develop and risks to be managed.

Trust, fairness and equity

From the chapters we can see that trust was an issue in virtual working at individual, team and inter-firm levels. For example, the trust that managers may have towards individual workers may be important in deciding whether they are allowed to adopt virtual forms of working and, if they are, how they will be managed. Whereas commitment strategies are adopted with some workers – especially skilled, knowledge workers – low-trust, control strategies are likely with more low skilled ones.

At the team-working level, two sources of trust were identified. Here, Nandhakumar distinguished between 'abstract structures' – where trust was based, for instance, on the expectation of others' professionalism – and 'personalised' sources of trust – i.e. that based on more social, 'back stage' encounters in face-to-face settings.

Both Harris *et al.* in the context of networking, and Campbell in the context of the Web enterprise, noted that in pooling resources and knowledge partners not only need to be able to trust each other but also be fairly rewarded. Moreover, this must be *seen to be fair*. Hence, open communications about the inputs and rewards of collaboration partners may be an important part of network relationship management. This is particularly so where, for example, 'commercialisable' knowledge is involved (i.e. that which can migrate relatively straightforwardly and offers sources of value). Only when organisations do not fear their openness will be exploited are they likely to share such knowledge.

Time and investment in virtual working

The dimension of time reveals some interesting analyses of virtual working, something of particular importance given the way issues of transience and agility are often taken to characterise virtual working. Nandhakumar pointed out, for instance, that for projects involving continuous virtual team working, *personalised* trust may need to be developed. In other words, the more enduring the arrangement, the more team members may want opportunities for face-to-face engagement to allow a deeper emotional connection.

In the area of inter-firm networks, Harris *et al.* suggest that because of the resources invested in getting a collaboration off the ground, the pay-back may not come from the initial networking project but from the second and subsequent ones. In other words, investments (in capital, resources and relationship-building) must sometimes be discounted over a longer period of time.

A similar point is made by Björkegren and Rapp. They noted that the dimension of time is particularly important in project-based organisations. If learning from one project is to be transferred to subsequent ones, or other parts of the organisation, efforts need to be made to ensure that knowledge does not simply remain the tacit preserve of the individuals who constituted erstwhile project teams.

Commitment and control

The chapters have shown that virtual forms of working demand methods of management and control that do not depend on face-to-face surveillance. Arrangements such as teleworking instead rely hugely on skilled, motivated and committed workers. As such, input controls – including recruitment, training, induction and socialisation – are important for building the right teleworking workforce. Where workers have developed appropriate skills, values and attitudes – through years of professional experience or company 'enculturation' – managers are more likely to afford them the autonomy needed to work flexibly in time and space.

Harris *et al.* also showed that in the case of team work, trust and autonomy may need to be combined with more rational management measures at times. This is especially so where there is a requirement to integrate work with people or teams as part of a larger project. Here, virtual teams may be coordinated with rigorous project management methods and technologies. This may include clear deadlines and goals – transparent to all members over IT networks – which create group pressures to meet obligations.

Learning and community building

In order to set the right context for learning, it was shown above that a sense of community may need to be put in place. This would allow trust, shared missions, and common values and norms to develop. Forming communities of practice (ensuring that individuals do not just keep in contact, but remain active members of work communities) is important here. In order to see where their efforts fit into wider organisational processes, storytelling opportunities may also be needed. This would allow such communities to exchange narratives about their work and the way it links to organisational rationales.

Storytelling then, helps to construct the context individuals operate in, assisting them to understand their role. Here, people can read and reproduce cultural norms, values and meanings, as well as codes of behaviour. This may also reaffirm a sense of identity connected to the (virtual) organisation, building a feeling of community. To function in a community, as Campbell notes, one must become an insider. This may also be important for overcoming the isolation associated with teleworking. Depickere suggested, for instance, that lack of contact with the organisation may produce a potential reduction in commitment to one's colleagues or employer. But the link between commitment and isolation is not unmediated and might also be reliant on narratives. To be in a community, feel part of it and be committed to it (as well as to one's peers and team members) may depend, in part, on the 'sense-making' that takes place through shared, community storytelling.

Relationship-building

For all forms of virtual working to develop and succeed, a certain amount of relationship-building is essential. This may be more important in some cases than others. Galpin and Sims, for instance, noted that knowledge workers frequently need to spend more time at the office building relationships. Indeed, a high level of strategic autonomy may be needed for those whose jobs involve boundary-spanning and relationship-building activities. The ability to do this may be limited by such factors as financial constraints (money to travel, attend conferences, exhibitions, etc.), as well as time and space barriers. Building a network of contacts is important, for instance, in creating virtual teams and undertaking the networking that can bring about inter-firm collaboration (Harris *et al.*). This is because networked organisations and Web enterprises may be born from (personal) networks that are formed at conferences, meetings and other occasions where face-to-face contact is made. Such situations also allow individuals to act out a professional role and engage in appropriate storytelling, profile maintaining, and so on. This will often take place in back-stage regions, where personalised trust is established, building stocks of goodwill to be drawn upon perhaps in later, more virtual, situations.

Contexts, places and knowledge management

One problem in virtual working is that such media as desktop conferencing and groupware may not present enough contextual clues for knowledge to be transferred effectively. In other words, virtual working can potentially de-contextualise knowledge, making it difficult to interpret properly. This is not simply a matter of the 'richness' of the medium but rather the *complexity of the context* in which knowledge is developed and in terms of which it must be understood. The more structured the problems and issues, the less important are physical, social and cultural factors. Certain knowledge work, though, since it is unstructured and complex – particularly that involved in technological and organisational innovation – may be difficult to transfer for these reasons.

Contexts, however, may influence the dynamics of virtual working in other ways. For example, the common threats faced by certain businesses, in Harris *et al.*'s example, meant that issues of confidentiality and being too open about 'commercialisable' knowledge became less important.

Nandhakumar also points out how certain places (informal, back-stage regions) allow for 'warm' relationships that promote social interaction, storytelling and general team bonding. Occasions such as social chats over coffee cannot be engineered (as Nandhakumar shows). While virtual coffee sessions may share time and a particular medium, the social context is simply not the same which may have important implications for knowledge creation and exchanges.

As we can see, the different forms of virtual working share many common dynamics. The problems and issues that have emerged from this analysis point to some tentative directions where new organisational thinking may be needed. This concerns both research work, in terms of theories, concepts and frameworks, as well as changing management strategies and corporate policies. Despite improvements in the technologies that support it, we can conclude that the social and organisational dynamics involved in virtual working will warrant serious and ongoing attention.

Index

Note: page numbers in italics refer to tables or figures where these are removed from the textual reference.